Educating the Catholic People

History of Early Modern Educational Thought

Editor-in-chief

Cristiano Casalini

Associate Editors

Anne Régent-Susini (*Université Sorbonne-Nouvelle*)
Christoph Sander (*Technische Universität Berlin*)

Advisory Board

Constance Blackwell† (*University of London*) – Paul Richard Blum (*Loyola University Maryland*) – Philippe Desan (*University of Chicago*) – Mordechai Feingold (*California Institute of Technology*) – Paul Grendler (*University of Toronto, emeritus*) – Maarten J.F.M. Hoenen (*University of Basel, University of Freiburg/Brsg.*) – Maryanne Horowitz (*Occidental College*) – Howard Hotson (*Oxford University*) – Richard Kagan (*Johns Hopkins University, emeritus*) – Sachiko Kusukawa (*Cambridge University*) – Francesco Mattei (*University of Rome iii*) – John W. O'Malley (*Georgetown University, emeritus*) – Vladimir Urbánek (*Czech Academy of Sciences*)

VOLUME 3

The titles published in this series are listed at *brill.com/hemet*

Educating the Catholic People

*Religious Orders and Their Schools in
Early Modern Italy (1500–1800)*

By

David Salomoni

BRILL

LEIDEN | BOSTON

Cover illustration: Vivir y morir con ellos_ fundador de los padres somascos, Vida de San Jeronimo Emiliani Patrono Universal de la niñez y juventud desamparada.

Library of Congress Cataloging-in-Publication Data

Names: Salomoni, David, author.
Title: Educating the Catholic people : religious orders and their schools in early modern Italy (1500-1800) / by David Salomoni.
Description: Leiden ; Boston : Brill, [2021] | Series: History of early modern educational thought, 2542-5536 ; volume 3 | Includes bibliographical references and index. | Summary: "In this book, David Salomoni reconstructs the complex educational landscape that arose in sixteenth-century Italy and lasted until the French Revolution. This book addresses this historigoraphical gap, providing a new chapter in the comparative study of pre-modern education"– Provided by publisher.
Identifiers: LCCN 2021017591 (print) | LCCN 2021017592 (ebook) | ISBN 9789004436466 (hardback) | ISBN 9789004448643 (ebook)
Subjects: LCSH: Catholic Church–Education–Italy–History. | Catholic schools–Italy–History. | Catholic universities and colleges–Italy–History. | Monasticism and religious orders–Education–Italy–History. | Religious education–Italy–History.
Classification: LCC LC506.I8 .S35 2021 (print) | LCC LC506.I8 (ebook) | DDC 371.071/20945–dc23
LC record available at https://lccn.loc.gov/2021017591
LC ebook record available at https://lccn.loc.gov/2021017592

Typeface for the Latin, Greek, and Cyrillic scripts: "Brill". See and download: brill.com/brill-typeface.

ISSN 2542-5536
ISBN 978-90-04-43646-6 (hardback)
ISBN 978-90-04-44864-3 (e-book)

Copyright 2021 by Koninklijke Brill NV, Leiden, The Netherlands.
Koninklijke Brill NV incorporates the imprints Brill, Brill Nijhoff, Brill Hotei, Brill Schöningh, Brill Fink, Brill mentis, Vandenhoeck & Ruprecht, Böhlau Verlag and V&R Unipress.
All rights reserved. No part of this publication may be reproduced, translated, stored in a retrieval system, or transmitted in any form or by any means, electronic, mechanical, photocopying, recording or otherwise, without prior written permission from the publisher. Requests for re-use and/or translations must be addressed to Koninklijke Brill NV via brill.com or copyright.com.

This book is printed on acid-free paper and produced in a sustainable manner.

To my mentors

Contents

List of Maps IX

Introduction 1
1 State of Research and Historiographical Problems 6

1 **Educating the Modern Catholics?: Roots of Catholic Schools in Renaissance Italy (15th–16th cc.)** 14
  1 The Last Phase of Communal Education in Italy 14
    1.1 *Complexity of the Renaissance Communal School System* 17
    1.2 *Weaknesses of the Renaissance Communal School System* 26
  2 The Catholicization of Italian Education 33

2 **Historical Paths: The Definition of Pedagogical Identities (16th–17th cc.)** 41
  1 Male Religious Orders 41
    1.1 *An Educational Benchmark: The Jesuits* 42
    1.2 *The Barnabites* 47
    1.3 *The Somascans* 54
    1.4 *The Piarists* 60
    1.5 *The Theatines and the Servites* 69
  2 Female Religious Orders 77
    2.1 *The Ursulines* 78
    2.2 *The Angelic Sisters and the Guastalla College* 84
    2.3 *Rosa Venerini and Lucia Filippini: The Pious Teachers* 89

3 **Schools and Colleges: Processes of Settlement in Italy and Contiguous Areas** 95
  1 From Lombardy to the Kingdom of France 96
  2 Schools for Northern Italy and Small Towns 100
  3 A Congregation for the Large Cities 105
  4 Between Central, Southern and Eastern Europe 111
  5 The Franciscans between Continuity and Rupture 116

4 **Different Types of Schools Operated by Religious Orders** 123
  1 Public Education Entrusted to Religious Orders and Secular Priests 123

    1.1   *Udine and the Barnabites: On the Outskirts of the Peninsula*   123
    1.2   *Jesuits and Piarists in the Duchy of Modena: A Competition between Local Networks*   131
    1.3   *Guastalla: A Multi-layered Religious Education for the Community*   139
  2   Episcopal Requests   145
    2.1   *The Somascans between Schools and Diocesan Seminaries*   147
  3   Other Types of Schools Operated by Religious Orders   151
    3.1   *Barnabite Schools Established by Notables and Aristocrats*   151
    3.2   *The Religious as Private Teachers*   154
    3.3   *Women, Nuns, Teachers: The 'Educandato' of Saint Charles*   155

5 **The End of an Educational Season: The Schools of Religious Orders between Scientific and Political Revolutions (17th–18th cc.)**   159
  1   The Scientific Culture: Religious Orders on the Eve of Modernity   160
    1.1   *Famiano Michelini and the Galilean Piarists*   162
    1.2   *Baranzano Redento*   167
  2   School Reforms in the Age of Enlightenment   169
    2.1   *The European Situation*   170
    2.2   *The Situation in Italy: The Italian States and the Religious Orders*   172
  3   Conclusion   181

Bibliography   185
Index   211

List of Maps

1 Map of Barnabite schools in Italy   100
2 Map of Somascan schools in Italy   104
3 Map of Somascan schools in Lombardy   105
4 Map of Theatine schools in Italy   112
5 Map of Piarist schools in Italy   116
6 Map of Jesuit schools in the Duchy of Modena   140
7 Map of Piarist schools in the Duchy of Modena   141

Introduction

Why publish a book on the history of religious teaching congregations and their schools between the sixteenth and the eighteenth centuries, a book focused on the Italian Peninsula, a declining historical and geographical context, according to early modern historians? The answer is twofold.

Firstly, there is a stainless relationship between historiography and the present; the recent expansion of various historiographical fields of investigation shows this clearly. From gender to queer studies, from the interest in Asian and Far Eastern history to the study of globalization to the history of ethnic minorities and religious groups, the past is always a mirror and a source of explanation for the most critical and relevant issues of our times. At first glance this may seem obvious, but its relevance should not be underestimated in the context of the history of education. In recent decades there has been no lack of research on the history of late-medieval pre-modern schools and educational institutions, with a particular focus on Italy;[1] however, it seems that historians' interest in this subject has not been as burning as for other themes. To a certain extent, the milder concern shown by historians is an indirect reflection of the expendability of schools and education on the priority scale of contemporary governments and societies. During the last decade, the first field to receive funding cuts in western countries facing budgetary and economic problems was public education. Nonetheless, the problem does not seem to relate only to the economic sphere and resources that governments can invest in education; the cause seems to lie deeper. It is truly an anthropological crisis. Education, particularly the liberal arts, is considered less important than remunerative disciplines, namely science, technology, engineering, and mathematics, also known as STEM. In the age of the *homo oeconomicus*, this is an example of the relationship between historiography and contemporary issues.

As will be shown in this book, however, it is precisely in times of social, political, and anthropological crisis that pedagogical paradigms start changing in an attempt to find new solutions for new problems. Social forces in the forms belonging to each historical age set out to redefine the identity and collective priorities of their time. This is exactly the story this book will tell. The cultural

---

1 In particular: Robert Black, *Humanism and Education in Medieval and Renaissance Italy. Tradition and Innovation in Latin Schools from the Twelfth to the Fifteenth Century* (Cambridge: Cambridge University Press, 2001); Paul Grendler, *Schooling in Renaissance Italy. Literacy and Learning 1300–1600* (Baltimore & London: The Johns Hopkins University Press, 1989).

crisis faced by sixteenth century Europe had few precedents in western history. In addition to the trauma represented by the rupture of Christian unity, a slow but profound change in cultural and scientific paradigms took place. The main changes concerned the slow and tormented overcoming of Aristotelianism and the new awareness of the shape and size of the world, thanks to the voyages undertaken by Portuguese and Spanish fleets in the fifteenth and sixteenth centuries, the gradual affirmation of heliocentric theories, and the first hints of the idea that the universe could be infinite and that the history of mankind and Earth could go beyond the Bible by hundreds of thousands, if not millions or billions of years.[2] These are but a few of the features of this epoch-making historical turning point. Within this context, and still dominated by an essentially religious concept of human beings, the Catholic Church, the strongest and broadest existing institutional structure, tried to respond to these problems through its most dynamic and organized components: its religious orders. As Mark Greengrass points out, "nothing was more challenging to both Catholic and Protestant Churches than the humanist notion that education can create pious and responsible citizens and change the world."[3] Both Protestants and Catholics wanted to make such a notion theirs. Like every historical crisis, the one that took place in the sixteenth century called into question both the religious and the civic identities of the people of that time.

In this sense, religious orders played an important role in redefining Catholic identity through the education they provided, superseding the earlier phase during which schools were run by secular authorities represented by municipal assemblies and princes (Chapter 1). The school system gradually created by religious orders merged pre-existing lay humanistic elements with new religious pedagogical paradigms that allowed space for new scientific discoveries, although this did not always happen without trauma (Chapter 2). These distinctions, however, are a simple heuristic model. From an institutional point of view, the new schools went through various hybrid forms and were mostly represented by cooperation between religious and secular teachers supported by lay authorities.

---

2   On the overcoming of Aristotelianism, refer to Charles B Schmitt, "Towards a Reassessment of Renaissance Aristotelianism," *History of Science*, 11, 3 (1973): 159–93. On the rupture of Christian unity, refer to: Mark Greengrass, *Christendom Destroyed. Europe: 1517–1648* (London: Penguin Books, 2014). On the affirmation of the concepts of deep history and the infinity of the universe, see Daniel Lord Smail, *Deep History and the Brain* (Oakland: University of California Press, 2008).
3   Greengrass, *Christendom Destroyed*, 481.

INTRODUCTION

At this point, we can try to offer an answer to the second question posed at the opening of this introduction: Why focus on the Italian Peninsula alone? For most of these religious orders, namely Barnabites, Somascans, Ursulines, and Piarists, Italy was the first country in which their educational projects were developed and their schools multiplied. During the sixteenth and seventeenth centuries, Italy was still the beating heart and driving force behind the continent's cultural and scientific progress (Chapter 4).[4] It was during these centuries that Europe experienced the 'Renaissance' and foreign monarchs visited the Peninsula. It is true that in some cases new, fresh forces arrived from other geographic contexts; Ignatius of Loyola and Joseph Calasanz, for instance, came from the Iberian Peninsula and passed through other countries such as France, but the ground on which they grafted their 'reforms' was Italy. It is also true, as Peter Burke pointed out,[5] that during the long European Renaissance the relational networks between individuals in every field of knowledge and spirituality were not necessarily 'Ital-o-centric,' but the fact remains that Rome housed the capital of Catholicism and every initiative within the universal Church had to pass through the Eternal City. In this sense, focusing on Rome and Italy during the Renaissance and Reformation overlaps with a global historical perspective.

It is equally true that discussing Italy before it became a political unity in 1861 leads to slippery ground. Neither the political nor cultural unity of the Peninsula was close to being achieved during the period considered here. Until the turning point represented by the gradual change in the pedagogical paradigms brought about by the religious orders, which slowly managed to bring a patina of uniformity to the institutional forms of education throughout the Italian area, every regional state, city and small town had autonomous and differentiated educational policies. Religious congregations had to struggle to fit into a diverse and extremely heterogeneous panorama of local political, economic, cultural, social, and geographical realities (Chapters 1 and 4). This process took place slowly and gradually; however, despite a long series of difficulties and setbacks that marked the course of the three centuries examined in this book, it could still be said that they succeeded.

---

4   Copernicus had studied in Italy at the University of Bologna from 1496 to 1501 under the professor of mathematics Domenico Maria Novara, and at the University of Padua, from 1501 to 1503. See André Goddu, *Copernicus and the Aristotelian Tradition* (Leiden: Brill, 2010); Richard Orson, *Science and Religion, 1450–1900: from Copernicus to Darwin* (Westport: Greenwood Press, 2004).
5   Peter Burke, *The European Renaissance. Centres and Peripheries* (Oxford: Basil Blackwell, 1998).

Nonetheless, the Italian diversity that existed during the pre-unification centuries and the historical processes that the Peninsula went through during that period, are to be counted among the reasons that makes this cultural and political area worth of attention.[6] Italy, between the fifteenth and eighteenth centuries, is probably one of the most interesting social and political European areas to observe. Some events, such as the loss of autonomy of the Duchy of Milan and the 1559 affirmation of Spanish hegemony over the entire Peninsula following the peace of Cateau Cambrésis, marked the sixteenth century in a decisive way. The Spanish governorate over Milan was joined by the viceroyalty of Naples, Sicily, and Sardinia; however, the remaining independent states did not decline in the manner in which a certain historiography emphasizes. The republics of Genoa and Venice and the Grand Duchy of Tuscany were still vital, as evidenced by the investments they made in the Iberian maritime expansion by arming ships and trading spices. Even the process of state centralization, begun in the fourteenth century, continued, as demonstrated by the State of the Church and its expansion into the Romagna region, to the detriment of Ferrara and the former territories of the Duchy of Milan.

The economic crisis of the seventeenth century should also be partially rethought. On closer observation, we can remark that only some areas of the Italian territory suffered from economic stagnation, while others grew and remained vital. The countryside of the northern plains was structurally reclaimed, allowing unprecedented agricultural and democratic development. Even from a political point of view there was no lack of vitality. The popular uprisings in southern Italy, such as that of Masaniello in 1647, were not simple riots; rather, they were a reflection of the social and cultural transformations of a proto proletariat demanding a political voice.[7] As we will see in this book, scientific and technological innovations were not extraneous to these transformations. Some of the most important exponents of Italian science, often members of religious teaching orders, were engaged in the development of hydraulic technologies for agricultural and economic development.

In the eighteenth century, the states on the Italian political chessboard had not changed much from those of the sixteenth century except for some shifts here and there in the dominant foreign power. Austria had replaced Spain as the hegemonic power. In addition, some states such as Venice and other small

---

6 On the vast topic of pre-unitarian Italian States, refer to Gaetano Greco and Mario Rosa, eds., *Storia degli antichi stati italiani* (Rome-Bari: Laterza, 2020.³)

7 On the birth of the proletariat in early modern Europe and America, see Peter Linebaugh and Markus Rediker, *The Many-Headed Hydra: Sailors, Slaves, Commoners, and The Hidden History of the Revolutionary Atlantic* (Boston: Beacon Press, 2000), 112–16.

dynastic lordships such as the Duchy of Mantua, were heading towards extinction. They were nothing but living fossils in a world launched into modernity. Other states acquired a more proactive role, such as the recently promoted Kingdom of Sardinia, which, in the nineteenth century, would lead to Italian unity. Overall, the northern part of the Peninsula was slowly moving towards an enlightened rationalization of state administration and economic resources, while southern Italy was still rather tied to backward forms of exploitation of resources. However, the best approach remains the analysis of individual micro-areas, the conditions of which were able to change significantly even at small distances.

The social changes that affected Italy during those centuries can help us to better understand the processes of the diffusion of the schools of religious orders which are the subject of this book. The closure of the aristocratic classes and the strong social stratification of this period suggest that we look at the birth of colleges for nobles. Connected with this phenomenon was the increasingly widespread diffusion, at least in northern Italy, of an artisan class requiring a precise technical-mathematical education.

For this reason, a study of the education provided by religious orders active in Italy between the sixteenth and eighteenth centuries must consider the political, economic and cultural framework of every town, village, rural region and regional state, along with their peculiarities and characteristics (Chapter 3). By connecting the puzzle pieces, we can create an overview from which it becomes possible to identify a common element. Italy had not yet achieved political unity in the way that it had been achieved (at least superficially) by kingdoms such as France, England or Castile, nor was it culturally united, as Germany had been by the Protestant Reformation. Only by recognizing the extreme internal Italian diversity can we grasp its lines of strength and unifying aspects.

Due to this book's limited space, it was not possible to consider every city and settlement in the Italian Peninsula where schools of religious orders were established. I have therefore taken into consideration some examples of the contexts in which religious orders settled with their schools. I use the term 'contexts' advisedly, rather than referring simply to cities or villages. Among the frames analyzed, I chose sub-regional areas, in particular Lombardy and the Po Valley area, the nerve center of the birth and diffusion of teaching orders such as the Barnabites and Somascans (Chapter 3) and regional states, in particular the Duchy of Modena, a limited political area in which it is possible to observe the competition on the educational market between orders such as the Piarists and Jesuits (Chapter 4). Some cities, of course, have also been considered, such as Udine, Reggio Emilia, Ferrara, Venice, Mantua and Milan, as well as several smaller centers throughout the Italian peninsular territory (Chapters 3 and 4). The most important cities were not always chosen, but rather those that were considered to be representative of the dynamics of the spreading of religious orders in each context.

At the end of the book, after analyzing the forms and times of settlement of each religious order, both male and female, we will have examined how the end of the *ancien régime* and the advent of the French Revolution brought about by Napoleon's troops in 1796 marked the end of this educational season. In particular, the attention will be focused on the different events experienced by each religious teaching order in this historical context, showing how the suppression or reduction of each group followed different patterns, without reference to a generalizing narrative (Chapter 5). On the other hand, the crisis represented by the Revolution, the collapse of the divine legitimacy of the European monarchs, and the rise of a new economic culture and an industrial civilization represented a crisis of values comparable to that of the sixteenth century. This new challenge triggered a new educational response, the birth within the Catholic world of new pedagogical projects, which has characterized the world to the present day.

1 State of Research and Historiographical Problems

The research on religious congregations devoted to education in Italy during the Renaissance and the Reformation has made considerable progress in recent years.[8] Historiography on this subject had long been dominated by scholars belonging to the congregations, who sometimes indulged in a celebrative tone. In this regard it is necessary to specify an important fact. The celebratory tone to which we are referring was typical of the nineteenth-century historiographic climate, particularly in the field of municipal history. Important local historical narratives have been produced since the end of the eighteenth century, even by important scholars. Let us consider Ireneo Affò, who wrote a monumental history of the city of Parma (*Storia della città di Parma*), and Girolamo Tiraboschi, who wrote the history of the men of letters of the Duchy of Modena, the *Biblioteca Modenese*. Despite their great methodological rigor, the celebratory tone with respect to the ducal authority of which these scholars were subjects is a structural part of these works; the two things

---

8   Maurizio Sangalli, "Le congregazioni religiose insegnanti in Italia in età moderna: nuove acquisizioni e piste di ricerca," *Dimensioni e problemi della ricerca storica*, 1 (2005): 25–47.

INTRODUCTION 7

are not divisible. Even local historians belonging to cities or villages produced important historical narratives of their towns, emphasizing their importance over the centuries.[9] The celebratory tone, however, takes nothing away from the documentary precision used by the authors. This indeed was the cultural climate in which the historians belonging to the religious orders also worked. This should not be forgotten. The religious order was for them the same as the towns or villages celebrated in municipal histories; documentary rigor is therefore assured. In more recent decades, however, historian members of religious orders have begun to increasingly align with academic and scientific research criteria. In particular, since the publication of William Bangert's *History of the Society of Jesus* in 1972, a fundamental step has been made in research on Jesuit schools and *Ratio Studiorum*, introducing a new standard in the study of the educational sphere in the Early Modern Catholic world.[10] The renewal introduced in the studies on Jesuit education has been accomplished by both lay researchers and members of the Society, leading to the creation of an utterly new disciplinary sector.

The names Paul Grendler, Thomas McCoog, John O'Malley, Claude Pavur, Sabina Pavone, Cristiano Casalini, and Maurizio Sangalli are found amongst the most important authors, but the list could be much longer.[11] Their works

---

9 On this topic, refer to Gian Maria Varanini, ed., *Storiografia e identità dei centri minori italiani tra la fine del Medioevo e l'Ottocento* (San Miniato: Firenze University Press 2013), 3–28.

10 William Bangert, *A History of the Society of Jesus* (Saint Louis: The Institute of Jesuit Sources, 1972). Other important but dated works on the history of Society are Pietro Tacchi Venturi, *Storia della Compagnia di Gesù in Italia*, 2 vols. in 4 parts (Rome: Civiltà Cattolica, 1910–'51), and Mario Scaduto, *L'epoca di Giacomo Lainez 1556–1565: Il governo* (Rome: La Civiltà Cattolica, 1964); *L'epoca di Giacomo Lainez, 1556–1565: L'azione* (Rome: La Civiltà Cattolica, 1974); and *L'opera di Francesco Borgia, 1565–1572* (Rome: La Civiltà Cattolica, 1992). For sources, refer to *Monumenta paedagogica Societatis Iesu, nova editio ex integro refecta*, ed. László Lukács, 7 vols. (Rome: Apud "Monumenta Historica Soc. Iesu," 1965–1992). For most recent bibliography on the Jesuit educational history see note 3, Chapter 2 of this book.

11 A list of the work of these scholars would be too long. I therefore refer to the most recent ones: Paul Grendler, *The Jesuits and Italian Universities 1548–1773* (Washington: The Catholic University of America Press, 2017) and Id., *The University of Mantua, the Gonzaga and the Jesuits, 1584–1630* (Baltimore: The Johns Hopkins University Press, 2009); Thomas McCoog, *A Guide to Jesuit Archives* (Saint Louis-Rome: The Institute of Jesuit Sources-Institutum Historicum Societatis Jesu, 1998); John O'Malley, *The First Jesuits* (Cambridge: Harvard University Press, 1993); Claude Pavur, *The Ratio Studiorum: The Official Plan for Jesuit Education* (Boston: Institute for Advanced Jesuit Studies, 2005); Maurizio Sangalli, *Cultura, politica e religione nella Repubblica di Venezia tra Cinque e Seicento. Gesuiti e Somaschi a Venezia* (Venezia: Istituto veneto di scienze morali, lettere ed arti, 1999) and Id., *Università, accademie, gesuiti. Cultura e religione a Padova tra Cinque*

led to renewed interest in the earlier research involving other religious congregations, now endowed with new critical tools thanks to recent historiography, especially regarding the Jesuits. To these developments we must add those that have taken place in Italy since the 1970s in regard to local powers and economies in the periods between the Middle Ages, the Renaissance, and the Reformation. Of particular interest were the processes of early modern regional state building and the proto-centralization of their governments.[12] These developments were made possible by the use of innovative research approaches on Catholic education mingled with social, political, and economic history but also with educational history, encouraging a more impartial evaluation of pedagogical experiences. Within this renewed interest, many publications on the history of Catholic education, especially Jesuit education, have seen the light over the past few years. Every related issue has been touched upon, such as global and women's education and Jesuits relations with other pedagogical traditions.[13] Maurizio Sangalli, in an important article written in 2005, underlines that comparative research on the educational activity of religious orders in early modern Italy is still to be completed.[14]

A comparative approach to the history of teaching congregations, nonetheless, still needs the previously mentioned scholarly research produced within the religious orders themselves. Particularly important are those books written between the last phase of the historical period considered here, the seventeenth and eighteenth centuries and the first decades of the twentieth century. The usefulness of these works lies in the portrait they offer of the current state of religious teaching orders in the time determined in this book to be the point of a centuries-old evolution. Among these books, which serve simultaneously

---

e Seicento (Padova: LINT, 2001); Sabina Pavone, *I gesuiti dalle origini alla soppressione* (Rome-Bari: Laterza, 2004).

[12] On that historiographical season, see Giorgio Chittolini, *La formazione dello stato regionale e le istituzioni del contado. Secoli XIV e XV* (Torino: Einaudi, 1979).

[13] To cite a few: John Brereton and Cinthia Gannet, eds., *Traditions of Eloquence: The Jesuits and Modern Rhetorical Studies* (New York: Fordham University Press, 2016); Sean Whittle, *A Theory of Catholic Education* (London: Bloomsbury, 2015); Elizabeth Petrino and Jocelyn Boryczka, eds., *Jesuit and Feminist Education: Intersections in Teaching and Learning for the Twenty-First Century* (New York: Fordham University Press, 2012); Edmund Cueva, Shannon Byrne, Frederick Joseph Benda, *Jesuit Education and the Classics* (Newcastle upon Tyne: Cambridge Scholars, 2009); Ernesto Diaz, *Jesuit Education and Mathematics: Review of Literature on the History of Jesuit Education and Mathematics* (Saarbrücken: VDM Dr. Müller, 2009); Martin Scroope, *Mission Formation Education: A Framework for Formation of Persons and Communities in Ignatian Education* (Pimble: Loyola Institute, 2006).

[14] Sangalli, "Le congregazioni religiose insegnanti in Italia," 25.

as both primary and secondary sources, we find mainly histories and descriptions of the congregation to which the author belonged.[15]

Other essential bibliographic tools of use in the examination of the history of early modern religious orders committed to education are the periodicals and journals of historical studies of these congregations. In the writing of this book, *Regnum Dei* (Theatines), *Barnabiti Studi* (Barnabites), *Somascha. Bollettino di Storia dei Padri Somaschi* (Somascans), and *Archivum Scholarum Piarum* (Piarists) were referred to. Although it can be said that the golden age of these periodicals was during the central decades of the twentieth century, these journals have continued to today, contributing significantly to the advancement of studies on the history of religious orders. Articles on their pedagogical history can be used in various ways. On the one hand they reconstruct a series of case studies, very often represented by the history of the orders in specific Italian cities and villages. Another recurrent subject is the historical evolution of the statutes that regulated the lives of the congregations.[16] Other

---

15   To cite a few examples in chronological order: *I barnabiti nel IV centenario dalla fondazione 1533–1933* (Genova: Tipografia Artigianelli, 1933); Luigi Zambarelli, *L'Ordine dei Chierici regolari Somaschi nel IV centenario della fondazione 1528–1928* (Rome: Tipografia Madre di Dio, 1928). For the Barnabites, we must also remember the three histories of Orazio Maria Premoli: *Storia dei barnabiti dal 1700 al 1825* (Rome: Società tipografica Aldo Manuzio, 1925); *Storia dei barnabiti nel Seicento* (Rome: Industria tipografica romana, 1922); *Storia dei barnabiti nel Cinquecento* (Rome: Desclee editore, 1913). See also: Giambattista Castiglione, *Istoria delle scuole della Dottrina Cristiana fondate in Milano e da Milano e nell'Italia altrove propagate* (Milan: Stamperia Malatesta, 1800); *Dizionario storico portatile degli ordini religiosi e militari e delle congregazioni regolari e secolari che contiene la loro origine, i loro progressi, la loro decadenza e le relative loro riforme* (Torino: Presso Francesco Prato, 1792); Luigi Barelli, *Memorie dell'origine, fondazione, avanzamenti, successi ed uomini illustri in lettere e santità della congregazione de' Chierici Regolari di S. Paolo*, Vol. II. (Bologna: Per Costantino Pisarri, 1707); *Chronologia Historico-Legalis Seraphici Ordinis Minorum Sancti Patris Francisci*, II Voll (Neapoli: ex Typographia Camilli Cavalli, 1650); Giambattista Del Tufo, *Historia della Religione de' Padri Chierici Regolari* (Rome: Presso Girolamo Facciotto e Stefano Paolini, 1609).

16   The list can be very long, but it's worth giving some examples. I refer to periodicals on the history of each religious order in alphabetical order: 1) Piarists: Joan Florensa, "La reforma de la sociedad depende de la diligente educación de los niños: el proyecto de Pere Gervàs de les Eres (1580)," *Archivum Scholarum Piarum* 83, XLII (2018): 139–202; Antonio Mursia, "'Per insegnare naturali le scienze.' A proposito delle Scuole Pie dei padri Scolopi ad Adrano." *Archivum Scholarum Piarum* 79, (2016): 109–17; "Numero delle provincie, luoghi e padri, dei Poveri della Madre di Dio delle Scuole Pie, raccolto con l'occasione del capitolo generale celebrato in Roma a 15 d'ottobre 1637," *Archivum Scholarum Piarum*, XIII, (1954): 31–79; Dario Pasero, "Per la storia delle Scuole Pie in Dalmazia. Documenti (1776–1854)." *Archivum Scholarum Piarum* XVIII, 36 (1994): 1–127; Osvaldo Tosti, "Ancora sulle Scuole Pie in Dalmazia." *Archivum Scholarum Piarum* XX, 31 (1996): 121–92. 2) Barnabites: Angelo Bianchi, "Le suole Arcimboldi a Milano nel XVII secolo: professori,

types of articles concern the biography of prominent personalities of the congregations. These articles are also important because they provide information on the educational and intellectual path of individual members. Another feature to remember when using this research is that it shows an erudite approach while maintaining a great documentary rigor, in addition to their use as references to local archives. In this way, these publications perform the essential function of documentary mediation. They also provide documental references to archives which otherwise would be difficult to spot and sometimes report sources that are now lost or destroyed.

Another central feature of historiography related to teaching congregations in Tridentine Italy is how their identity was shaped. Maurizio Sangalli pointed out that this process of identity building is still problematic and especially important. The identity of each group of regular clerics could be influenced by internal elements, such as the different orientations and charisms existing within each congregation. Even external factors could reveal important, such

---

studenti, cultura scolastica," *Barnabiti Studi* 19, (2002): 55–78; Filippo Lovison, "Le scuole dei barnabiti a Udine (1679–1810)," *Barnabiti Studi* 15 (1998): 91–211; Id., "Le scuole dei barnabiti. Pietà e scienza nell'età dei lumi," *Barnabiti Studi* 26 (2009): 111–57; Sergio Pagano, "Le biblioteche dei barnabiti italiani nel 1599. In margine ai loro più antichi cataloghi," *Barnabiti studi* 3, (1986): 26–39. 3) Theatines: Julian Adrover, "I Teatini in Monaco di Baviera," *Regnum Dei* 9, (1953): 3–18; Francesco Andreu, "I Teatini e l'Oratorio del Divino Amore a Venezia," *Regnum Dei* 99, (1973): 53–76; Id., "La regola dei Chierici Regolari nella lettera di Bonifacio de' Colli a Gian Matteo Giberti," *Regnum Dei* 2, (1946): 38–53; Donato De Capua, "I Teatini a Bitonto," *Regnum Dei* 25, (1969): 3–143; Pietro De Leturia, "Il papa Paolo IV e la fondazione del Collegio Romano," *Regnum Dei* 10 (1954): 3–16; Ferrari, S., Frecassetti E., Galli O., Gilardi R. "La chiesa e la casa teatina di Sant'Agata in Bergamo alta," *Regnum Dei* 46, (1990): 81–106; Cleto Linari, "Contributo dell'Ordine Teatino al Concilio di Trento," *Regnum Dei* 4, (1948): 203–29; Costanza Longo-Timossi, "I teatini e la riforma cattolica nella Repubblica di Genova nella prima metà del seicento." *Regnum Dei* 43, (1987): 3–104; Maulucci, Vincenzo. "I teatini a Barletta." *Regnum Dei* 49, (1993): 3–58; Maulucci, Vincenzo. "I teatini a Foggia," *Regnum Dei* 51, (1995): 57–172; Gian Ludovico Masetti-Zannini, "I teatini in Rimini," Regnum Dei 21, (1965): 87–47; Franco Molinari, "I teatini a Piacenza," *Regnum Dei* 35, (1979): 171–204; Paola Oleari, "L'interesse per la geografia tra i secoli XVI e XVII alla biblioteca dei teatini di Sant'Agata in Bergamo alta," *Regnum Dei* 50, (1994): 297–24; Michele Paone, "I teatini in Lecce." *Regnum Dei* 21, (1965): 148–72; Vincenzo Porta, "I teatini a Vicenza," *Regnum Dei* 16, (1960): 85–143; Jaime Prohens, "Los teatinos en Mallorca," *Regnum Dei* 4, (1948): 121–71; Litterio Villari, "I Padri teatini nella città di Piazza Armerina," *Regnum Dei* 40, (1984): 91–46. 4) Somascans: Giovanni Alcaini, "Origini e progressi degli istituti diretti dai Padri Somaschi," *Somascha. Bollettino di Storia dei Padri Somaschi* 4, (1979): 70–175; Stefano Casati, "I preti riformati di Santa Maria Piccola e i Somaschi," *Somascha. Bollettino di storia dei padri somaschi*, XI, (1986): 55–72; Attilio Gabrielli, "I padri somaschi a Velletri," *Somascha. Bolletino di storia dei padri somaschi*, III, 2 (1917): 3–27.

as the perceptions that contemporary urban or rural societies had of these groups of religious. Other important elements in defining the identities of regular clerics were the economic and political reasons for which they were called to a city or a state, after which the clerics were expected to adapt and cope. In addition, we shall not forget the interactions, meetings and clashes with the other direct competitors in the educational market, as in the case of the Jesuits and Piarists within the Duchy of Modena (Chapter 4).[17] Another feature connected to the progressive definition of religious orders' identities in Modena is the evolution of their educational aims. Sangalli highlights how these purposes changed over time; for example, it became clear that the Piarists of Modena, over the course of a few decades, soon targeted the education of the local nobility and notables as a response to the competition with the Jesuits, despite Calasanz having initially identified poor children as their primary educational target. Just like today, in fact, it was market demand that guided the response (Chapter 4). These aspects also contributed to the restoration of a non-monolithic and non-uniform image of religious teaching orders' lives. Their acting and interacting, their movements throughout the territory and consequently their physiognomy were influenced by many aspects, which I will bring to light.

Another important element I will address is the role of the female teaching orders (Chapter 2). While it is true that the male teaching congregations have not yet received all the attention they deserve, female orders have received even less. The most famous example is perhaps Angela Merici (1474–1540), a native of Desenzano del Garda in the Lombardy region, who, in 1535, after becoming a Franciscan tertiary, informally founded the first female teaching order, the Company of Saint Ursula, bringing together twenty-eight virgins in Brescia under the protection of the homonymous sainted woman, patroness of medieval universities.[18] As we shall see, the Ursulines were not the only

---

17 Sangalli, "Le congregazioni religiose insegnanti in Italia." 35–47. See also: Bert Roest and Johanneke Uphoff, ed., *Religious Orders and Religious Identity Formation, ca. 1420–1620* (Leiden-Boston: Brill, 2016).

18 On Angela Merici's Ursulines see Querciolo Mazzonis, "The Impact of Renaissance Gender-Related Notions on the Female Experience of the Sacred: The Case of Angela Merici's Ursulines," in *Gender, Catholicism and Spirituality: Women and the Roman Catholic Church in Britain and Europe, 1200–1900*, ed. Laurence Lux-Sterrit and Carmen Mangion (London: MacMillan, 2010), 51–67; Silvia Evangelisti, *Nuns: A History of Convent Life* (Oxford: Oxford University Press, 2007), 105; Id., "A Female Idea of Religious Perfection: Angela Merici and the Company of St. Ursula (1535–1540)," *Renaissance Studies*, 18 (2004), 391–411; Danielle Culpepper, " 'Our Particular Cloister': Ursulines and Female Education in Seventeenth Century Parma and Piacenza," *Sixteenth Century Journal*, 4 (2005): 1017–37; Charmarie J. Blaisdell, "Angela Merici and the Ursulines," in *Religious*

female teaching order. In 1685 in the city of Viterbo, for example, the nun Rosa Venerini (1656–1728) established a society of common (or apostolic) life without vows dedicated to the education of poor girls, a task formalized in 1692 by Cardinal Marcantonio Barbarigo. The Pious Venerini Schools soon spread throughout the Italian Peninsula, particularly in the center. From this congregation another female educational institute was created. Cardinal Barbarigo, in fact, did not want the pious Venerini teachers to spread outside his diocese, and so it was that a disciple of Rosa Venerini, Lucia Filippini (1672–1732), opened an autonomous school in Rome in 1707, giving rise to an independent branch of the Venerini Schools.[19]

Another example of an educational institution being opened by women for women chronologically precedes the above examples, and is worth citing here before delving into the book. In 1530, Ludovica Torelli, Countess of Guastalla, founded the *Angeliche* sisters in Milan, a non-cloistered female religious order. In 1539, she sold her fief to the Mantuan nobleman Ferrante Gonzaga in order to devote herself totally to her nuns, who were very closely linked to the Barnabites. Their common spiritual father was the Dominican friar Battista Carioni, former spiritual director of Gaetano da Thiene, the founder of the Theatines and confessor of Saint Anthony Maria Zaccaria, founder of the Barnabites. However, with the imposition of the cloistered life decided by the Council of Trent in 1565, the *Angeliche* had to reinvent themselves, and so it was that in 1557 they opened one of the first boarding schools for girls in Italy, the *Collegio della Guastalla*, in Milan.[20] This example remains among the most

---

Orders of the Catholic Reformation, ed. Richard L. DeMolen (New York: Fordham University Press, 1994), 98–136; Gabriella Zarri, "Ursula and Catherine: The Marriage of Virgins in the Sixteenth Century," in *Creative Women in Medieval and Early Modern Italy: A Religious and Artistic Renaissance*, ed. Ann J. Matter and John Coackley (Philadelphia: University of Pennsylvania Press, 1994), 237–78; Grendler, *Schooling in Renaissance Italy*, 392; Thérèse Ledochowska, *Angèle Merici et la Compagnie de Ste. Ursule* (Rome-Milan, Ancora, 1967).

19 On Rosa Venerini and Lucia Filippini, refer to: Nicola D'Amico, *Un libro per Eva. Il difficile cammino dell'istruzione della donna in Italia: la storia, le protagoniste* (Milan: FrancoAngeli, 2016) and Grendler, *ivi*, 392. See also: Maria Mascilongo, *Ho creduto nell'amore. Itinerario spirituale di Rosa Venerini* (Rome: Città Nuova, 2006).

20 On Ludovica Torelli and her religious and educational experience, see Renée Baernstein, *A Convent Tale: A century of Sisterhood in Spanish Milan* (New York: Routledge, 2002); Paul Grendler, "Man is Almost a God: Fra Battista Carioni Between Renaissance and Catholic Reformation," in *Humanity and Divinity in Renaissance and Reformation: Essays in Honor of Charles Trinkaus*, ed. John W. O'Malley, Thomas M. Izbicki and Gerald Christianson (Leiden-New York-Cologne: Brill, 1993). 227–49; Id., *Schooling*, 393. See also: Elena Bonora, *I conflitti della Controriforma. Santità e obbedienza nell'esperienza dei primi barnabiti* (Florence: Le Lettere, 1998).

significant; indeed, the identity and nature of the female orders show how certain elements played decisive roles, such as the mythical figure of the founder, their relationship with cities and towns, and their links with other religious orders, both female and male.

In this book, the main religious orders, both male and female, will be considered. They will include the male Barnabites, Somascans, Theatines and Piarists, and the female Ursulines, Pious Teachers Venerini, the Pious Schools of LuciaFilippini , and the *Collegio della Guastalla* established by Ludovica Torelli. The evolution of the general educational guidelines of the orders will be followed, using the statutes and the deliberations of the chapters of each order as primary sources. For single case studies, archival sources of various types have been used, from notarial deeds to the accounts of the convents, from municipal deliberations to didactic sources. However, in the overall panorama of religious education in Italy during the Renaissance and the Reformation, catechism schools and the role played by secular priests who never ceased to perform a specific pedagogical function will also be considered.

The Society of Jesus will remain an essential benchmark in the background of this research; in fact, the Jesuits represent an inevitable point of reference for most of the religious teaching orders that only, with the passing of time, came to the full awareness of their commitment to education. This is valid not only for the religious who, between the sixteenth and seventeenth centuries, arose in the wake of the renewal represented by the Catholic reformation, it is also valid today. This is because, from a historiographical point of view, interpretative tools developed for the study of Jesuits are especially useful for deepening historians' understanding of other educational congregations.

CHAPTER 1

Educating the Modern Catholics?
Roots of Catholic Schools in Renaissance Italy (15th–16th cc.)

1 **The Last Phase of Communal Education in Italy**

In 1552 the Society of Jesus entered without fuss into Modena. A rich town in northern Italy located in the eastern part of the great floodplain of the Po River, Modena was situated on the crossroads of important arteries of communication and commerce between Italy and northern Europe. The group of fathers who settled there was led by the Spaniard Francisco Scipion, who had previously studied in Salamanca and Paris. Scipion managed to obtain the establishment of a new convent by the church of San Bartolomeo, to which a small school was annexed.[1] The first decades of this school, however, were not easy ones. Despite the emerging economic crisis caused by the Italian Wars between Habsburg and Valois, the municipal institutions of Modena considered the presence of a free school harmful because it threatened to rob the city of a source of prestige, along with one of the few prerogatives of self-government left by the ducal authority, namely education.[2] The Jesuit school caused discontent even amid some groups of students. First, the gratuity of the new school's education increased the rigor and independence of the institution. This gave rise to acts of vandalism and damage: "We also had many persecutions of the *putti* and young people, damage to the doors and to the windows of the college, cutting the ropes and tearing the chains of the bell."[3]

---

1 At that time the city of Modena was part of the Venetian Jesuit province. See Gian Paolo Brizzi, "Scuole e collegi nell'antica Provincia Veneta della Compagnia di Gesù (1542–1773)," in *I Gesuiti e Venezia. Momenti e problemi di storia veneziana della Compagnia di Gesù*, ed. Mario Zanardi (Padova: Gregoriana Libreria Editrice, 1994), 474.
2 Signs of difficulty in the management of schools in Modena, for example, emerged as early as 1538, when the municipality lowered the salaries of public masters by increasing the fees to be paid by the families of school children, and in 1544, when the closure of some schools caused the revolt in city of groups of students. The documents relating to these facts can be consulted at the Municipal Historical Archives of Modena in the public education fund, envelopes 23 December 1538, 20 June 1544.
3 Original quote: "Habbiamo adonche havuto molte persecutioni de' putti et gioveni insino a romperci le porte et fenestre del collegio, tagliar la fune e straciare le catene della campanella." Brizzi, "Scuole e collegi," 477.

Another effect of the religious education on pupil behavior was to render them a recognizable group that aroused the aversion of their peers. The pupils of the small college annexed to the church of San Bartolomeo were publicly mocked in 1555, sarcastically nicknamed the 'saints' by other boys. Circumstances such as these were not new to the Jesuits, who struggled to enter other Italian towns. It was for these reasons that the Jesuit school of Modena was closed a few years later.[4]

In the following decades, however, the attitude of the municipal authorities towards the Jesuits, and especially their schools, suddenly changed. In a 1581 deliberation of the city council, we find that

> for a while now, public instruction has lapsed mainly due to the lack of preceptors who teach grammar and the other necessary principles. Wishing for the best interests of our children, on the example of some famous cities, we would like to introduce a school with three orders or three classes for three Reverend Fathers of Jesus.[5]

In 1591, in a further act of collaboration by the city authorities, the seats of the convent and the Jesuit school were moved from the small church of San Bartolomeo (later beautifully rebuilt by the Jesuits in 1607) to the larger and more suitable church of the Annunciation. Later, in the eighteenth century, the erudite Jesuit Girolamo Tiraboschi reported in his *Biblioteca Modenese* that in 1591 the

> priests of Jesus began to hold school in Modena in their convent, and made two classes, one of grammar, the other of rhetoric, where many pupils participated, both because the school was free, and for the beautiful and useful order that was held.[6]

---

4 Paul Grendler, *The Jesuits and Italian Universities 1548–1773* (Washington: The Catholic University of America Press, 2017), 115–53.
5 Original quote: "per difetto di precettori che insegnano grammatica e li altri principi necessari, desiderando per interesse dei propri figli, ad esempio di alcune famose città, si vorrebbe introdurre una scola con tre ordini o per tre classi di tre R. Padri del Gesù," Archivio Storico Municipale di Modena, Fondo educazione pubblica, *Ex Actis*, 1581.
6 Original quote: "I preti del Gesù cominzarono a tenere scola in Modena nel suo monastero e fecero due scole, una di gramatica, l'altra di rettorica, ove molti scolari concorsero, sì perché non si pagava la scola, sì anche per il bello e utile ordine, che si teneva," Girolamo Tiraboschi, *Biblioteca Modenese*, Vol. 1 (Modena: Società Tipografica, 1781), 62.

What happened, then, between 1555 and 1581 to change the attitude of the public authorities towards the Jesuit college to such a degree? The answer is complex, so it is necessary to proceed in order. Let us look carefully at two sources in order to get some useful insights. The first source, Modena's 1581 deliberation, shows us that the city council followed the example of other Italian cities, suggesting that Modena was part of a large-scale transformation movement. The second source, Tiraboschi's quotation referring to 1591, provides us with some insights into the nature of the ongoing transformation. On the one hand, we note the gratuitousness of the new scholastic model that was being established; it no longer represented a threat to the prestige of the city, which wished to maintain control over the activities of the schools. Another important aspect of the source concerns what Tiraboschi defines as "the beautiful and useful order that was held there." Beyond the obvious Foucaultian suggestions, quite easy to spot in the thought of the eighteenth-century Enlightenment figure of Tiraboschi, a general process of reorganization and rationalization of the school structures was taking place in the second half of the sixteenth century. It reflected the profound and pervasive changes in the society, politics, economy, and religious sphere of that time.

The example presented here concerns a Jesuit college in a deeply studied city. As mentioned in the introduction, the comparison with the Jesuits is an important element for understanding both the paths to education of other religious orders that arose in the atmosphere of the Catholic Reformation and the educational renewals within the existing medieval congregations. The example of Modena, therefore, is paradigmatic of a series of transformations underway in Italy during the transitions between the late Middle Ages, the Renaissance, and the Reformation.[7] As will be shown, these changes were due to a series of tensions that originated between the end of the fifteenth and the beginning of the sixteenth century. Among these tensions we can spot the breaking up of Christian unity in Europe caused by the Protestant Reformation but also the loss of autonomy and self-government of Italian cities. Another factor was the protest led by the urban humanist school teachers deprived of their pedagogical function for the ruling classes. These schoolmasters sometimes embraced the new Protestant doctrines in order to give expression to their political and social demands. In short, before examining the religious dimension related to the affirmation of the collegiate model brought by religious orders, we must

---

7 Fabrizio Ravaglioli, "L'educazione umanistica nel passaggio dalla città stato tardomedievale alla città-capitale," in *Vittorino da Feltre e la sua scuola: umanesimo, pedagogia, arti*, ed. Nella Giannetto, (Florence: Olschki, 1981), 95–108.

look at how the previous model of municipal schooling, established between the twelfth and thirteenth centuries, collapsed.[8]

1.1 Complexity of the Renaissance Communal School System

When we refer to the Italian Communal age, we usually think of the political tradition of self-government that characterized the cities of the Peninsula between the eleventh and fourteenth centuries; however, with the advent of the *Signorias*, which gave rise to political aggregations often reaching supra-regional size, the Italian cities did not immediately lose all the political privileges they had acquired during previous centuries.[9] Among the tasks that the cities had strenuously tried to keep under their control, sometimes succeeding and sometimes not, we find the governing of public schools, often administered and financed by the city council. In fact, the scholastic model born in Italy and in those areas of Europe in which cities had played an important political and economic role had made pre-university schools a distinctive element of medieval urban society, together with enlarged social classes that, over time, began to participate in the city's political life.[10] It must also be specified that this type of school funded by the public authority was not exclusive to city centers alone but was widespread even in rural and small-scale settlements.

During the Renaissance and the Reformation (approximately between 1400 and the beginning of 1600) this type of communally ruled school remained widespread in Italy.[11] We find this system not only in the centers that became the capital cities of larger state formations, as in 1598 in the case of Modena, but also in those towns that did not assume the role of capital, such as Reggio Emilia. This system had persisted despite the Este dukes' rule over both cities

---

[8] On the history of the school in Italy in the middle and late Middle Ages, refer to Paul Grendler, *Schooling in Renaissance Italy. Literacy and Learning 1300–1600*, (Baltimore & London: The Johns Hopkins University Press, 1989); Carla Frova, *Istruzione e educazione nel medioevo*, (Torino: Loescher, 1973).

[9] The reference goes to state formations such as the Visconti-Sforza dukedom of Milan, the Republic of Venice and the Estensi Aemilian states, as opposed to mono-city state formations such as the Gonzaga dominion over Mantua. On the topic, the most recent and complete work is represented by Andrea Gamberini and Isabella Lazzarini, eds., *The Italian Renaissance State*, (Cambridge: Cambridge University Press, 2012).

[10] Peter Denley, "Governments and schools in Late Medieval Italy," in *City and Countryside in Late Medieval and Renaissance Italy. Essays presented to Philip Jones*, ed. Trevor Dean, Chris Wickham (London: The Hambledon Press, 1990), 93–108. See also: Paolo Rosso, *La scuola nel Medioevo: secoli VI–XV*, (Rome: Carocci, 2018).

[11] In general, see Carla Frova, "La scuola nella città tardomedievale: un impegno pedagogico e organizzativo," in *Le città in Italia e in Germania nel Medioevo: cultura, istituzioni, vita religiosa*, ed. Reinhard Elze and Gina Fasoli, (Bologna: Il Mulino, 1981), 119–43.

and had centralized all forms of higher education in their capital.[12] In the archives of both cities in the middle of the sixteenth century, we find impressive amounts of correspondence between municipal councils and teachers who wanted to reach the towns to work in their public schools.[13]

However, this educational system based on communal initiative was not limited to the Estense State. Between the fifteenth and the sixteenth centuries, we find municipal schools in many towns located within the Papal States. In the pontifical legation of Romagna in 1410, the civic statutes of Faenza provided for the recruitment of a schoolteacher by the representatives of the town's neighborhoods. The same circumstance occured in Imola, Forlì, Cesena, Ravenna, and Rimini, while in the middle of the Papal State we find important public schools in average sized towns such as Macerata, Recanati, Foligno and Viterbo.[14] During the same period, Rome, a metropolis in the making of the Italian Renaissance, never lacked public teachers, known as *maestri rionali* (neighborhood masters). Overall, their numbers did not exceed fifteen, and even though they were publicly salaried, these *maestri* received small fees from their pupils to supplement their wages.[15]

---

12 For Reggio Emilia, refer to David Salomoni, "Maestri e studenti alla fine del Medioevo: il caso emiliano," in *Città, campagne e castelli. Cultura, potere e società nel Medioevo padano*, ed. Carlo Baja Guarienti, (Reggio Emilia: Antiche Porte, 2016), 101–18 and Odoardo Rombaldi, "Maestri e scuole in Reggio Emilia nel secolo XV," in *Bartolomeo Spani 1468–1539. Atti e memorie del Convegno di studio nel V centenario della nascita*, (Modena: Aedes Muratoriana, 1970), 91–125.

13 The documentation concerning the schools of Reggio Emilia is now kept in the public State Archives (Archivio di Stato), as a part of the municipal archives, envelope *Scuole (1273–1789)*. In the case of Modena, a list of 200 public school teachers working in the city between the fifteenth and the fifteenth centuries, produced for Girolamo Tiraboschi, working on the preparation of his History of Italian literature, is kept in the Estense Library (collocation: It, alfa, H.1.14).

14 On the cities of Romagna see Maurizio Tabanelli, *Una città di Romagna nel Medioevo e nel Rinascimento*, (Brescia: Magalini Editrice, 1980), 173–81, and Adamo Pasini, *Cronache scolastiche forlivesi*, (Forlì: Valbonesi, 1925). For Macerata, Recanati, Foligno and Viterbo, see respectively Luigi Colini Baldeschi, "L'insegnamento pubblico in Macerata nel '300 e nel '400," *Rivista delle biblioteche e degli archivi* 9, (1900): 19–26; Maria Rosa Borraccini Verducci, "La scuola pubblica a Recanati nel sec. XV," *Università di Macerata. Annali della facoltà di lettere e filosofia* 8, (1975): 121–62; Agostino Zanelli, "Maestri di grammatica in Foligno durante il secolo XV," *L'Umbria, rivista d'arte e letteratura* 2, 13/14 (July 1899): 102–03; Marta Materni, "Il precettore pubblico in una città italiana di provincia del Cinquecento," *Annali di Storia dell'Educazione e delle Istituzioni Scolastiche* 17, (2010): 247–64. In general, see Grendler, *Schooling* […], 138.

15 Still in the seventeenth century, the public authority had failed to bring under its full control this large number of masters. See "Communal supervision of Roman Schools," in Grendler, *Schooling* […], 83–86.

In 1420 in the northern part of the Italian Peninsula in the Duchy of Savoy, which includes the current Italian region of Piedmont, we find a schoolteacher hired by the city council of Moncalieri. Public school activity is also documented in Turin, Ivrea, Chivasso, Pinerolo and Vercelli.[16] In the Republic of Venice, in addition to the public schools located in the huge capital city, we find public teachers hired in small communities such as Palazzolo sull'Oglio (1460), and in bigger towns, such as Treviso (1475, 1524, 1542), Brescia (1545) and Verona (until 1580), while in Bassano a public school was opened in 1590.[17] Within this educational scene, there was no lack of important profiles among public teachers; for example, in 1443 the city council of Vicenza hired Ognibene Bonisoli da Lonigo, illustrious former student of Vittorino da Feltre. Vittorino himself started his teaching career in Padua, together with his equally famous colleague, Guarino of Verona. We find traces of public schools even in the Venetian overseas territories in the Adriatic, the so-called *Stato da Mar* (State of the Sea). Throughout the fifteenth century in Ragusa, the current Dubrovnik, the municipality salaried teachers for public schools came mostly from Venice and its surroundings.[18]

Schools open to the public existed also in the other political giant of Renaissance Italy, the Visconti-Sforza dukedom of Milan, from whose territory the smaller Duchy of Parma and Piacenza was excluded in 1545.[19] Because of

---

16   Ferdinando Gabotto, *Lo Stato sabaudo da Amedeo VIII ad Emanuele Filiberto I (1451–1467)*, Turin-Rome: Luigi Roux Editore, 1892, see in particular the chapter: "Dizionario dei maestri di grammatica che insegnarono in Piemonte prima dell'anno 1500", 288–349, and Id., "Supplemento al dizionario dei maestri che insegnarono in Piemonte fino al 1500," Bollettino storico-bibliografico subalpino 11, (1906), 102–41. See also Anna Maria Nada Patrone, *Vivere nella scuola. Insegnare ed apprendere nel Piemonte del tardo medioevo*, (Torino: Gribaudo, 1996) and Grendler, *Schooling* [...], 104.

17   For Venice, see "Venetian Schools in High Renaissance" in Grendler, *Schooling in Renaissance Italy*, 42–70. For Palazzolo, Treviso, Brescia, Verona and Bassano, see respectively: Franco Chiappa, *Una pubblica scuola di grammatica a Palazzolo nella seconda metà del '400*, (Brescia: Tipografia Fiorucci, 1964); Giuseppe Liberali, *Le origini del seminario diocesano*, (Treviso: Editrice Trevigiana,1971), 75–76; Simone Signaroli, *Maestri e tipografi a Brescia 1471–1519*, (Brescia: Eduzioni Torre d'Ercole, 2009), Paolo Guerrini, "Scuole e maestri bresciani del Cinquecento," *Commentari dell'Ateneo di Brescia* 121, (1922): 167–244 and Agostino Zanelli, *Del pubblico insegnamento in Brescia nei secoli XVI e XVII*, (Brescia: Apollonio, 1896); Celestino Garibotto, *I maestri di grammatica a Verona dal '200 a tutto il '500*, (Verona: La tipografia veronese, 1921).

18   Nicolò Villanti, "Maestri di scuola a Ragusa (Dubrovnik) nel Medioevo 1300–1450," *Dubrovnik annals* 22, (2018): 7–50.

19   Although at the time of its creation in 1545 the territories of the Duchy of Parma and Piacenza were part of the Church State, to which they had been annexed in 1521, throughout the late Middle Ages they had been part of the Duchy of Milan.

its great size, the city of Milan always had different types of educational institutions. In addition to confraternal schools, there were also public schools. These were open to anyone who wanted to attend but were not financed by the city. The civic statutes in force under the governments of the Visconti and the Sforza families (who ruled Milan from the end of the fourteenth to the beginning of the sixteenth century) established that teachers' wages had to be paid by the pupils. There were also free schools, such as the one founded by Tommaso Grassi in 1473.[20] Nonetheless, between the end of 1400 and the beginning of 1500, new schools were founded for private initiatives but with a charitable purpose: the Cicogna schools in 1481, the schools of Charity in 1491 and the Piattine schools in 1503.[21] Municipally funded public schools, based on the classic model, were present in all the towns and villages of the duchy. Among these were important communal schools in Pavia, Vigevano, Cremona, Piacenza, Parma, Casalmaggiore, and Viadana, just to cite a few.[22]

If the public schools of *abaco* in the Tuscan cities have so far been the most studied by historians of education, the public educational institutions of the cities of southern Italy and the islands of Sicily and Sardinia deserve even greater attention.[23] We know that public schools were also present in the cities of the Kingdom of Naples and in the vice-kingdoms of Sardinia and Sicily. In 1477 a teacher was publicly salaried in Palermo while in Catania it was the university that set up lower schools open to the population in collaboration with the municipality and the cathedral. Southern Italian schools were not lacking illustrious students either. In Messina, which in 1548 would be the seat of the first Jesuit College, we find Pietro Bembo attending Greek classes at the end of the fifteenth century. southern Italy also had no lack of particular forms of public schools in smaller centers, as in the case of Miletus in Calabria, where

---

20   On the Milanese Renaissance schools, a large number of documents are preserved in the "Studi parte antica" fund of the State Archives of Milan. In general, see Marina Gazzini, "Scuola, libri e cultura nelle confraternite milanesi fra tardo medioevo e prima età moderna," *La Bibliofilìa* 103, 3 (2001): 215–26.

21   Marina Gazzini, "Cultura e *Welfare*: l'istruzione gratuita per fanciulli e giovani nella Milano sforzesca," in *Maestri e pratiche educative in età umanistica (Italia settentrionale, XV secolo)*, ed. Monica Ferrari, Federico Piseri and Matteo Morandi, (Brescia: Morcelliana, 2019), 141–58.

22   For other examples of minor centers, see David Salomoni, "Fragments of Renaissance schools on the banks of the Po River," *Educazione. Giornale di pedagogia critica* 6, 1 (2017): 7–30.

23   For Tuscany, see Robert Black, *Education and Society in Florentine Tuscany. Teachers, Pupils and Schools, c. 1250–1500*, (Leiden-Boston: Brill, 2007); Id., *Humanism and Education in Medieval and Renaissance Italy. Tradition and Innovation in Latin Schools from the Twelfth to the Fifteenth Century*, (Cambridge: Cambridge University Press, 2001).

in 1447 a free school was partially funded by the will of Pope Niccolò V and partially supported by local monasteries.[24] There were even municipal schools in Sardinia, though they were not widespread. Schools were financed by the municipality in Sassari and Cagliari starting from 1530, as well as in smaller communities such as Nuoro, Busachi and Mandas.[25]

This quick overview does not exhaust the entire list of public schools existing in Italy between the end of the Middle Ages, the Renaissance and the Reformation, but it shows how this scholastic model was widespread throughout the Italian territory. Yet, in addition to the archetype of public educational institutions described here whereby schools were financed by communal governing bodies, there were other types of schools open to the populations of hamlets and villages. Forms of consortia between notables and aristocrats of smaller towns or rural villages were able to create schools designed for the children of the contractors, and these schools were also open to other young people in the community. The purpose of these small schools, in addition, of course, to imparting knowledge by teaching the alphabet and numbers, was to reaffirm the social pre-eminence of the individuals who financed them. Similar types of schools could be found in many villages in the countryside around Milan. These centers were composed of a few hundred inhabitants that often did not reach a thousand people before 1500, such as Castiglione Olona, Tradate, Caravate, Gavirate, Besozzo, Carnago, Solbiate Arno and Nerviano.[26] On the high Apennine Mountains of Modena, we find the case of the castle of Montecuccolo where in 1484 the humanist and schoolteacher Pomponio Tribraco was commissioned by three local nobles. Among these men was Giacomo Albinelli, the local mayor representing the owners of the castle, namely the Montecuccoli counts. Tribraco was hired to "teach reading and writing to twenty schoolchildren, all living in Montecuccolo, of whom four children were of Albinelli's family, five of Melchiorre, one of Ser Raimondo

---

24 Domenico Taccone-Gallucci, *Regesti dei romani pontefici per le chiese di Calabria*, (Roma: Tipografia Vaticana, 1902), 221.
25 Francesco Manconi, *La Sardegna al tempo degli asburgo. Secoli XVI-XVIII*, (Nuoro: Il Maestrale, 2010), 289–94 and Francesco Floris, *Storia della Sardegna*, (Rome: Newton Compton, 2008), 329–32.
26 On the small schools of the Milan countryside, see Federico Del Tredici, "Maestri per il contado. Istruzione primaria e società locale nelle campagne milanesi (secolo XV)," in *Medioevo dei poteri. Studi di storia per Giorgio Chittolini*, ed. Maria Nadia Covini, Massimo Della Misericordia, Andrea Gamberini and Francesco Somaini (Rome: Viella, 2012), 275–99 and Id., *Un'altra nobiltà. Storie di (in)distinzione a Milano. Secoli XIV–XV*, (Milan: FrancoAngeli, 2017), 185–86.

and the others of prominent families of the place, such as the Riccis, the Montesanis and the Bonvicinis."[27]

Although still playing an important role, the Renaissance Italian public schools were teaching a smaller fraction of the school age population because of the rise of new types of educational institutions, including court schools, which, during the fifteenth century, were often open to the public. Such schools were financed by the lord of the city or by a local aristocrat to emphasize their social distinction and their civic role towards their subjects.[28] Among the most famous examples of this type of school are the *Ca 'Zoiosa* or *Casa Giocosa* (The Joyful House) of Vittorino da Feltre, opened in Mantua between 1423 and 1446 at the behest of the Marquis Gianfrancesco Gonzaga, and Guarino Veronese's school in the city of Ferrara, ruled by the Este family, active between 1430 and 1460.[29]

As for Mantua, we know that public schools already existed in this city during the fourteenth century. We know of the presence of a certain Venturino, public reader of Virgil, in 1398, while in 1407 the master Francesco from Parma was rector of the municipal public schools.[30] It was with the consolidation of the Gonzaga family that things changed, including in the educational field. The founding of a school by the dominant *signoria*, in fact, was part of an affirmation of power. We can observe this process from more than one perspective.

---

27 Original quote: "ammaestrare nel leggere e nello scrivere 20 scolari tutti residenti in Montecuccolo, dei quali 4 figli dell'Albinelli, 5 di Melchiorre, uno di ser Raimondo e gli altri di cospicue famiglie del luogo, come i Ricci, i Montesani, i Bonvicini." See Albano Sorbelli, *Il comune rurale dell'Appenino emiliano nei secoli XIV e XV*, (Bologna: Zanichelli, 1910), 358. The act by which the conduct is stipulated is kept at the Modena State Archives, Fund: *Archivio Jacoli*, Acts of Giacomo Albinelli, 1484. On the schoolteacher Pomponio Tribrarco, see Anita Della Guardia, *Gaspare Tribraco de' Trimbocchi. Maestro Modenese della II metà del secolo XV*, (Modena: Antica tipografia Soliani, 1910).

28 The sovereigns of the early Italian Renaissance states sought to legitimize their power through the assumption of communal elective offices. For example, in 1328 Luigi Gonzaga, in order to legitimize himself as the lord of Mantua state, had himself elected *Capitano del Popolo* (Captain of the People) to underline the continuity between his government and the communal liberties of the city.

29 The bibliography on the *Zoiosa* is very large. I will cite here the main works: Federico Piseri, in "L'educazione civile come problema pedagogico: il caso di Vittorino da Feltre tra continuità e innovazione," in *Maestri e pratiche educative in età umanistica (Italia settentrionale XV secolo)*, ed. Id., Monica Ferrari and Matteo Morandi (Brescia: Morcelliana, 2019), 53–72; Nella Giannetto, ed., *Vittorino da Feltre e la sua scuola: umanesimo, pedagogia, arti*, (Florence: Olschki, 1981).

30 Stefano Davari, *Notizie storiche intorno allo studio pubblico ed ai maestri del secolo XV e XVI che tennero scuola in Mantova tratte dall'Archivio Storico di Mantova*, (Mantova: Tipografia Eredi Segna, 1876), 4.

On the one hand, this gesture was typical of renaissance aristocratic patronage of the arts that brought prestige to the lordship. In addition to the opening of the court school for the most deserving young people of the city following the judgment of Master Vittorino, the institution fulfilled a principle of service exerted by the lord towards the population. Such a demonstration of power aimed at creating a direct link between the ruler and the governed as well as establishing international prestige. The Gonzaga family could not establish a university because of the high costs, despite the imperial diploma of 1433 that allowed it. Nonetheless, a court school could attract students and intellectuals both from inside and outside Italy, with the additional advantage of creating a parallel and informal diplomacy alongside the official one. Culture, after all, has always been at the mercy of politics.

The same dynamic was taking place simultaneously in nearby Ferrara, dominated at that time by Niccolò III of Este. The duke of Ferrara, following in the footsteps of Mantua, wanted to call on Guarino of Verona to create a prestigious court school.[31] As Paul Grendler points out, Guarino "conferred distinction on the Este city and court" and "added considerable intellectual luster to the city. He attracted many pupils from Italy and abroad and induced many humanists to visit Ferrara."[32] Even in smaller centers we find the same model of court schools open to the young people of the community. In the small county of Novellara, for example, there was a school governed by a cadet branch of the Gonzaga of Mantua. In 1503 there was a Mantuan teacher, Cristoforo Savi, hired by the local lords as a preceptor for their children; however, the school was also open to other children of the town.[33] As we will see later, the role played by the seigneuries in the shaping of educational policies within Italian political realities, both major and minor, was very important in the transition of the late Renaissance communal school model to the Trindentine one. The tensions between the princes and the municipal governing bodies regarding the control of educational institutions were powered by a new conception of the role of humanist intellectuals in society. This conflict had strong repercussions on the self-representation of their proper function that many schoolteachers developed from the mid-fifteenth century onwards. Such context gave rise to social,

---

31 On Guarino the bibliography is extensive but, in general, a little dated. The most recent essay that puts order to the historiography is: Enrica Guerra, "Guarino Veronese. Cenni storiografici e di ricerca," in *Maestri e pratiche educative in età umanistica*, cit. (Brescia: Morcelliana, 2019), 239–52.
32 Grendler, *Schooling in Renaissance Italy*, 128.
33 David Salomoni, "Le scuole di una comunità emiliana nel Rinascimento tra religione e politica. Il caso di Novellara," *Educazione. Giornale di pedagogia critica* 5, 2 (2016): 17–42.

economic and political claims that translated into religious terms and found fertile ground in the crisis opened up by the Protestant Reformation. After all, it was Italian humanism that represented one of the most powerful intellectual fertilizers for the rise of a more intimate and direct relation with the divinity (*Devotio Moderna*), an essential premise for the spread of Protestant doctrines.[34] In other words, it was not uncommon that teachers who felt cheated of their civic role preferred to adhere to the teachings of Martin Luther.

Before focusing on this dimension, however, we need to consider the third essential component of the Renaissance school network, namely the *Studia* of the mendicant orders, the Dominicans and Franciscans. The long-lasting presence of these orders proves that during the late Middle Ages, the Renaissance and the Reformation period, the link between school and church had never been broken, although its physiognomy had changed.[35] Among the most characteristic elements of the Italian medieval urban society, in fact, was the existence of Franciscan and Dominican convents in urban conglomerates. The presence of at least one of these two congregations has even become a historiographical criterion to define whether an inhabited center can be defined as a city, showing the importance of mendicant orders in *ancien régime* societies.[36] After their birth, these orders soon equipped themselves with powerful and highly stratified educational systems. The first schools were set up by Dominicans. Each convent was obliged to contain a school where novices began the study of liberal arts, logic and rhetoric and then natural philosophy and theology. After these courses, the best students passed to a higher level, either the *Studium Solemne*, open to friars of the same province, or the *Studium Generale*, open to friars of the whole order.[37] The Franciscans based their *Scholae* on the Dominicans' model, but a little later, reaching a greater extensiveness of presence. Their schools were organized into lower provincial schools for the start of studies (*Studia Artium*, *Studia Philosophiae*, and *Studia Theologiae*), more widespread in the territory, and schools of a higher level

---

34 William Naphy, *The Protestant Revolution: From Martin Luther to Martin Luther King Jr.*, (London: BBC Books, 2007), 7–16.

35 For the Franciscan order, see Bert Roest, *Franciscan Learning, Preaching and Mission c. 1220–1650*, (Leiden-Boston: Brill, 2015) and Id., *A History of Franciscan Education 1210–1517*, (Leiden-Boston: Brill, 2000).

36 Roberto Lambertini, "Il sistema formativo degli *Studia* degli ordini mendicanti: osservazioni a partire dai risultati di recenti indagini," in *Die Ordnung der Kommunikation und die Kommunikation der Ordnungen. Bd. 1 Netzwerke: Kloster und Orden im Europa des 12. und 13. Jahrhunderts*, ed. Cristina Andenna, Klaus Herbers, Gert Melville (Stuttgart: Fraz Steiner Verlag, 2012), 135–46.

37 Rosso, *La scuola nel Medioevo*, 173.

(*Studia Generalia*) for the most promising students to access the highest academic degrees.

Although the mendicant *Studia* have never primarily addressed people not belonging to their orders, the role played by Franciscans and Dominicans was of enormous importance in defining, at a theoretical and practical level, the meaning of education in the life of a Christian before the Reformation, and of a Catholic after it. The mendicant schools had never been closed to the laity, which introduced a powerful factor of acculturation to Italian cities at the end of the Middle Ages. Even into the seventeenth century, as Bert Roest points out, "explicit reference to the public character of a number of these schools is rather striking."[38] Franciscan conventuals, for instance, "continued the late medieval tradition of providing lectors to public schools, colleges and faculties outside the order" and "also continued the late medieval tradition of allowing outsiders to attend lectures."[39] Another aspect of great importance, as we will see in the following chapters, was the educational role played by members of these orders in external schools. From the second half of the sixteenth century, it often happened that Franciscan or Dominican friars were called upon by municipal administrations or princes to teach in public schools in cities and smaller towns. In cases where a convent could not guarantee adequate education in grammar, rhetoric, and logic to the novices within it, novices were sent to external schools held by lay teachers.[40]

Even at the height of the apogee of the lay school at the turn of the high and late medieval period right up to the Renaissance and Reformation period, the link between religion and education never stopped. Even in the secular schools of the fifteenth century religion was essential, inseparable from everyday activities. In municipal schools there was often an image of the Virgin and Child hung on a classroom wall. School days usually began with students praying while facing an icon, as described by Bonvesin de la Riva in his famous manual written at the end of the thirteenth century, *De vita scholastica*. The prayer started with the invocation "O Christ, for love of your Mother, may I have your grace, because my tongue gives praise in your name."[41] After all, in the period

---

[38] Roest, *Franciscan Learning*, 162.
[39] Ibidem.
[40] Alfonso Maierù, "Formazione culturale e tecniche d'insegnamento nelle scuole degli Ordini Mendicanti," in *Studio e Studia: le scuole degli ordini mendicanti tra XIII e XIV secolo*, (Spoleto: Centro Italiano di Studi sull'Alto Medioevo, 2002), 3–32.
[41] Original quote: "Per l'amore di tua madre, la tua grazia sia con me, oh Cristo, affinché la mia parola fruttifichi in tuo nome." The book *De vita scholastica*, also known as *De discipulorum preceptorumque moribus*, or *Scolastica moralis*, became extremely popular in the fifteenth and sixteenth centuries. Between 1479 and 1555 there were twenty editions

considered here, a clear distinction between sacred and profane, religious and secular, ordinary and extraordinary would have been too rigid, even blasphemous for the people of the time.[42] As we shall see shortly, it would have been a particularly zealous adhesion to the demands of reform of the Church and religion by both lay and religious teachers, which would have undermined the school system.

1.2   Weaknesses of the Renaissance Communal School System

As was mentioned in the previous paragraph, the strengthening of Italian regional states, both princely and republican, caused violent clashes regarding municipal liberties that the cities had jealously defended. These tensions were particularly traumatic for Venetian humanists. This superimposition upon traditional municipal institutions, namely city councils, of a princely governor or vicar as a new political leader questioned the principle of active citizenship and political participation so dear to Italian medieval city populations. These political transformations also influenced the role of the intellectuals who worked in communal schools as teachers for the urban governing ranks. The most representative example of this phenomenon can be found in the Venetian occupation of most of northeastern Italy during its expansion between 1404 and 1420. During these years, the main intellectuals of that area abandoned conquered cities such as Padua to go to other capitals in northern Italy which were governed by princes, namely Mantua, Ferrara, and Milan. Among these men were Vittorino da Feltre, Guarino of Verona and Gasparino Barzizza. They were all teachers, eager to train the ruling classes in civic virtues, but they were disappointed in their pedagogical expectation by the indifference shown by the Venetian state. For Venice, its patriciate with its traditional values was enough to govern the new territorial state, but these humanists wanted to forge the characters of Italian princes, the 'heads' of state, and the elite, the limbs of the state body, in light of classical culture.[43] For these men,

---

in northern Italy. See Valentina Iodi, *La "Vita Scolastica" di Bonvesin de la Riva*, Master Dissertation, University of Bologna, 2014–2015. For the English translation, see Lisa Pon, *A Printed Icon in Early Modern Italy. Forlì's Madonna of the Fire*, (Cambridge: Cambridge University Press, 2015), 107.

42   Pon, *A Printed Icon*, 102, and Edward Muir, "The Virgin on the Streetcorner," in *Religion and Culture in the Renaissance and Reformation*, ed. Steven Ozment (Kirksville: Sixteenth Century Journal Publishers, 1989), 25–106.

43   Giuseppe Zago, "Maestri di Umanesimo nell'Italia nord-orientale del Quattrocento," in *Maestri e pratiche educative in età umanistica*, cit. (Brescia: Morcelliana, 2019), 183–202. See also: Eugenio Garin, ed., *Il pensiero pedagogico dello umanesimo*, (Florence: Giuntine-Sansoni, 1958), 1–19.

a traditional aristocratic education such as that of Venice's, based essentially on familism and mercantilism, was not enough. They dreamed of an ideal state with a philosopher prince in which their role would be as exalted as that of the intellectuals of antiquity.

The same aspirations and frustrations, however, remained for generations of other humanist teachers who grew up on the examples and values of the most famous of this category. This was the case throughout the fifteenth and a good part of the sixteenth century. In 1540 the humanist Sebastiano Corradi from Reggio Emilia was called by the city council of his town to take service in public schools. In a letter sent to the city council, Corradi expresses his thought on the usefulness of the city youth being educated by a native teacher who cares about the fate of his "country." Corradi says that,

> foreigners usually care about the gain and not the good of the city, so it often happens, and perhaps always, that they are lost in money and then nothing is done. But this does not happen when one has a good teacher of the fatherland, because he puts all diligence so that his citizens learn, and where he lacks the doctrine, with hard work and study he learns it.[44]

However, Reggio Emilia, like many other cities, was no longer an autonomous homeland; it was part of the Duchy of Modena. For this reason, the civic sensibility committed to educational service for the hometown would no longer receive due acknowledgment. In the new political order, there was no need to train legal experts for a political life in the city; the need was now to prepare a controllable number of technicians for the administration of the interests and possessions of the lord. Many schoolteachers, with the first shocks brought to the foundations of Italian society by the Lutheran Reformation, transformed their pedagogical commitment from civic to religious. The claim of an active role in shaping their society had passed from the political forum to that of an individual conscience. Schoolteachers soon became one of the most insidious and uncontrollable categories on inquisitorial tribunals. In 1525 Ludovico Ariosto, in his satire on the search for a private teacher for his son Virginio,

---

44   Archivio di Stato Reggio Emilia, Fondo archivio comunale, *Scuole (1273–1789)*, letter of Sebastiano Corradi to the city council from Venice, October 10th, 1540. Original quote: "i forestieri solamente hanno l'occhio al guadagno, e non alla utilità della città, e profitto de' scolari. Onde avviene spesso, e forse sempre, che si perdono in danari, e nulla si fa; il che non suole accadere così di leggero, quando si ha buon lettore della patria, perché egli mette ogni diligentia che i suoi cittadini imparino: e dove gli manca la dottrina con studio e fatica supplisce."

alluded to the *Peccadiglio di Spagna* (the Spanish Sin), namely the rather widespread anti-Trinitarian tendency of schoolteachers.[45] The profession of faith imposed in 1564 by Pius IV on all schoolteachers was just the formalization of the generalized suspicion of the ecclesiastical world towards humanists, who were generally considered to be responsible for the initiation of many young pupils into Protestant and anti-Catholic doctrines.[46]

During his 1560 mission in Piedmont, a northwestern border area close to the very Protestant Geneva and therefore under special surveillance, the young Jesuit Antonio Possevino identified schoolteachers as a group on which to exert special pressure for his campaign of systematic Catholicization. He distributed among them the catechism of his fellow Jesuit Peter Canisius. In 1561, Possevino wrote from Vercelli that he had given 500 copies of Canisius' catechism "to schoolteachers to give to schoolchildren." In 1563 he obtained an edict from the Duke of Savoy, Emanuele Filiberto, obliging all teachers to make a public confession of faith. This happened a year before the general profession imposed by Pope Pius IV, whose text had to be copied and posted in every classroom and explained by teachers in both male and female schools.[47] In 1621 Eliseo Masini's *Sacro Arsenale*, one of the most durable and influential inquisitorial manuals in early modern Italy, stated that "doctors, schoolteachers, and confessors who have abjured, as suspects, must not return to their first offices, if not on express order and *gratia* of the Supreme Pontiff."[48]

The professions listed by the famous inquisitor were placed in the delicate intersection between care of the body and soul. Schoolteachers did both, taking care of the intellectual and therefore moral education of the individual, in addition to his physical activity in society. The role of schoolteachers in

---

45 "Et oltra questa nota, il peccadiglio di Spagna gli danno anco, che non creda in unità del Spirto il Padre e il Figlio"; Mario Santoro, ed., *Opere di Ludovico Ariosto Carmina, Rime, Satire, Erbolato, Lettere*, Vol. III, (Torino: UTET, 1962), 425.

46 Adriano Prosperi, *Tribunali della coscienza. Inquisitori, confessori, missionari*, (Torino: Einaudi, 2009), 608.

47 On Possevino's mission in Piedmont between 1560 and 1563, see Prosperi, *Tribunali*, 611–13. The quotation of the letter written in 1561 is reported both in Prosperi, 612, and in Mario Scaduto S.I., "Le missioni di A. Possevino in Piemonte. Propaganda calvinista e restaurazione cattolica 1560–1563," *Archivum Historicum Societatis Iesu*, XXVIII (1959): 51–191. Translation: "Alli mastri di scuola che ne facciano pigliare a scolari."

48 Eliseo Masini, *Sacro arsenale ouero prattica dell'Officio della Santa Inquisitione*, (Genova: Giuseppe Pavoni, 1621), 270. Original quote: "medici, maestri di scuola, e confessori che havranno abiurato, come sospetti, non sogliono restituirsi, o habilitarsi a' loro primieri uffici, se non d'espresso ordine e gratia del sommo pontefice." On inquisitorial manuals in early modern Italy, see Christopher Black, *The Italian Inquisition*, (New Haven & London: Yale University Press, 2009), 123–24.

the diffusion of Protestant doctrines in sixteenth century Italy, in fact, proceeded in two ways. On the one hand, these humanists possessed the intellectual tools to understand and access books containing the ideas of German reformers. Sometimes the more cultivated among them even participated in intellectual gatherings, often hosted in aristocratic houses, where these ideas were discussed. By doing so, they served as a transmission belt between the elites in which the principles of Reformation took root within urban populations, where such ideals spread like wildfire.[49] On the other hand, schoolteachers had the pedagogical tools to introduce many young people to the ideas of the Protestant Reformation. The Modenese schoolteacher Giovanni Maria Tagliati, known as Maranello, a fervent anti-Trinitarian and a devoted reader of the Spanish physician and theologian Miguel Serveto,[50] was reported to be an initiator of the new spirituality. He was also the author of a grammar text, the *Compendium rei grammaticae maxime ex Linacro*. The text was published in 1540 by the printer Gadaldino, and it shows the existence of a real production of "reformed" schoolbooks.[51] Maranello was repeatedly denounced to the authorities as a heretic. In 1551 he secretly abjured in the hands of the Dominican theologian Egidio Foscarari (1512–1564) but from 1566 to 1567 he was sentenced to perpetual prison. Maranello died in 1574.[52]

As shown by the case of Maranello, "an assorted heretical world of artisans, carpenters, mask makers, weavers, cobblers" and even prostitutes orbited around the school teachers.[53] The trial papers of these heretical teachers, such as those from the prosecution against the humanist Ludovico Poliziano

---

49   David Salomoni, "Pedagogia eretica. Note di ricerca su alcuni processi a maestri di scuola nella Modena del '500." *Educazione. Giornale di pedagogia critica* 7, 2 (2018): 7–32.
50   Miguel Serveto (1511–1553), more familiar to English-speaking readers as Michael Servetus, was a Spanish humanist, physician, theologian and mathematician mainly active in France during the early phases of the Protestant Reformation. After rejecting Catholicism and Trinitarian doctrine, he fled to Calvinist Geneva where he was burned at the stake after preaching a sermon in which he affirmed his strong Anabaptist and anti-Trinitarian ideas. See "Verdict and Sentence for Michael Servetus" in *A Reformation Reader*, ed. Denis R. Janz (Minneapolis: Fortress Press, 1999), 268–70.
51   The *Compendium rei grammaticae* (Mutinae: Antoniium Gadaldinum, 1549) is preserved at the Augusta Municipal Library of Perugia. On heretics in the city of Modena, see Matteo Al kalak, *L'Eresia dei fratelli. Una comunità eterodossa nella Modena del Cinquecento*, (Rome: Edizioni di storia e letteratura, 2011) and Id., *Gli eretici di Modena. Fede e potere alla metà del Cinquecento*, (Milan: Mursia, 2008).
52   Matteo Al Kalak, *Il riformatore dimenticato. Egidio Foscarari tra Inquisizione, Concilio e governo pastorale, 1512–1564* (Bologna: Il Mulino, 2016), 95.
53   Massimo Firpo, *Juan de Valdés and the Italian Reformation*, trans. Richard Bates (New York: Routledge, 2016), 99.

imprisoned at the end of 1579, divulge dense relational ties with the Italian and foreign spiritual communities thanks to the circulation of students from beyond the Alps.[54]

Years later, during other pastoral visits carried out in the 1590s in Casale Monferrato, Mantua and Reggio Emilia, Antonio Possevino continued to distribute pious devotional books to schoolteachers. He strongly admonished them to eradicate pagan antiquities from their teaching and suggested reading only Horace, Cicero, Virgil and Terence, who he himself had studied. These warnings demonstrate a certain obstinacy of the humanist masters in imparting their traditional teachings. Further proof is provided by the bishop of Reggio Emilia, Benedetto Manzoli (1530–1585). At the beginning of the 1580s in his diocesan statutes, Manzoli insisted on the importance of reforming the contents of school teachings, requiring the masters to observe the profession of faith of 1564.[55] It is clear from these brief observations that the school system during the Renaissance and Reformation period, with its love for the classical world, was kept under special surveillance by the forces that sought to contain the expansion of Lutheran doctrine.

Even within the mendicant orders, violent clashes on the role of schools and education broke out. Once again this was in relation to the new religious climate, which called for a more rigid morality and a response to the growing threat of Protestant heresy. Since the second half of the fifteenth century within the Franciscan order, the birth of the Observance as a response to a perceived decline of customs by the Conventuals had powerfully challenged the need of such a refined internal school network. The accusation was that this system favored the pursuit of honors and academic qualifications to the detriment of spiritual elevation. Initially, the reaction of the Observant faction to the Conventual academic worldliness had condemned the pursuit of learning by fostering the ideal of a religious life of eremitical withdrawal; however,

---

54 Archivio di Stato di Modena (Modena State Archives), Fondo inquisizione, envelope 2 (1489–1549); fasc. II (1503–1523); n. 23. The process chart is entered chronologically into the wrong envelope due to a storage error. The year in which the proceedings began, 1579, was confused with 1519.

55 On the 1590s missions of Possevino, see Prosperi, *Tribunali*, 616–17 and Id., "Educare gli educatori. Il prete come professione intellettuale nell'Italia tridentina," in *Problèmes d'histoire de l'éducation* (Rome: École Française de Rome, 1988), 123–40. See also Mario Scaduto, "Le 'visite' di Antonio Possevino nei domìni dei Gonzaga (contributo alla storia religiosa del tardo Cinquecento)," *Archivio storico lombardo* 10, LXXXVII (1960): 336–410.

from the 1420s the need for a more active apostolate put an emphasis on the need for adequate theological education.[56]

This need led to the foundation of the first Observant *Studium* for moral theology in the convent of Monteripido in Perugia in 1440. This was only the starting point for a brilliant ascent of a series of foundations. Eventually, the Observant Franciscans took control of many Conventual *Studia*, of which the *Grand Couvent* of Paris, *de facto* as early as 1502, was the most illustrious. The new Observant foundations in Italy followed one another rapidly. In the fifteenth century schools were opened in Bologna, Ferrara, Mantua, Fabriano, Florence, Pavia, Milan, Verona and Venice, and from the early 1500s in Brescia, Lucca, Naples, Rome, Siena and Vercelli.[57] With the Bull *Ite et vos*, promulgated in 1517 by Pope Leo X, the Reformed and Observant groups of the Franciscan family were brought together, making the Observants the dominant force within the Franciscan world. This change made it more difficult for the members of the Conventuals to access the important *Studia* that had fallen under strict Observant guidance. This lessening of the Conventual status was reinforced by the loss of many of their schools and convents in the areas of Europe where the Lutheran and Calvinist Reformation was taking hold, namely Germany, Switzerland, England, and Scandinavia. Moreover, the Conventuals had brought their study houses under Observant control in the Franciscan provinces of Spain and Portugal.

The rapid rise of the Observant faction to the top of the Franciscan order was a sign of the changing times, namely the growing need for spiritual renewal which represented the same ground in which the Protestant Reformation took root. In other words, the internal reforms in the organization of the Franciscan schools were not determined by the challenge brought by Lutheranism, but by the Franciscan need for morality to which even Luther and the Protestant reformers sought to respond. When the Protestant Reformation came, its effect was to accelerate the reorganization of studies, both for Conventuals and Observants.

A clear example of this dynamic is given by the third main branch of the Franciscan family, namely the Capuchins. The group was founded in 1525 and approved by Clement VIII in 1528. Their aim was to return to original Franciscan

---

56   In general, see Roest, *Franciscan Learning*, 138–39. For more details, see Dionisio Pacetti, "La necessità dello studio. Predica inedita di S. Bernardino da Siena," *Bullettino di Studi Bernardiniani* 2, (1936), 310–21; Mario Fois, "La questione degli studi nell'Osservanza e la soluzione di S. Bernardino da Siena," in *Atti del Simposio Cateriniano-Bernardiniano*, eds. Domenico Maffei, Paolo Nardi (Siena: Accademia degli Intronati, 1982), 477–97.

57   Bert Roest, *A History of Franciscan Education (1210–1517)*, (Leiden-Boston: Brill, 2000), 164.

spirituality, with respect to which even the Observants' policies were considered degenerate. Initially, the Capuchins refused to provide themselves with an educational structure since the first members of the group were educated adults coming from the Observants or Conventuals; however, the Capuchins soon had to deal with many uneducated young people. The major problem occurred when the twice Capuchin vicar, General Bernardino Ochino, had to flee to Switzerland because of his adherence to Protestant doctrines. Thus, the main factors for the transformation and reorganization of schools within the Franciscan family were the desire for moral reform and the loss of control over the development of these spiritual needs.

To close this survey concerning the main weaknesses of the Italian Renaissance Reformation school system, we must not forget the chronic financial weakness of the cities and Renaissance regional Italian States. When faced with a military or food emergency which could have remarkably high costs, the first service cut by public authorities was education.[58] This situation was exacerbated by the continuous movement of armies and by the sieges of the first half of the sixteenth century, during which Italy was the main theater for the wars between Habsburg and Valois. By the end of the Italian Wars in 1559 the public finances of the Italian states had been bled dry; they were required to supply, without excessive expenditure, a series of functions that could not be guaranteed at times of emergency, not least of which was the educational system that had flourished in the relative political stability of the second half of the fifteenth century.

To the strictly economic perspective must be added the subversive threat, from a political point of view, of the widespread religious dissent of schoolteachers. In the eyes of Italian princes, the spread of heresy meant risk of social disruption, just as revolutionary and anarchist forces had threatened European societies between the end of the nineteenth century and the beginning of the twentieth. This threat drove Emanuele Filiberto of Savoy, among others, to entrust the struggle against Protestantism in Piedmont to Possevino.[59] The inability to control the religious situation within their domains, however, threatened a loss of political legitimacy (and therefore a loss of the state) before the pontiff, who, between the end of the fifteenth and the first half of the sixteenth century, was busy affirming his role as a state maker.

---

58   See the chapter "Un mondo che cambia. La rottura degli equilibri," in Salomoni, *Scuole, maestri e scolari*, 363–71.
59   Prosperi, *Tribunali*, 611–12.

2 The Catholicization of Italian Education

The role played by schoolteachers adhering to Protestant doctrines in guiding the choice of Italian Renaissance states to assign public education to new post-Tridentine religious orders has never been taken into due consideration by scholars, perhaps because of the total success of these congregations in eradicating modern "heresies" from their classrooms. The impression is that this reading is affected by a teleological approach. In addition, in regard to internal conflicts of mendicant orders concerning the role of education and culture, let us understand how the real question at the beginning of the sixteenth century was how to educate the modern Christian. Only later, in response to the Protestant challenge, came the need to define how to educate the modern Catholic.

During the fifteenth century, as we have seen, the presence of the Church in the world of education never lapsed, and priests who carried out the profession of schoolmaster, especially in the countryside, never disappeared; however, from the beginning of the sixteenth century, the weight carried by priests in the school world began to increase. This growth was taking place both in cities and in villages. In 1582 in Venice, for instance, priests made up 65 percent of all the teachers in the city. In the whole of the State of Milan in 1574, 35 percent of the teaching body was composed of priests. However, the percentage rises when we look at the more modest country settlements where the reports of diocesan pastoral visits reveal that almost all the teachers paid by the communities in public schools were priests. Between 1579 and 1580, in the communities of Carnago, Bollate, and Rosate, all active teachers were priests. As for lay masters in Melegnano, "there were none." We find the same situation in Arsago, Somma, Decimo, Casorate, Lecco, Settala, Corneliano, Tre Valli (Three Valleys) and Marliano, where "there is no layman who teaches."[60] Even in the smaller centers where the city council had not yet hired or could no longer afford to pay for a public teacher, the so-called *Gratis et Amore Dei* schools were set up completely for free.[61] This phenomenon is more frequently observed in

---

60   The data and the quotations reported here on the State of Milan come from: Angelo Turchini, *Sotto l'occhio del padre. Società confessionale e istruzione primaria nello Stato di Milano*, (Bologna: Il Mulino, 1996), 240. The quotations are taken by the author from the Diocesan Historical Archive (*Archivio Storico Diocesano*) of Milan, section VI, 137.
61   These schools anticipate and in a certain sense represent a model for the future Schools of Christian Doctrine created by Castellino Da Castello, with which they would merge.

hilly or mountainous areas, particularly in northern Lombardy and the territories of Como, Milan, Bergamo, Brescia, Lario, Verbano and Ticino.[62]

Among the reasons for this increase in the number of priests engaged in the role of teacher, we find the moralizing need to decrease pagan content in lessons and to increase devotional material. Another reason for the increased presence of priests in schools was the need for artisans and technicians, at a time of economic crisis in the seventeenth century, to develop individuals with a better education in mathematics and more solid professional skills. We frequently find village craftsmen in the territories of Como and Varese who explicitly ask parish priests to keep existing schools open or to open new ones.[63] The main reason for this boost of teacher priests, however, remained the moral issue. The sources supporting this are widespread and can be found in most of the historical archives of Italy, even the smaller ones; for instance, in the tiny Renaissance state of Guastalla, located halfway between the cities of Mantua and Reggio Emilia, bought by the imperial captain Ferrante Gonzaga in 1539, we find much relevant information. In 1578, for example, the municipality hired the priest Orazio Ruggeri, a native of Pizzighettone near Cremona, as a public teacher. He was given a salary and a house, together with the possibility of requesting further payment from students.[64]

The rewording of the contract would have remained the same throughout the sixteenth and seventeenth centuries, with the teacher priest in all respects dependent on the community and authorized to demand a small payment

---

[62] In general, see Xenio Toscani, "Ruoli del clero, canali e strumenti di apprendimento nella Lombardia dei secoli XVI–XIX," in *Formare alle professioni. Sacerdoti, principi, educatori*, ed. Egle Becchi and Monica Ferrari, (Milan: FrancoAngeli, 2009), 70–118, inter alia 89–90; and Maurizio Piseri, ed., *L'alfabeto in montagna. Scuola e alfabetismo nell'area alpina tra età moderna e XIX secolo*, (Milan: FrancoAngeli, 2012). For singular cases, see Daniele Montanari, *Gregorio Barbarigo a Bergamo (1657–1664). Prassi di governo e missione pastorale*, (Milan: Glossa, 1997), 59–77; and Giovanna Gamba's works: "Catechesi e scuole di alfabetizzazione," in *A servizio del Vangelo. Il cammino storico dell'evangelizzazione a Brescia. Vol. II L'età moderna*, ed. Xenio Toscani, (Brescia: La Scuola, 2007), 143–73; *La scoperta delle lettere. Scuole di dottrina e di alfabeto a Brescia in età moderna*, (Milan: FrancoAngeli, 2008); "Guidati alla virtù. Le scuole di dottrina cristiana a Brescia," in *Dalla virtù al precetto. L'educazione del gentiluomo dal '500 al '700*, Maurizio Tagliaferri, ed., (Brescia: Fondazione Civiltà Bresciana, 2015), 71–100.

[63] Toscani, "Ruoli del clero [...]," 90.

[64] Archivio Comunale di Guastalla, *Delibere dei consigli comunali*, Vol. 1 (1556–1606), April 7th, 1578. Original quote: "Convocato il consiglio in n. 6 consiglieri nel solito luogo elessero per l'anno venturo 1579 in Maestro di scuola Messer Orazio Ruggeri di Pizzighettone coll'emolumento di 40 scudi all'anno e la casa di Bando con facultà di esigere pagamento dagli scolari secondo il loro potere e perché il suddetto Maestro era sacerdote, la Principessa offriva a Lui una Cappellania nel Duomo di questa terra."

from pupils who were not declared too poor (*miserabili*) with a suitable certificate. Between the sixteenth and seventeenth centuries, 70 percent of the public teachers active in Guastalla were religious, including diocesan priests and regular clerics. Over the course of the sixteenth century, however, customary dispositions were increasingly affirming the obligation for school teachers "to educate the children who will go to the School both in the Letters, as well as in the good customs, and all the Sundays teach them the Christian Doctrine."[65] At the beginning of the seventeenth century, in the deliberations of the municipal councils of two other communities in the territory of Mantua, Canneto Sull'Oglio and Goito, we respectively read requests addressed to the schoolteacher to "take good care of the pupils and educate them in the good discipline of life, in the good customs and fear of God" and "to instruct them in the dogmas of Holy Mother Church and in the duties of a true Roman Catholic."[66]

Perhaps the only discrepancy in the increasing number of priests in classrooms can be found between cities attached to the old forms of humanistic education, and small communities which were more permeable to new religious needs. However, even in the cities the process of clericalization of schoolteachers was evident. In Milan, in the aforementioned Cicogna schools founded by Tommaso Grassi and attended by 250 pupils, the only active teachers were priests who officiated at monastic churches, parish churches or in the cathedral.[67] In addition, other movements of religious education were developing in the first decades of the sixteenth century aimed at the urban classes, especially the poor. Among these movements, one of the most distinctive was created by a priest, Castellino da Castello. During the 1530s Castellino had felt the need to create a place of Catholic literacy and moralization for the poor children of Milan.[68] The congregation created by Castellino was composed of

---

[65] Municipal Archives of Guastalla, *Delibere dei consigli comunali*, Vol. 2 (1556–1606), November 30th, 1615. Original quote: "ammaestrare educare li figliuoli che andranno alla Scuola tanto nelle Lettere, quanto anche nelli boni costumi, et tutte le Domeniche insegnarli la Dottrina Christiana nel Domo di questa Terra."

[66] Original quote: "di prendersi buona cura degli allievi e di educarli nella buona disciplina della vita, ai buoni costumi e al timor di Dio, e di istruirli ai dogmi della Santa Madre Chiesa e ai doveri del vero cattolico romano." Xenio Toscani, *Scuole e alfabetismo nello Stato di Milano da Carlo Borromeo alla Rivoluzione*, (Brescia: La Scuola, 1993), 126–27.

[67] Turchini, *Sotto l'occhio del padre*, 103.

[68] On Castellino da Castello and the Schools of Christian Doctrine, see Grendler, *Schooling*, 333–62 and Turchini, *Ibid.* 173–75. See also Claudia Di Filippo, "The Reformation and the Catholic Revival in the Borromeo's Age," in *A Companion to Late Medieval and Early Modern Milan. The Distinctive Features of an Italian States*, ed. Andrea Gamberini, (Leiden-Boston: Brill, 2014), 93–117, inter alia 98–99; Miriam Turrini, "Catechismi e scuole della dottrina cristiana nell'Italia del Cinquecento," in *L'educazione religiosa in Russia*

both lay people and the religious who, on Sundays and during religious feasts, taught children the gospel, the alphabet and the rudiments of mathematics. The teaching activities of the group began in 1536 in the oratory of the Milanese church of Saints James and Philip. The initiative was a great success and grew to the point of requiring a more formal structure that was built in 1539. Castellino created a congregation named *Compagnia della Reformatione Christiana in Charità* (Society of the Christian Reform in Charity). This name, however, echoed too closely the ongoing struggle between the Roman Church and religious Reformation in progress in Germany. This earned Castellino a summons by Giovanni Maria Tosi, vicar of the Archbishop of Milan, in order to clarify his position. Once the doubts about the activity of the congregation were resolved, the name was changed in 1546 to *Compagnia dei Servi di Puttini in Charità* (Society of the Servants of Children in Charity). From that moment on the group's success was unstoppable.

In a few years, a network of Schools of Christian Doctrine was formed in northern and central Italy. The stages of this expansion proceeded as follows: Pavia (1538); Genoa, Verona, Vigevano and Piacenza (1541); Mantua and Parma (1542); Lodi (1545); Cremona (1547); Varese (1550); Novara (1553); Bergamo and Brescia (1554); Rome (1560); Monza, Asti and Ascoli (1562); Desio, Belgioioso, Savona, Turin and Ferrara (1563); and Como (1565).[69] The opening of a new school usually took place on the initiative of a confrere, who spontaneously went to a new city or small town. It could also happen that a municipality requested the opening of one of their schools. The company's rule (*Regola de la Compagnia dei Servi di Puttini in Charità*), published for the first time in 1555, was successful. It was reprinted several times in Milan (1555, 1566, 1568, 1579, 1582, 1595); Cremona (1583, 1595); Brescia and Ferrara (1590).

---

e Europa. XVI secolo, eds. Evghenia Tokareva and Marek Inglot, (Saint Petersburg: Casa editrice dell'Accademia russa cristiana umanistica, 2010), 60–80; Angelo Bianchi, "Le scuole di dottrina cristiana: linguaggio e strumenti per una azione educativa 'di massa,'" in *Carlo Borromeo e l'opera della "Grande Riforma." Cultura, religione e arti nella Milano del pieno Cinquecento*, ed. Franco Buzzi and Danilo Zardin, (Milan: Credito Artigiano, 1997), 145–58; Luigi Cajani, "Castellino da Castello," *Dizionario Biografico degli Italiani*, vol. 21, (1978): 786–87; Alessandro Tamborini, *La compagnia e le scuole della dottrina cristiana*, (Milan: Daverio, 1939); Giuseppina Achilli, "Castellino da Castello e le scuole della dottrina cristiana," *La scuola cattolica* LXIV, (1936): 35–40; Eleuterio Chinea, *Le scuole di dottrina cristiana nella diocesi di Milano (1536–1796)*, (Gallarate: Stabilimento Tipo-Litografico Carlo Lazzati, 1930).

69   Cajani, "Castellino da Castello," 786.

The rule explicitly stated that boys and girls should be educated without distinction.[70] Of course, things did not always go well, and there were incidents and inconveniences. The recruiting activity by the Company was sometimes labelled as "fishing for poor children" to send to school, sometimes leading to violent and coercive acts.[71] It is interesting to note that the success of the schools of doctrine was stronger in those areas where mercantile culture was more widespread.[72] During the second diocesan council of Milan in 1569, Carlo Borromeo imposed the obligation to establish a school of Christian doctrine in all the cities and villages. In 1585, moreover, the new *Constitutioni et regole della Compagnia et scuole della Dottrina christiana* (Constitutions and rules of the Society and schools of the Christian Doctrine) were also promulgated in Milan. The structure of this educational institution became more and more centralized.[73]

Without going into the details of the teaching programs which have already been extensively studied by historians,[74] what interests us most is that the education provided in these schools met the needs of the artisan class of one of the most advanced agricultural and manufacturing areas in sixteenth century Europe, namely Lombardy and central northern Italy. Alongside the requirements of religious moralization emerged the formative needs of the local economy. These material needs show the complex physiognomy of the modern Italian Christian, namely the "counter-reformed" Catholic, around which a new school system was being created. Some historians, speaking of the Catholic confessional education of the sixteenth century, stated that the schools held by laymen and the religious, such as those cited above, "were more than literacy places of the subordinate classes, occasions for 'collective

---

70 "This is the Rule of the Society of the Servants of Children in Charity, who teach good Christian customs on the days of festivities to boys and girls and to read and write for free." Translation: "Questa è la Regola della compagnia delli servi dei puttini in carità, che insegna nei dì delle feste à puttini e alle puttine li boni costumi christiani e legere e scrivere gratis." In *Regola della Compagnia dei Serui di Puttini in Charità*, (In Ferrara: appresso Francesco de' Rossi da Valenza, after 1555), 1.
71 In the city of Monza, near Milan, it was attested that "two men go with the whips to send the children to school." Translation: "vanno doi homini con le fruste a caciar li putti alla schola." The information is taken from the Diocesan Archives of Milan (section IV, n. 65, files 18 *recto*-23 *verso*; 29 *recto*-31 *recto*) and is reported in Turchini, *Sotto l'occhio del padre*, 164.
72 Turchini, *Sotto l'occhio del padre*, 165 and Jean Hébrard, "La scolarisation des savoirs élémentaires à l'époque moderne," *Histoire de l'éducation* 38, (1978): 7–58, *inter alia* 49.
73 Bonaventure Racine, *Storia ecclesiastica divisa per secoli con riflessioni*, Vol. 15, (Florence: Francesco Pisoni, 1781), 199–200.
74 See note 65.

indoctrination, ritualized and sung' by means of which the texts were 'listened to and memorized, recognized rather than deciphered.' "[75] Yet, the data illustrate a much more complex and diversified situation. We know with certainty that the education given in the ever more structured schools of Christian doctrine did not reach the same degree of refinement for all pupils, many of whom only learned to read; however, we find the same habit in the Medieval and Renaissance schools and in many other sixteenth century educational institutions. The simple learning of religious formulas for basic literacy appears more like an element of continuity with the previous humanistic world than a counter-reformist novelty. In addition to this, as we shall see, the schools of religious orders in post-Tridentine Italy, in particular their colleges, would have taken free education to unimaginable levels in the fourteenth and even in the fifteenth centuries. If, on the one hand, some have said that the schools of doctrine did not reveal a true community dimension beyond the Sunday lesson in church,[76] other historians have recognized that these schools were at the center of the life of communities, both large and small. These institutions offered a new professional role to the early modern laity who helped religious teachers, allowing us to know more of a large and extensive voluntary activity growing over time, not only for religious purposes.[77]

The Schools of Christian Doctrine arose before the advent of all the modern religious orders that, either immediately or after a period of gestation in search of their true vocation, dedicated themselves to scholastic activity from the sixteenth century forward. We can affirm that the Schools of Doctrine represented, if not a model, at least a fundamental premise that highlighted the critical issues of the Mediterranean Catholic society in search of a strong identity to face the challenges posed by an uncertain future.

In 1536, while Castellino da Castello was starting his first school in the Milanese Oratory of Saints James and Philip, the new Clerics Regular of Saint Paul, future Barnabites, were defending themselves against the suspicion of Pelagianism. The reason for this suspicion came from the posthumous accusations raised in 1535 against one of the main spiritual inspirations of the Barnabites, the Dominican priest Fra' Battista Carioni da Crema. Carioni, who died in 1534, had been the spiritual guide of some of the founders of the

---

75 Elena Bonora, *La Controriforma*, (Rome-Bari: Laterza, 2005), 87, and Marina Roggero, *L'alfabeto conquistato. Apprendere e insegnare nell'Italia tra Sette e Ottocento*, (Bologna: Il Mulino, 1999).
76 Danilo Zardin, "Confraternite e comunità nelle campagne milanesi fra Cinque e Seicento," *La scuola cattolica* 112, (1984): 698–732, *inter alia* 716.
77 Cfr. Turchini, *Sotto l'occhio del padre*, 174.

Barnabites, namely Ludovica Torelli, countess of Guastalla, and Antonio Maria Zaccaria. He emphasized the freedom of man who, through the *Imitatio Christi*, could achieve grace autonomously. Carioni also expressed harsh criticisms against the moral habits of the clergy, praising instead a religiosity founded on charity and with little attention to dogma and ceremony. Even though he was never condemned as a heretic while alive, after his death Pope Paul IV placed his works on the *Index Librorum Prohibitorum*. All this did not fail to have repercussions on the early stages of the Clerics Regular of Saint Paul, whose beginnings were not easy. Only much later, during the pontificates of Pius V and Gregory XIII (1566–1572 and 1572–1585 respectively), the papacy explicitly exhorted the Barnabites to engage in education. This eventually led to the definitive entrance of their congregation into the educational world between the end of the sixteenth and the beginning of the seventeenth century.[78] Even the Somascan fathers, at the beginning of their activity in the 1530s, did not have education as their primary pastoral goal; their main interest was the care of orphans and prostitutes. Only at the end of the sixteenth century was the educational mission more clearly defined.[79] As for the Piarists, whose activities were immediately addressed by the educational sphere, these actions arose later in the 1590s when the general outline for the commitment of Catholic congregations within the school world had already been traced.[80] Only Jesuits had a better-defined involvement in educational activity as early as the 1540s.

In conclusion, the Schools of Christian Doctrine laid the groundwork for the arrival on the educational market of the new religious orders, namely Jesuits, Barnabites, Somascans, Theatines, and Piarists. These Schools of Christian Doctrine defined not only the essential pedagogical paradigms of their time, i.e. religious teaching and scientific-technical/literary education, they also paved the way from an institutional point of view. This aspect should not be

---

78   On Fra' Battista Carioni, see Paul Grendler, "Man is Almost a God: Fra Battista Carioni Between Renaissance and Catholic Reformation," in *Humanity and Divinity in Renaissance and Reformation: Essays in Honor of Charles Trinkaus*, ed. John W. O'Malley, Thomas M. Izbicki and Gerald Christianson (Leiden-New York-Cologne: Brill, 1993), 227–49. On the accusations of heresy against the Barnabites see Elena Bonora, *I conflitti della Controriforma. Santità e obbedienza nell'esperienza religiosa dei primi barnabiti*, (Florence: Le Lettere, 1998). On the first Barnabite schools see *I barnabiti nel IV centenario dalla fondazione 1533–1933*, (Genoa: Tipografia Artigianelli, 1933), 243–47.

79   *L'ordine dei Chierici Regolari Somaschi nel IV centenario della sua fondazione (1528–1928)*, (Rome: Presso la Curia Generalizia, 1928), 195.

80   Paul Grendler, "The Piarist of the Pious Schools," *Religious Orders of the Catholic Reformation: In Honor of John C. Olin on his Seventy-Fifth Birthday*, ed. Richard L. DeMolen, (New York: Fordham University Press, 1994), 252–78.

taken for granted if we think of the steadiness with which the cities defended their prerogatives in the educational sphere. The three most common settlement methods through which religious orders came to create new schools or colleges in Italian centers were the call of a municipal council, a private initiative (often aristocratic) and spontaneous foundation by members of the order. These methods were all anticipated by the members of the Society of the Servants of Children in Charity, with burdens, challenges, and suspicions as well as honors connected to them. In the next chapter, we will analyze the ways in which the new sixteenth-century religious congregations defined and redefined their educational vocation. There could have been exogenous factors such as eschatological anxieties, social needs, the Protestant Reformation and the Catholic response, as well as endogenous factors, such as disciplinary reorganization and responses to internal tensions. These congregations were initially a motley crowd. Even for their contemporaries it could sometimes be hard to distinguish one from another. For this reason, during the first decades of their history religious congregations needed to refine their individual identities. In doing so, they expressed both a new pedagogical and social model destined to last for centuries (in some respects even up to the mid-twentieth century) and an ecclesial model and a new identity for the Catholic Church, lasting until the threshold of the Second Vatican Council.

CHAPTER 2

Historical Paths

The Definition of Pedagogical Identities (16th–17th cc.)

1   Male Religious Orders

As it was shown in the previous chapter, the forms taken by educational institutions between the end of the Middle Ages and the Renaissance and Reformation period changed significantly. In the following chapter, the primary ways in which educational vocations developed within the various religious orders will be outlined. Among these dynamics, some common points can be identified. The most evident is the reluctance of the majority of religious orders to immediately and unreservedly embrace the educational cause and cultural commitment.

A high level of cultural, doctrinal, and scientific commitment, in fact, was perceived as risky to the spiritual renewal projects of these congregations. Culture was perceived as a potential tool for pride and religious deviation. Such fear was felt as much for the education of the internal members of each order, particularly the novices, as for the educational activity to be offered to the outside world. This distinction is a key point to keep in mind when approaching the processes of identity creation of the teaching orders. The acquisition of a full awareness of the importance of an internal educational system for their members was more problematic, in particular for the Barnabites, Somascans, and Capuchins. The fear was that an excessive level of education would lead young religious people towards overly autonomous thought and put them at risk of falling into heresy. Even while remaining in the ranks of orthodoxy, a refined education would contrast with the intentions of moral reform. Soon, however, it became clear that not having internal schools exposed the orders to an even greater risk of heresy, especially in their expansive phases when many young people without any theological training asked to be admitted.

Similar reasons led to an initial diffidence towards full educational commitment. While basic education for poor children was unanimously seen as good and just, anything more than this was sometimes perceived as potentially dangerous.[1] Even in this regard, however, it was clear that the best way to

---

[1] In this regard, we have seen in the first chapter how in certain urban contexts Protestant doctrines were widespread and how this had an undeniable link with the relatively high levels of urban literacy of the late Middle Ages.

avoid the spread of Lutheran ideas was to develop an effective educational system, replacing and partly merging with the previous municipal one. The attitude towards education, especially of the social elites, which required greater preparation on the part of teachers in the various fields of knowledge, gradually changed in each religious group. This could happen under the exhortation of religious authorities, sometimes in response to internal needs of the order. In general, however, it can be said that in the early decades of the seventeenth century the transition to a complete educational vocation was accomplished for all congregations of regular clerics. As we shall see, from the seventeenth century onwards within each order, the number of individuals involved in the various fields of science would grow considerably. This led to the creation of real and specific traditions of scientific research for some of these orders, and in other cases to results of condemnation by the Church, as in the case of the Barnabite astronomer Baranzano Redento.[2]

In this chapter I will try to outline with a comparative approach the paths undertaken by religious congregations towards a full educational identity. Among the main objects of investigation used for this purpose are the rules of study which were slowly developed by religious orders over the years. As we shall see, these were inspired by the Jesuit *Ratio Studiorum*. Other important sources for this analysis are the constitutions, statutes, and deliberations enacted by the councils and chapters that regularly met for the governance of the religious Orders. From these sources it is possible to better understand the historical framework in which religious congregations matured their educational vocation. These paths were often tormented and stormy, oscillating between eschatological anxieties, aspirations for moral reform and pastoral desires.

1.1 An Educational Benchmark: The Jesuits

The educational history of the Society of Jesus is undoubtedly the best known and the most studied among historians.[3] There are many reasons for this

---

2 Baranzano Redento (1590–1622), as we will see in chapter 5, was a Barnabite philosopher and astronomer. In his work *Uranoscopia seu de coelo* (1617) he supported the heliocentric doctrines of Copernicus. For this he was condemned, and he retracted in the work *Nova de motu terrae copernicaeo iuxta Summi Pontificis mentem disputatio* (1618). The *Campus philosophicus in quo omnes dialecticae quaestiones agitantur* (1622) is what remains of his activity as a philosopher.

3 It is impossible to summarize in one single note the amount of excellent scholarly work produced in recent years on the Jesuit educational history. For this reason, references will be limited to the most accessible works which have been used for this book. For the history of the first Jesuits, always refer to John O'Malley, *The First Jesuits* (Cambridge: Harvard University Press, 1993). For a comprehensive history of Jesuit education, see Paul Grendler, *Jesuit Schools*

success. The narrative of a worldwide engagement to the service of the faith, largely produced by Jesuits, has exerted a strong appeal for research. In addition, the anthropological implications of a global missionary commitment, the tenacious theological struggle against Protestantism and the tensions and contradictions of cutting-edge scientific thinking have provided further elements for the Jesuit legend. As mentioned in the introduction, however, this book will not look directly at Jesuits, and yet, as is clear from the first chapter, Jesuits will be a constant point of reference for the understanding of other religious orders. For this reason it is useful to provide the reader with a very brief summary of the educational path of the Jesuits, and some keys points with which to view their history as a useful comparison tool when looking at other congregations of regular clerics.

After the definitive approval of the Society in 1540, the arrival in the educational sphere was not a foregone conclusion. The first Jesuits had already been defined by Pope Paul III as *"in artibus Magistri, Universitate Parisiensi graduate,"*[4] but even for the followers of Ignatius the approach to education was not immediate, albeit precocious. The first members of the Society of Jesus initially imagined themselves on other paths, namely the mission to the Holy Land, or engaged in other charitable activities. As Paul Grendler pointed out, the Jesuits "had not intended to become educators," since Ignatius "had in mind more

---

    and Universities in Europe 1548–1773 (Leiden-Boston: Brill, 2019). For the hard relation between the Jesuits and the University world, refer to Paul Grendler, *The Jesuits and Italian Universities 1548–1773* (Washington: The Catholic University of America Press, 2017). For an interesting case study, see Paul Grendler, *The University of Mantua, the Gonzaga and the Jesuits, 1584–1630* (Baltimore: The Johns Hopkins University Press, 2009). The most comprehensive recent work on the production of the *Ratio Studiorum* is represented by Cristiano Casalini, and Claude Pavur, eds., *Jesuit Pedagogy, 1540–1616: A Reader* (Boston: Institute for Advanced Jesuit Studies, 2016). Concerning the early stages of Jesuit pedagogy, see Cristiano Casalini, *Benet Perera and Early Jesuit Pedagogy. Human Knowledge Freedom Superstition* (Rome: Anicia, 2016) and Id., *Aristotle in Coimbra: The Cursus Conimbricensis and the education at the College of Arts*, trans. Luana Salvarani (New York: Routledge, 2017). See also Thomas M. McCoog, ed., *The Mercurian Project: Forming Jesuit Culture 1573–1580* (Rome: Institutum Historicum Societatis Iesu, 2004). For the worldwide outreach of Jesuit philosophy, see Cristiano Casalini, ed., *Jesuit Logic and Late Ming China: Lectures on the Cursus Conimbricensis* (Boston: Institute of Advanced Jesuit Studies, 2019). On the Jesuit expansion in Italy, refer to Sabina Pavone, "I Gesuiti in Italia 1548–1773," in *Atlante della letteratura italiana*. Vol. 2: *Dalla Controriforma alla Restaurazione*, ed. Sergio Luzzatto, Gabriele Pedullà, Eriminia Irace (Torino: Einaudi, 2011), 359–73.

4 Gian Paolo Brizzi, "Scuole e collegi nell'antica Provincia Veneta della Compagnia di Gesù (1542–1773)," in *I Gesuiti e Venezia. Momenti e problemi di storia veneziana della Compagnia di Gesù*, ed. Mario Zanardi, (Padova: Gregoriana Libreria Editrice, 1994), 467–511, quote page 470.

dramatic service to God." Nonetheless, Grendler continues, "events conspired to bring schooling to their attention," and this was the story of all the orders who eventually committed to school instruction.[5] It is always Grendler, in his recent and fundamental synthesis of Jesuit school history,[6] who highlights how the Society's first steps in the educational world responded more to momentary contingencies than to a concerted plan. Proof of this lies in the scattered nature of the very first schools opened or taken over by society.

The first experiments took place in Goa, India, in the Portuguese colonial empire. After the Franciscans' refusal to take care of the schools opened by the colonial authorities in 1541, Francis Xavier appointed one Jesuit in 1543, and a second in 1545 to teach Latin and grammar and to administer the sacraments. Another experiment, which later failed, took place in the Spanish town of Gandía, in 1545, in response to the call of some Jesuits by Francisco de Borja to open a school later to be transformed into a university. More successful was the arrival of the Jesuits in Messina, where in 1548 they opened what is conventionally considered the first true Jesuit college.

These examples immediately reveal one of the most distinctive traits of the Jesuits: their global reach. The development of the Jesuit educational commitment from the college of Messina onwards was amazing. Already at the death of Ignatius of Loyola, in 1556, the schools of the order numbered forty-six. It is difficult to see such development in little more than ten years in other religious orders. It is evident how the pedagogic zeal of these religious people responded to the educational needs bequeathed by the world of communal schools described at the end of the previous chapter. However, this is not the place to go into the details of the Society's educational policies, nor the pedagogical choices related to teaching, nor even the professional paths of Jesuit teachers. For this reason, the reader may refer to Grendler's recent synthesis, namely *Jesuit Schools and Universities in Europe 1548–1773*. What is useful here is to bring to light the dynamics in which the Jesuits represented a necessary reference point for other religious orders on their way to education.

Since his arrival in Messina, it was immediately clear to Ignatius and his early followers that education would be one of the main fields of Jesuit practice. In this early awareness we can find many of the aspects that the other teaching congregations would also face. For Barnabites, Somascans, and Piarists, the direct or indirect confrontation with Jesuits would always be present, both virtuous and problematic. Despite their great enthusiasm, the death

---

5   Grendler, *Schooling in Renaissance Italy*, 363.
6   Grendler, *Jesuit Schools*, 1–6.

of Ignatius had left his successors with enormous problems related to the lack of teachers to meet the great demand for schools and an increase in the number of students.[7] The Piarists found themselves in a remarkably similar situation in the first decades of their history. In the face of great development they did not have enough teachers. It is no coincidence, as we shall see, that a Jesuit was appointed to investigate such problems.

On the other hand, Jesuits were the forerunners of many of the most original educational solutions in Tridentine Italy. From an institutional point of view, among the most important examples of this innovative capacity was the development of a school model inherited from Renaissance humanism, the college. The college, as an institution, was born between the fourteenth and fifteenth centuries as an educational alternative to medieval universities. Within it the emphasis was placed on the moral education of the individual on the basis of classical authorities. Universities insisted on a more technical type of education aimed at the legal professions or theological teaching. Jesuits were able to take this humanistic invention and make it an instrument for the application of their mission in the service of the Church. Within Jesuit colleges, young people from the urban bourgeoisie were generally accepted free of charge and were educated according to the classical authorities and the dictates of the post Tridentine Church. The model of the college had a strong influence on other religious orders, which adapted the model to their needs, but always kept the Jesuit example in mind.[8]

In addition, it is worth noting the creation of boarding schools specifically intended for the aristocracy, the Colleges of Nobles.[9] These were schools reserved for young nobles destined to form the ranks of government of the *ancien régime* in Europe. The Colleges of Nobles began to appear at the beginning of the seventeenth century and gave rise, despite internal opposition, to the founding of similar institutions in other religious orders. The Colleges for Nobles were usually opened by the monarchs at the head of Italian states, of which the first was the College of Parma founded by Duke Ranuccio I Farnese in 1601 and taken over by Jesuits in 1604.[10]

In general, some boarding schools and Colleges of Nobles during the sixteenth and seventeenth centuries became particularly important institutions,

---

7   Grendler, *Jesuit Schools*, 10.
8   Grendler, *Jesuit Schools*, 12–14.
9   Grendler, *Jesuit Schools*, 45–48.
10 Cristiano Casalini, "Building a Duchy to the Greater Glory of God. The Jesuits and the Farnesian Educational Policy in Parma (1539–1604)," *Educazione. Giornale di pedagogia critica* IV, 1 (2015): 29–48.

comparable in prestige to universities. This was clearly due to the prestige of their professors, in some cases among the best trained in Europe, but also because they provided an alternative for Jesuits who had encountered challenges in entering universities as teaching staff. Despite initial difficulties often due to the jealousy with which both secular and religious authorities defended the autonomy of university institutions, the Jesuits managed to enter European universities, in some cases founding their own. The models of these educational partnerships could vary. In Italy, for example, where cities still played an important role in the seventeenth century, a Jesuit-civic university model was the most successful.[11] Despite this, the religious orders never had the determination of their Jesuits counterparts to enter the university system, but the presence of the Society of Jesus was not irrelevant in their stories. In many cases, in fact, future members of religious teaching congregations who attended universities had Jesuit professors. In other cases, individuals belonging to religious teaching orders became professors in civic universities.

The aspects of Jesuit history described so far are simple heuristic tools, useful to better understand some comparative aspects to be developed later. The one presented here is a framework into which to insert the frequent comparative references between various religious orders and the Jesuits. The most striking aspect of the educational history of the Society of Jesus, however, was the constant and fervent internal debate on the most effective and appropriate educational practices to be adopted in schools. The most important result of this tireless educational planning was the *Ratio atque Institutio Studiorum Societatis Iesu* (The Official Plan for Jesuit Education) completed in 1599.[12] As Paul Grendler states,

> The complete Jesuit course of studies had three ascending parts intended for three different student constituencies. At the same time, it was a remarkably unified and coherent plan of studies that Jesuits believed enabled everyone to learn.[13]

---

[11] Grendler, *Jesuit Schools*, 85–91. See also Paul Grendler, *The Jesuits and Italian Universities 1548–1773* (Washington: The Catholic University of America Press, 2017).

[12] Cristiano Casalini and Claude Pavur, eds., *Jesuit Pedagogy, 1540–1616: A Reader* (Boston: Institute for Advanced Jesuit Studies, 2016). See also Allan P. Farrell, *The Jesuit Code of Liberal Education: Development and Scope of the Ratio Studiorum* (Milwaukee: Bruce Publishing Company, 1938), 25–27.

[13] Grendler, *Jesuit Schools*, 15.

This fundamental document, as we shall see, exerted a decisive influence on the educational forms of all religious orders born in the sixteenth and seventeenth centuries. All the congregations dedicated to teaching developed their own rule of study more or less directly inspired by that of the Jesuits. Let us now turn our attention to the educational paths of the other religious orders and how they were inspired by or interacted with the previous pedagogical experience of the Jesuits.

1.2 *The Barnabites*

The educational story of the Clerics Regular of Saint Paul, also known as Barnabites, begins in a strange way.[14] Their history has even been defined as "a strange paradox in the history of education."[15] During their initial years, perhaps more so than in other orders, transformations and contradictions, characteristic traits of an era of lacerating and radical changes, increased. In addition, their first steps contained elements of continuity between the two phases of Italian cultural and scholastic history, as discussed in the first chapter. It is for this reason that it is worth beginning the discussion of the history of the educational vocations of the sixteenth century religious orders with the Barnabites. In their story, the symbol of both continuity and rupture was the Dominican friar Battista Carioni, inspirer and spiritual director of the founder of the Barnabites, the *cremonese* nobleman Antonio Maria Zaccaria. Carioni, Paul Grendler said, "linked Renaissance and Catholic Reformation."[16] This definition is based on Carioni's ability to combine the Florentine Renaissance Platonism of Marsilio Ficino and Pico della Mirandola with the eschatological and reform needs of his time, which enabled him to attract "educated upper-class Italians searching for a new religious direction."[17] This attitude passed from Carioni to Zaccaria and deeply defined the physiognomy of the first Barnabites. The order, founded in 1530 and approved by Clement VII in 1533,

---

14 The name 'Barnabites' (*Barnabiti*) derives from the donation of the ancient convent of San Barnaba to the order in 1538 as their main seat. See Antonio Maria Gentili, *Les Barnabites. Manuel d'histoire et de spiritualité de l'Ordre des Clercs Réguliers de Saint Paul Decapité* (Rome, 2012), 70.
15 Rocco Pititto, "Teorie pedagogiche e pratica educativa. La Ratio Studiorum dei Barnabiti," *Barnabiti Studi* 26, (2009): 85–109.
16 Paul Grendler, "Man is Almost a God: Fra Battista Carioni Between Renaissance and Catholic Reformation," in *Humanity and Divinity in Renaissance and Reformation: Essays in Honor of Charles Trinkaus*, ed. John W. O'Malley, Thomas M. Izbicki and Gerald Christianson, (Leiden-New York-Cologne: Brill, 1993), 227–49.
17 Ivi, 249.

was steeped in reforming zeal through works of charity and deeply inspired by the *Devotio Moderna*.

How did this order move from zealous spiritual reform to the world of school and teaching? It was perhaps its own commitment that triggered the chain of events that led to this precise charism. The ability of Carioni and his first followers to attract young and educated nobles soon led to great success among the social elites of northern Italy, particularly in Veneto and Lombardy where the Barnabite movement rapidly expanded. However, the radical attitudes of some early members of the congregation, particularly the spiritual mother Paola Antonia Negri, aroused the suspicion of the Venetian government. Venice, in fact, saw in any religious order outside its borders the potential for foreign spies.[18] Paola Antonia Negri, an early follower of Fra' Battista Carioni, together with Ludovica Torelli, had founded the order of the Angelic Sisters (*Angeliche*). These nuns were a sort of female counterpart to the Barnabites, like a twin congregation, without a precise distinction. The accusations made by Venice against Sister Negri covered a range of arrogant and unwomanly acts. Among them was the charge of giving orders to Barnabite priests, bizarre spiritual abuses such as trying to separate wives from husbands, and even the attempt to steal state secrets of the Republic through the frequent confession of members of the ruling class. Based on these accusations, more or less instrumentally used by Venice, the Barnabites were expelled from the Republic in 1551.[19] The investigations, however, did not stop there, and reached Rome. Two fathers of the clerics of Saint Paul were arrested in 1552 in the papal capital and the works of Battista Carioni were examined for possible heretical propositions. At the end of the investigation, the *Angeliche* and the Barnabites did not suffer further serious consequences and the two priests were freed; however, measures were taken in Rome both to reassure Venice and to inject order into a group of religious people with habits verging on heresy. The two congregations had to separate in a clear and total way without being able to

---

18 The *Angeliche*, like the Barnabites, were also a Lombard congregation, based in Milan, potentially at the service of Spain. Moreover, the imperial governor in Lombardy was Ferrante Gonzaga, a personal friend of Ludovica Torelli, the other founder of the Angelic Sisters, of whom Carioni was a confessor and spiritual guide for many years. See Elena Bonora, *I conflitti della Controriforma. Santità e obbedienza nell'esperienza dei primi barnabiti* (Florence: Le Lettere, 1998). On the Barnabite expulsion from Venice, see also: Gabriella Zarri, "Living Saints. A Typology of Female Sanctity in the Early Sixteenth Century," in *Women and Religion in Medieval and Renaissance Italy*, ed. Daniel Bornstein, Roberto Rusconi (Chicago and London: The University of Chicago Press, 1996), 219–304, in particular 274.

19 Grendler, *Man is almost a God*, 247.

have further relations with each other aside from confessors for the nuns. The Angelic Sisters became subject to strict rules of cloistering, putting an end, as we shall see later in the chapter, to their educational experiment in Milan aimed at educating young girls.

It is within this context that an increase in the awareness and need to give themselves an adequate education so as to no longer run the risk of being theologically unprepared occurred amongst the Barnabites. Similar to other orders, the congregation was until then mainly composed of educated adults; only at the beginning of the 1550s did a sufficient number of young people begin to open internal schools for the training of novices. The first school was opened in 1553 at the Milanese convent of *Santa Maria della Pace* and another in 1557 in Pavia. Among the first people to complete their training with the Barnabites was the Genoese nobleman Alessandro Sauli, a key figure in turning the congregation towards the creation of a school curriculum. In the 1560s, in fact, Sauli was a professor of theology and philosophy between the newly established schools of Pavia and Milan, before becoming confessor of San Carlo Borromeo.[20] Sauli created a first circle of university students within the Clerics of Saint Paul, but the attitude of the congregation toward higher education was still fluctuating and its identity as a teaching order was far from reaching fruition. It was for this reason that Sauli was later forbidden to accept positions at the University of Pavia.

The real turning point in the order came with the Constitutions of 1579.[21] These rules established that the father general should elect a prefect of studies. They also introduced the scholastic discussion regarding what should take place on holidays to accompany the normal course given by the teacher. The duration of studies was lengthened and the time when young fathers could be available for schooling activities was delayed. In return, they were more educated and better prepared for practicing in the ministry. Father Giovanni Pietro Besozzi, a prominent promoter of this study reform, said that "wanting to move fast makes you go slowly and creates delays." Even the pope, Pius V, explicitly expressed his desire for the Barnabites to be specifically involved

---

20   Alessandro Sauli was beatified in 1741 by Pope Benedict XIV and canonized in 1904 by Pius X. See Simona Negruzzo, "Alessandro Sauli: il professore santo," in *Almum Studium Papiense. Storia dell'Università di Pavia*, I: *Dalle origini all'età spagnola*, II, (Milan: Cisalpino, 2013), 975–76; Pietro Grazioli, *Della vita, virtù e miracoli del Beato Alessandro Sauli* (In Bologna: Per Giovanni Antonio Ghidini, 1741); Francesco Luigi Barelli, *Vita del Venerabil Servo di Dio Alessandro Sauli* (In Bologna: Per Costantino Pisarri, 1705).

21   "Rules of the Study": Third Book, Fifth Chapter of the COSTITUZIONI DEI CHIERICI REGOLARI DI SAN PAOLO DECOLLATO. PRIMA EDIZIONE DELLE COSTITUZIONI DEL 1579. Ed. Giovanni Scalese. In Barnabiti Studi 31, (2014), 241–58.

in school activities: "Our Lord (the Pope), in discussing your Congregation, expresses what he would like: that it be more attached to studies than it is to what it does, so that it can be all the more useful for the salvation of souls."[22]

As far as the approach to knowledge is concerned, the Constitutions of 1579 express a triple criterion to be followed: reason, authority, and the holy spirit (*rationem, auctoritatem et Spiritus sancti ductum libere sequantur*). Man's reason is put first, a decisive aspect in determining the opening of the next generation of Barnabites to the world of scientific discoveries and the new cultural paradigms of the seventeenth century. In this period, the general of the Order, Agostino Tornielli, definitively established in Pavia the seat for theological, philosophical, and Jewish studies, while Latin and Greek studies were concentrated in Cremona. Another key figure was Carlo Bascapé, the future general of the order, who reorganized literary studies, without which, he claimed, no other study could exist.[23] The wound caused by the doctrinal troubles of the mid-sixteenth century was still open, however, and the greatest emphasis in education was placed on theology. The general chapter of 1662 thus decreed the opening of a school of theology in Rome at the church of Saints Blaise and Charles in Catinari, where each province of the order was required to send two students.

A 1665 decree of the congregation informs us of the internal organization of the probation houses. The Roman province had one novitiate in Zagarolo, a second in Macerata for philosophy and another in Rome for theology. For both theology and philosophy, the novices had to attend for at least three years. The Lombard province, on the other hand, had its first novitiate in Monza and the second in Saint Barnaba for theology. The number of clerics for each of these houses was not to exceed ten.[24]

So far, we have focused on the evolution of internal studies of the order, which in the seventeenth century assumed their definitive physiognomy, but how did things go with the schools for the external world? As briefly mentioned, the Barnabites went through a rough process in acquiring full identity as a teaching order, though this did not prevent them from becoming one of the most successful and complete examples of these orders on the Italian

---

22 Quotes by Besozzi and Pio V are also reported in Gentili, *Les Barnabites*, 142.
23 Carlo Bascapé was elected general of the Barnabites for the first time in 1586, a position renewed twice. He was also elected bishop of Novara in 1593 and became promoter of the cause of canonization of St. Charles Borromeo. See Dorino Tuniz, *Carlo Bascapé. Un vescovo sulle orme di san Carlo* (Novara: Interlinea, 2015); Innocenzo Chiesa, *Vita di Carlo Bascapè: barnabita e vescovo di Novara, 1550–1615* (Florence: Olschki, 1993).
24 Gentili, *Les Barnabites*, 143.

educational scene. A first attempt to open schools to lay society was made by the newly elected general of the order, Carlo Bascapé, in Cremona in 1586. The initiative, however, failed because of the strong internal opposition of the congregation, demonstrating a very ambiguous attitude towards the role of educators. As we shall see, other attempts to open a boarding school in Pisa, one at the invitation of the Grand Duke Ferdinando de Medici, and another in Ragusa in 1608 at the request of the Pope Clement VIII, were unsuccessful. The reason given by the fathers was always the same. In the letter of refusal sent to the pope by Cosimo Dossena, Procurator General of the order, in which he refused to open a school in Ragusa, it was stated that the Congregation of Saint Paul had not been founded to teach letters.[25] Education, it was explained, distracted the fathers from their religious offices and, it was claimed, the order did not have enough teachers. However, the refusal given to the pope had to shake the souls of the fathers. In Father Dossena's tone there is more frustration than annoyance at not being able to accept the commission.

Under this circumstance, therefore, there was perhaps a psychological turning point within the congregation to take a decisive step towards assuming full educational commitment. As Antonio Maria Gentili explains, there was already a favorable current among the Barnabites to open schools for the outside world as an apostolate activity. At the head of this movement was Candido Poscolonna.[26] As Poscolonna claimed, even the ancient medieval Benedictine schools were open to the laity, but this did not prevent monks from fulfilling their religious offices. Poscolonna attacked the widespread feeling that the educational vocation did not structurally belong to the Barnabites. He recalled that from the origins of the Barnabites, their founding fathers had combined spiritual and literary education, evoking the humanistic spirit of Battista Carioni. He added, moreover, that the missionary approach at the very basis of Saint Paul's spirituality found education to be a central tool. This was true even in the use of profane texts that opened one to revealed truths and to the exercise of honest profession. After all, Poscolonna concluded, if one of the reasons against the opening of schools was that nothing was mentioned in this regard in the very first constitutions of the sixteenth century, then nothing had been said against their institution either.[27] The breach was definitively opened by two events. In 1603, the Milanese nobleman Giambattista Arcimboldi left in

---

25 Cosimo Dossena served as bishop of Tortona from 1612 to 1620. See Bartolomeo Gavanti, *Vita del venerabile Cosimo Dossena vescovo di Tortona* (Milan: Ditta Boniardi Pogliani di Ermen. Besozzi, 1860).
26 Gentili, *Les Barnabites*, 144.
27 *Ibidem*.

his will a large sum of money for the opening in the city of a school for youth to be led by the Barnabites. In 1605, during a memorable general chapter of the order, which was still shocked by the refusal given to the pope but galvanized by the unrepeatable Milanese opportunity, it was decided to embrace the educational apostolate without reservation. In 1608, under the generalate of Cosimo Dossena, the Arcimboldi schools were opened in Milan. From this moment the expansion of the Barnabites into the educational market proceeded very quickly.[28]

In order to govern the rapidly growing field of public lay schools, it became necessary for the Congregation to draw up rules for studies. The Barnabites felt the need to give themselves a *Ratio Studiorum*, following the example of the Jesuits. The comparison with the Society of Jesus is not incidental or dictated by the historiographic popularity of their famous *Ratio*. At the time we are discussing, in fact, the rule of study of the followers of Ignatius, finally defined in 1599, had already become a pedagogical paradigm that inspired both lay and religious schools.[29] The rules of study of the Barnabites, the *Exterarum Scholarum disciplina apud Clericos Regulares S. Pauli in Provincia Mediolanensi*, were promulgated in 1666, drafted by Father Melchiorre Gorini. A key moment in the development of the rules was the experience of the Arcimboldi schools. As Angelo Bianchi underscores, despite the influence of the Jesuit *Ratio* on the first *Regulae* made at the Arcimboldi, these two rules differed visibly.[30] The Barnabite rule did not fix content and teaching methods, two elements of great importance in the Jesuit *Ratio*. The *Ratio Studiorum*, in fact, established authors to be explained, exercises to be assigned, content and methods, objectives of teaching methods and examinations. The Arcimboldi rule established only the duration of the lessons, indicating that the two professors must be "well trained" (*bene periti*) and that in case of absence they must provide a substitute at their own expense. The only suggestion made regarding teaching methods was to follow the custom of the professors whose disciplines were practiced in the city schools.[31]

---

28 For the expansion of the Barnabite schools, refer to the third chapter of this book.
29 On the *Ratio Studiorum* of the Regular Clerics of Saint Paul, see Rocco Pititto, "Teorie pedagogiche e pratica educativa. La Ratio Studiorum dei Barnabiti," *Barnabiti Studi* 26, (2009): 85–109.
30 Angelo Bianchi, "Le suole Arcimboldi a Milano nel XVII secolo: professori, studenti, cultura scolastica," *Barnabiti Studi* 19, (2002): 55–78.
31 Some more information on the contents of the teaching is reported in a text preserved in the Archivio Storico dei Barnabiti in Milan, the "Orders and Rules for good governance and profit of the college infrascribed" (*Ordini et Regole per il buon governo et profitto dell'infrascritto collegio*, ASBMi, B, cart. II, fasc. IV): "The master of humanity will compose

The 1666 rule, on the other hand, had a more marked and conscious pedagogical imprint. This time every aspect of the student's life, from a pedagogical, cultural, disciplinary and medical point of view, was carefully considered.[32] The Barnabites showed themselves to be attentive pedagogists, aware of the universality of their educational mission. In addition, they were conscious that if they wanted "the student to succeed as an excellent Christian, as an excellent citizen, useful to society," they had to follow "what the natural inclination, or his special condition calls him to."[33] However, despite this careful structuring, the Barnabite schools always maintained a lower social profile than the Jesuit schools. The Regular Clerics of Saint Paul never attempted to rival the Jesuits or establish new universities, and they remained more flexible to the different socio-economic needs of individual micro-areas as we will see in the next chapter. Such flexibility made the Barnabites less suspect to the monarchs of the eighteenth century and allowed them to survive the expulsions and suppressions that various religious orders experienced in the European states of that time.[34]

In the meantime, the Barnabites were able to innovate further. In the wake of the writings of authors such as Ludovico Antonio Muratori and Antonio Genovesi, the Regular Clerics of Saint Paul partly abandoned the traditional

---

every day or letters or verses in addition to the lesson, repetitions, examinations, and disputes. The Master of Rhetoric shall have recited more often than he can declamations and prayers, ensuring that his pupils in such exercises put into practice the precepts of the Rhetoric with good judgment and diligence, warning each of them respectively their pupils of what they have missed." Original quote: "Il maestro dell'humanità farà comporre ogni giorno o epistole o versi oltre alla lettione, repetitione et esamini, over dispute. Il maestro della Rettorica faccia recitare più spesso che potrà declamationi, orationi o crie, procurando che li suoi scolari in tali esercitij metino in pratica li precetti di essa Retorica con buon giuditio e dilligenza, avisando cadauno di loro rispettivamente li loro scolari di quello in che havranno mancato." The source is also reported in: Bianchi, "Le scuole Arcimboldi a Milano," 63n.

32 The disciplinary rules were very strict, and regulated the behavior of the boarders at school, at the table, in their studies, in public places, in their relations with the teachers, with the security staff, with the parents themselves, in their way of dressing and even in the linguistic expression to be used in interpersonal relations. It was intended to create in the students the habits necessary to reach certain behavioral standards required by the contexts of life, specific to each of the students and the boarders. Cfr. Bianchi, "Le scuole Arcimboldi a Milano," 70–71.

33 Pititto, "Teorie pedagogiche e pratica educativa," 95.

34 The expulsion of the Jesuits from the Iberian and the Borbonic states occurred between 1759 and 1767, and their suppression in 1773 is the most famous of these reductions but the expulsion of the Somascans from the Republic of Venice in 1769 should not be forgotten either.

humanistic-rhetorical structure. They broadened their approach to a type of school which was more focused on technical-scientific subjects.[35] In this way the Barnabites gave further vent to the scientific research carried out in the past within the order, which will be the subject of further analysis. In this regard, the story of Baranzano Redento is only one of the most famous examples.[36] It was thanks to this innovative and self-critical force that in the second half of the eighteenth century the Barnabite schools did not undergo the school reforms undertaken in Austrian Lombardy by Count Carlo di Firmian. The Barnabite pedagogy had already been implemented and only the Napoleonic suppressions of religious orders in 1810 would be able to stop this path.[37]

1.3   The Somascans

The path of the Somascan fathers towards a full awareness of their own educational vocation, just like the Barnabites, was not without uncertainties and doubts. The initial aim of the company, created in 1532 by the former Venetian soldier Girolamo Emiliani (1486–1537), is well defined by the first name adopted by the congregation: *Compagnia dei Servi dei Poveri di Cristo* (Company of the Servants of the Poor in Christ). Initially, the goal of the Somascans was to care for people living in poverty and misery, including children and especially orphans. In general, throughout the sixteenth century, a certain reluctance to unreservedly embrace the post-Tridentine educational cause remained in the order. Once again, the reasons for this reticence were to be found in the fear of falling into an intellectual pride and the search for idle knowledge.

As evidence of this, we note that in 1557 only two of the twenty-one houses of the congregation were dedicated exclusively to schools, (those in Milan and Merone in the territory of Como) while the remaining houses were for orphans, *converse* (girls rescued from the streets) and virgins.[38] Of course, even

---

35   Ludovico Antonio Muratori (1672–1750) and Antonio Genovesi (1713–1769) are two key figures of the Italian Enlightenment. Both were presbyters, philosophers, and intellectuals trained in a wide variety of disciplines. Muratori, however, was more focused on historical-philological studies, to the point of being considered the father of Italian historiography and in particular of medieval studies, while Genovesi concentrated more on economic studies. Their thinking had a strong impact on Italian education. In 1754 Genovesi activated the first university course in economics at the University of Naples, while Muratori revolutionized the critical approach to historical sources. See Franco Venturi, *Settecento Riformatore: Da Muratori a Beccaria, 1730–1764* (Torino: Einaudi, 1976).
36   On Baranzano Redento, see Footnote 4 in Chapter 2 and Chapter 5.
37   Pititto, "Teorie pedagogiche e pratica educativa," 97–98.
38   ACTA CONGREGATIONIS, 1557, I (1528–1602). The school in Merone wasn't opened until 1551, when, "On October 12, the Company gathered [...] and it was resolved that for a year they would try to hold a school in Merone, estimating this to be necessary for the

in orphanages children were given some form of education. During a chapter held in 1560, it was stated that "in all the houses children of talent must be trained in reading the table, the grammar of Donato and in writing."[39] The 'table' (*tavola*) was usually a board with the alphabet and some prayers used between the thirteenth and the sixteenth century for basic literacy. The grammar of Donato was a manual used for the elementary teaching of Latin. In this way, education for orphans followed the more traditional and simple forms of basic education, similar to the Lombard Schools of Christian Doctrine.

However, during the first decades of their history, there was still no trace of a clear Somascan identity as a religious teaching congregation. The constitutions and deliberations made on scholastic matters during the Chapters of the Order show caution in making a clear educational commitment. In 1544, at the very beginning of the internal debate on whether or not to undertake a full educational enterprise, it was decided "that only children who were suitable for serving God and whose relatives wanted to be educated in religion and piety should be accepted, having them observe the established school rules."[40] Moreover, in order to avoid making education the major purpose of the Order and to maintain their mission of helping the poor in 1547, a chapter held at the Venetian convent of Saint Nicholas decided to exclude children of the rich (*li figliouli de' gentiluomini*) from the schools in order to help those of the poor.[41]

Nonetheless, things gradually started to change and in 1580 a decree, issued in Venice, proclaimed that "no one will study other than those sciences that will be determined and each student shall give an account of the study done in the past year." Some years later in 1585 during the chapter held at the convent of San Majolo near Pavia, it was urged that "at least some students had to be held in all the colleges."[42] We do not know whether this last decree referred to external students, namely lay boys who were not Somascans, or to internal

---

good footing of the congregation; and in case that in this place the school was not going to last, it would move elsewhere." Original quote: "Li 12 ottobre si unì poi in Merone la Compagnia e fu risoluto, che per un anno si provasse a tenere Scuola in Merone, stimandosi ciò necessario per il buon incaminamento dell'Opera; che quando pure in tal luogo non si conoscesse durevole la detta scuola, si trasferisse altrove." Acta, I, 1551.

39 Original quote: "In tutte le opere li Putti d'ingegno si ammaestrino nel leggere a tavola, nella grammatica del Donato e nello scrivere." ACTA, I, 1560.
40 Original quote: "Nel Capitolo di quest'anno in Somasca fu stabilito che si continuasse la scuola, ma non si accettassero che figliuoli atti a servire a Dio e di cui i parenti piacer avessero che s'instruissero nella pietà, facendo loro osservar le regole della scuola stabilite." ACTA, I, 1544.
41 General chapters, *Archivio Storico dei Padri Somaschi*, Roma. Venice, October 1st, 1547.
42 Original quote: "Che nessuno studi se non quelle scienze che saranno lui determinate e che ciascuno renda ragione ogni anno dello studio fatto l'anno passato." Orders and up to

novices; however, it was a clear symptom of how education was not yet the central element of the Somascan mission as their schools were not yet able to attract enough students. Despite the gradual change of trend, however, there was continued resistance to committing to the field of education. In 1581, the fathers refused to take charge of the schools of Biella because they only wanted to focus on the care of orphans. In 1587, fathers who refused to teach grammar, arts or sciences lost their right to vote in the capitulary seat for a period of two years and could also be imprisoned, an unequivocal sign of resistance to schooling by many Somascan Fathers.[43]

From the 1590s onwards, however, things moved towards an increasingly perceptible educational turning point. The fact that in 1587 the same punishments continued to be imposed on those who refused to teach testifies to the will of the order to strengthen its educational offering. In 1590, a new decree stipulated that lessons should be given to all the young novices in the houses of the order, and that the houses of greatest observance should be placed under the direction of a teacher.[44] Perhaps the most evident sign of this change was the request made to the Somascans in 1595 by Pope Clement VIII to establish a school for nobles in Rome, namely the Clementino College.[45] In this act, we see a convergence with the path undertaken by the Jesuits more or less in the same period. Although most of the Jesuit noble boarding schools in Italy were to be founded later, namely in the seventeenth century, this was now the direction being pursued by religious teaching orders. Even the prototypical Jesuit noble school, the College of Parma, was founded by a duke in 1601, the Jesuits not taking direction of it until 1604. Similarly, in the case of Parma, the creation of the Clementino, whose activity began only in 1601, was still an exception or at least an early case. It was symptomatic of an alignment with the Roman Catholic world that counterbalanced the Lombard-Venetian center of gravity of the Somascan congregation. It is perhaps not by chance that right at that moment we start finding references in Somascan sources to Jesuit schools. In some cases it is even possible to see a hint of educational competition between the fathers of the Society; in 1597 two young boys were admitted to the school

---

1591, *Archivio Storico dei Padri Somaschi*, Roma. April 16th, 1580. Patriarchal Seminary of Venice; May 6th, 1585, San Majolo, Pavia.

43   ACTA, I, 1581, 1587.
44   ACTA, I, 1590.
45   For the Clementino College, refer to Luigi Mascilli Migliorini, ed., *I Somaschi* (Rome: Edizioni di Storia e Letteratura, 1992), 92–94. See also Ottavio Maria Paltrinieri, *Elogio del nobile e pontificio Collegio Clementino di Roma* (Presso Antonio Fulgoni, 1795).

in Genoa, although it was specified that they "attended the Jesuit school."[46] It was during these years that the foundations of new Somascan schools started increasing. This process concerned not only the acceptance of municipal schools; the growing Somascan commitment to education related also to the opening of colleges and boarding schools for nobles, such as the Clementino of Rome. Boarding schools for nobles were also founded in Lugano in 1597, again at the behest of Pope Clement VIII, and in 1614 in Rivolta d'Adda near Cremona in northern Italy. In the latter case, the college was established by the will of the noble Maino family. The management of the school had initially been given to the Franciscan order, but it was soon deemed incapable of running the college because of its policy of living from charity and donations, so it passed to the Somascans, this time at the behest of Pope Paul V.[47] These colleges for nobles remained the spearhead of Somascan education in Italy for a long time. It is interesting to note that not only the Clementino of Rome, but also the provincial colleges represented an excellence in the educational landscape of the Peninsula; in 1775, the college of Rivolta had ninety boarders and a few years later would be attended by Alessandro Manzoni, the father of the Italian language.

At the beginning of the seventeenth century, therefore, the educational vocation of the Somascans became more and more marked. Their activity quickly spread to public education through the hiring of Somascan teachers in municipal schools, as in the cases of Melfi and Velletri (1616), Orzinuovi (1626), and Lodi and Salò (1627). As we see from certain place names, the congregation had also arrived in central and southern Italy. During this period, the founding of boarding schools for nobles increased, as in the cases of Santa Maria degli Angeli College in Fossano, Piedmont (1623), the College of San Carlo in Albenga, Liguria (1625), the College of San Clemente in Monferrato, then part of the Gonzaga States (1626) established under the authority of Pope Urban VIII, the Caracciolo College in Naples, and the College of Nobles in Brescia (1628).[48]

---

[46] Original extended quote: "Accettati furono alla probazione: Pantaleo de Conti genovese d'anni 60, con due figlioli, due cittadini da Brescia che frequentano le scuole de Padri Gesuiti." ACTA, I, 1597.

[47] On the Somascan boarding school of Rivolta, see Migliorini, *I Somaschi*, 39–40; Maurizio Sangalli, *Per il Cinquecento religioso italiano. Clero, cultura, società* (Rome: Edizioni dell'Ateneo, 2003), 339.

[48] ACTA CONGREGATIONIS, II, (1603–1663). On the spreading of Somascan schools, refer to Giovanni Alcaini, "Origini e progressi degli istituti diretti dai Padri Somaschi." *Somascha. Bollettino di Storia dei Padri Somaschi* 4, (1979): 70–175. For the history of education in

In spite of this, we see the pedagogical dimension of these new institutions still strongly linked to the humanistic paradigm of "rhetoric, humanity, grammar and abecedary," at least as far as public schools were concerned. A driving force in the definition of Somascan pedagogy was the Clementino College of Rome. The educational system issued in 1600 for this school, *Le regole circa lo studio*, was clearly inspired by the Jesuit *Ratio Studiorum* and was aimed primarily at the education of social elites. In this pedagogical rule, Latin, disputations and theater played fundamental roles.[49]

Novices, after two years of rhetoric, studied logic and, after a further examination, philosophy and theology for three years. Theology was learned mainly through treatises, namely *De Deo Trino et uno, De Angelis, De incarnatione, De fide, spe et charitate, De actibus humanis, De gratia, De Sacramentis in genere et in specie*, and *De poenitentia et Eucaristia*, on which the young Somascans were examined. Based on the outcome of their examinations, the religious could be assigned to preaching or teaching activities, provided that all were serving in lower-level schools.[50]

Between the end of the seventeenth and the first decades of the eighteenth century, therefore, we see how Somascan pedagogy remained very linked to traditional humanistic curriculum. Nonetheless, things were changing. As Antonella Barzazi underlines, the second half of the seventeenth century had experienced a profound transformation in the teaching of philosophy and its traditional instruments. Aristotelianism, driven out by Baconian induction and Cartesian doubt, was declining, although it always maintained the function of an exhibition scheme for disciplines that were in fact increasingly autonomous and endowed with their own canons.[51]

Thus, in 1738, the Somascan general Giovanni Battista Riva promoted the production of an updated pedagogical manifesto for the Somascan congregation, the *Methodus studiorum ad usus Congregationis de Somascha per rei litterarie moderators exhibita atque anno 1741, iussi domini Johannis Baptistae Riva, Prepositi Generalis insinuate*.[52] This extremely complex document represents one of the most advanced points of pedagogical reflection of the

---

Velletri, see Attilio Gabrielli, "I padri somaschi a Velletri." *Somascha. Bolletino di storia dei padri somaschi*, III, 2 (1917): 3–27.

49 Antonella Barzazi, *Gli affanni dell'erudizione. Studi e organizzazione culturale degli ordini religiosi a Venezia tra Sei e Settecento* (Venice: Istituto veneto di scienze, lettere ed arti, 2004), 155.

50 ACTA, II, 1648.

51 Barzazi, *Gli affanni dell'erudizione*, 131.

52 Edoardo Bressan, Marco Bona Castellotti, Paola Vismara, eds., *Politica, vita religiosa, carità. Milano nel primo Settecento* (Milan: Jaca Book, 1997), 280.

early eighteenth century. It was profoundly influenced by French educational thought, from Arnauld to Lancelot and from Fleury to Rollin.[53] All the current orientations of European culture merged, from the importance of the study of the national language of Muratorian imprint to the condemnation of mechanical learning, up to the demolition of the fences between disciplines and the return to a Lockian conception of knowledge as a common matrix of derivation. Furthermore, a Cartesian philosophical teaching was affirmed, and an attempt was made to reconnect with the world of the humanism of the fifteenth and sixteenth centuries through an ethical conception of philological research and the study of classical letters.[54]

Within the theoretical and epistemological boundaries set by the *Methodus*, the talents of the Somascan congregation were able to flourish. As we shall see later in this chapter, they were to have great results not only in literature and philosophy but also in science. The openness to Cartesian rationalism and to the theoretical and experimental acquisitions in the field of natural philosophy and technology developed during the seventeenth and early eighteenth centuries and inspired the minds of both internal and external students of the order. Between the sixteenth and eighteenth centuries, even in the absence of an important theological tradition and with the middle-gymnasium main scholastic objective, the congregation of the Regular Clerics of Somascha transformed from an institution responsible for the care of the poor and orphans into one of the most distinctive and characteristic schools of the Italian educational panorama. Both the external context and the internal forces within the congregation were fundamental for this evolution. On the one hand, as mentioned, all the forces within the Catholic world deemed education necessary for the success of the Tridentine Reformation. The same confrontation, and in some cases competition with the advanced forces of this educational effort, especially with the Jesuits, contributed to the refining of pedagogical principles from simple literacy (grammar) to the adoption of educational tools such as theater and the integration of Cartesianism and Newtonianism.

---

53   Antoine Arnauld (1612–1694), Claude Lancelot (1615–1695), Claude Fleury (1640–1723), and Charles Rollin (1661–1741) were French intellectuals, mostly exponents of Jansenism, who were active in various fields of knowledge, from historiographic erudition to law, from science to mathematics, from theology to pedagogy. Their pedagogical ideas, sometimes in conflict with Jesuit educational methods, which were very widespread in seventeenth century France, represented an element of strong innovation. See Frédéric Delforge, *Les petites écoles de Port-Royal: 1637–1660*, préface de Philippe Sellier (Paris: Editions du Cerf, 1985).

54   For a meticulous and detailed analysis of the *Methodus*, refer to Barzazi, *Gli affanni dell'erudizione*, 155–72.

The changes that took place, however, did not only concern the cultural setting of educational practices, but also the way in which the Somascans lived. Although the capitulars of 1547 decided to admit only the children of the poor to the schools, in 1787 the advisory of the Information for Admission into the College of Fossano (*Notizie per l'ingresso nel Collegio di Fossano de P.P. Somaschi*), explicitly established that only "young people of noble birth or at least distinctly civilian" were to be admitted to the college.[55] As we will see in the last chapter, it was with the suppression of the small convents decreed by the Republic of Venice in 1769 and subsequently with the suppressions decreed by Joseph II of Habsburg and Napoleon in 1810 that the order experienced a decline from which it recovered only at the beginning of the twentieth century.

1.4   The Piarists

Among all the congregations we have seen so far, the Piarists were the order whose educational identity was defined in the shortest time.[56] This does not mean that the development of this identity was not without problems and difficulties; rather, it means that the educational charism of the new congregation was immediately clear to its founder, Joseph Calasanz.[57] The Piarists, to a certain extent, closed the great propulsive phase of post-Tridentine educational innovation begun by the Jesuits in the mid sixteenth century. As stated by Paul Grendler, the Piarists, together with the Jesuits, "reorganized a part

---

55   *Notizie per l'ingresso nel Collegio di Fossano de P.P. Somaschi* (Torino: Presso Giammichele Briolo, 1787).

56   After the Jesuits, the Piarists are the teaching order that has received most attention from recent historiography. For a general but detailed overview of the congregation's history, see Antonio Lezàun, *Storia delle Scuole Pie* (Madrid: Instituto Calasanz de Ciencias de la Educación, 2011). Another important narrative on the educational vocation of the Piarists can be found in Paul Grendler, *Schooling in Renaissance Italy. Literacy and Learning 1300–1600* (Baltimore & London: The Johns Hopkins University Press, 1989), 381–90; Id., "The Piarist of the Pious Schools," in *Religious Orders of the Catholic Reformation: In honor of John C. Olin on his Seventy-Fifth Birthday*, ed. Richard DeMolen (New York: Fordham University Press, 1994), 252–78. Many important analyses on the local presence of the Piarists have also been carried out. For the northeastern area see Maurizio Sangalli, *Le smanie per l'educazione. Gli scolopi a Venezia tra Sei e Settecento* (Roma: Viella, 2012); Id., "Gli scolopi e la Serenissima. Verso il riconoscimento 1630–1730," *Studi veneziani* 50, II (2005): 173–96; Osvaldo Tosti, "Ancora sulle Scuole Pie in Dalmazia," *Archivum Scholarum Piarum* XX, 31 (1996): 121–92. On the 1646 reduction of the Piarists, see Joseph-Marie Timon-David, *Une victime des Jésuites. Saint Joseph Calasanz* (Paris: Librairie Moderne, 1922).

57   On the founder figure, see Mario Spinelli, *Giuseppe Calasanzio: il pioniere della scuola popolare* (Rome: Città Nuova, 2001). Dated but still worthy, see the work of Giovanni Giovannozzi, *Il Calasanzio e l'opera sua* (Florence: Le Monnier, 1930).

of Italian Pedagogy and helped Renaissance education become Old Regime schooling."[58]

The first steps taken by the congregation are well known. The founder was probably born in 1557 in an Aragon village, the son of a fallen hidalgo. After university studies and priestly ordination in 1592, he went to Rome in search of a prebend. In the capital of Catholicism, Calasanz immediately committed himself to works of charity; in particular, he undertook teaching in the Roman company of the Schools of Christian Doctrine, becoming its president in 1593. In the course of his educational activity, Calasanz was struck by the large number of illiterate children who were too poor to afford an education even from the modest local teachers of Rome (*maestri dei rioni*). To find a solution, Calasanz called on the municipal authorities to increase funding for lay teachers, but the city replied that it did not have enough money. He then asked the Jesuits, who justified their refusal by reiterating that they only accepted those who had already studied the rules of Latin. He received a similar response from the Dominicans, who declared themselves too busy preaching to take on this commitment.

The only solution for Calasanz was to take matters into his own hands. In 1597, he started teaching the poor boys of Rome for free in two rooms at the church of Santa Dorotea in Trastevere in what he immediately called the Pious Schools (*Scuole Pie*). From this moment on, the growth of the Pious Schools was fast. New material and financial resources were given to Calasanz in the wake of this success, and by 1602 enrolment had risen to 500 students.[59] The school system built by Calasanz can be seen in its pedagogical and institutional features as an original synthesis of the various educational models existing in Italy at that time. Its chronological setting at the end of the post-Tridentine scholastic innovations makes it interesting. In the Piarists' case, unlike other congregations, we see how their founder had a clear idea of the educational identity of the congregation to be. It is interesting to see how this identity was made up of various elements already existing in the institutional and pedagogical fields at the beginning of the seventeenth century.

Among these components, we find gratuity of attendance. In the Calasanzian schools, students were admitted for free upon presentation of a certificate of poverty issued by their parish priests. This practice, however, had

---

58 Grendler, *Schooling in Renaissance Italy*, 382.
59 As Paul Grendler points out: "Popes Clement VIII and Paul V, Cardinals Cesare Baronio and Silvio Antoniano, and others provided the funds to rent additional rooms, to hire teachers when volunteers could not be found, and to buy the paper, pens, ink, and books furnished without charge to the students." Grendler, *Schooling*, 383.

long been in use, at least since the fifteenth century, and was still in use in the time of Calasanz. It was mainly lay municipal schools that made use of the system of poverty certificates for free admission of schoolchildren.[60] The system of poverty certificates, however, was not unknown to other religious teaching orders; for instance, we have seen that throughout the sixteenth century the Somascans tried to exclude children of the wealthy from their schools. Calasanz probably knew this mechanism and thought it could be useful for his idea of a school. The other component that we find incorporated into the Pious Schools is represented by the model of the Schools of Christian Doctrine. As mentioned above, Calasanz, before embarking on his own pedagogical initiative, had worked intensively in the Schools of Christian Doctrine in Rome, and learned their method. The religious component of basic indoctrination was very important in Piarist schools. As Grendler points out, Calasanz "judged inculcating good morals and saving souls to be as important as learning."[61] During the school day, comprised of two and a half hours in the morning and two and a half hours in the afternoon, the students attended various religious offices, from morning mass to the litany and perpetual prayer, with groups of nine students and a priest alternating every fifteen to thirty minutes. The Piarists had great hope that their children, thanks to this perpetual catechism, would instruct their parents in religious matters; in fact, it was the fathers of the Pious Schools who involved the parents of their students more than any other religious order. These fathers were often consulted by teachers to find out whether the young people should be educated in the *abacus* (commercial arithmetic for a career as a craftworker, shopkeeper or merchant), or in the rules of Latin.

From this fusion of elements, we can see how Calasanz was able to merge institutional and pedagogical features of existing school models. Like Barnabites and Somascans, Piarists maintained a lower and more flexible

---

60   In the public schools of the Lombard community of Guastalla, for example, in 1586 the teacher's contract with the community stipulated that he could not "demand anything from the truly poor, who, however, would justify their poverty with a certificate from the municipality." In this case the teacher was a diocesan priest dependent on the community, confirming the substantial confessionalization of the Italian school system, even in hybrid forms. In 1608 the town of Guastalla hired a lay teacher, Antonio Bologna of Pontremoli. In the contract it's stated that he would accept "at his school free of charge those that by the town were declared miserables (*miserabili*)." These examples reflect a widespread practice in the Italian school of the sixteenth century. The cited sources are taken from the Archivio Comunale di Guastalla, Registro delle Deliberazioni del Consiglio Comunale (1556–1651), February 1st, 1586 and July 5th, 1608.

61   Grendler, *Schooling*, 383.

social profile than Jesuits, who were successfully launched as educators of social élites. Such flexibility contributed to their rapid affirmation and diffusion both in Italy and abroad.[62] It was perhaps the hard line held by the Pious Schools in focusing on the education of the poor, however, that caused some cracks in their structure before the reduction of the order in 1646. Despite some significant exceptions, Calasanz always insisted on marginalizing the education of nobles and the rich as much as possible.[63] This uncompromising observance of a free education for the poor, even in Latin, was viewed with suspicion by many who believed that a sophisticated education could cause disorder in the *ancien régime* highly hierarchical society. If the poor, the populace and the peasants decided to subvert the established order, it would be an insult to God and a great problem for mankind. Despite the defence of the Pious Schools made by Tommaso Campanella, who claimed that educating the simple would allow them to better perform their duties instead of creating a subversive school system, the doubts about the work of the Piarists remained, creating a strong element of structural weakness in the congregation.

A further difficulty encountered by the congregation was the internal evolution of the educational structure. From 1617 on, the obligation to provide the certificate of poverty in order to attend the Pious Schools lapsed, opening enrolment to anyone, though poor children remained the backbone of the Piarist's student population. This, however, led the Piarists into more direct competition with other religious teaching orders. In addition, there were problems within the school organization; the rapid expansion of the Pious Schools increasingly required the recruitment of new teachers. Adequately trained teachers were few, especially those willing to teach in a stimulating and rapidly growing educational context that was certainly not as prestigious as that offered by Jesuit schools. For this reason, the new teachers hired for the Pious Schools were increasingly younger and less prepared. The problem, in short, was of an internal educational nature. Though many religious orders had arrived at the education of young people after concentrating deeply on the education of their members, for the Piarists it was the opposite; they threw

---

62 Giuseppe Lorenzo Moncallero, *La fondazione delle Scuole degli Scolopi nell'Europa centrale al tempo della Controriforma* (Bologna: Edizioni Domenicane, 1972).

63 One of the most important exceptions was the opening in 1638 of a class for nobles within the Piarist School in Florence. This was a single class for about twenty noble boys, probably created at the behest of the Grand Duke Ferdinand II. The exceptionality of this case is underlined by the fact that the class for nobles was only one amidst seven or eight classes for non-nobles.

themselves into the education of the laity without concentrating adequately on the training of their novices.

There was also a problem of spiritual formation. The Jesuits had spiritual exercises with which they scrupulously prepared their young people, but the Piarists often threw students into classrooms before they had completed their novitiate. In addition, many teachers were simple laypeople who had not studied religion. They were called "brother workers" (*Fratelli Operai*), and taught grammar in the lower classes alongside older priests who taught Latin. Calasanz began to admit brother workers for priestly ordination, causing resentment in older, educated priests. In response, the founder discontinued the practice, but this raised serious doubts concerning his leadership ability. It is in this context of rapid growth and major problems that we must frame the turning point of how we define the educational identity of the Piarists, namely their 1646 reduction from a religious order to a simple congregation of secular priests subject to the jurisdiction of local bishops.[64]

A spark was lit in 1641 when fellow Piarist Mario Sozzi (1608–1643) arrived in the previously mentioned community of Florence. It was his eighth move in eight years; as Paul Grendler said, "a sure sign of a trouble-maker."[65] His Florentine stay was no exception; Sozzi was immediately involved in disagreements with his brothers, on whom he decided to take revenge. A pretext was provided by the close attendance of five Piarists from the convent in Florence at the house of Galileo Galilei in Arcetri who, in 1633, had been condemned to the abjuration of his scientific theses in support of heliocentrism. In 1641, Sozzi denounced the five clerics for teaching heretical theories, including heliocentrism, atomism and the denial of God's omnipotence. Among the accused brethren was Famiano Michelini, future algebra teacher at the Medici court. The accusation arrived at the Holy Office, which soon dropped the accusations of heresy but in December 1641 it began an investigation into the internal problems of the order that was to last more than four years. The first result was the dismissal of Calasanz as General of the Order and his replacement by Sozzi in 1642. In 1643, however, the Jesuit Silvestro Pietrasanta was commissioned to carry out investigations to assess the internal state of the order. For health reasons, Pietrasanta could not move from Rome, so to conduct his investigations he had to rely mainly on external advice. Among the judges he relied on was Mario Sozzi himself, certainly not the most neutral! Pietrasanta's first report was released on October 1st, 1643. He substantially denounced the problems

---

64   Paul Grendler, "Did the Jesuits Cause the Reduction of the Piarists?" (Paper presented at the Renaissance Society of America Annual Meeting in Toronto, March 4th, 2019).
65   *Ibid.*

listed above, recommending the expulsion of the internal troublemakers and the convening of a general chapter to make decisions and resolve current issues. The investigations continued until the papal brief of reduction *Ea quae pro felici* was issued by Innocent X on March 16th, 1646, in which the Piarists were demoted to a simple association of clerics subject to bishops and could no longer accept novices.

For the Piarists, this was a real shock. Reactions began to rain from Pious Schools all over Italy as well as from central Europe, where the order was spreading fast. Calasanz wrote from Rome on April 28th, 1646: "Here in Rome everyone feels compassion for us, but no one wants to be the first to face this question with the Pope."[66] In smaller towns as well as larger cities, moans of anger and fear arose. From the village of Pieve di Cento near Ferrara, where the Piarists had arrived in 1641, the fathers wrote: "You can't imagine the great sorrow these villagers have in general and they would be even more sorry if we had to leave." A father wrote to Calasanz from Cagliari: "Here we have been discredited more than we can believe, and we do not know what to do. For God's sake, do not cease to console us with some advice, because amid so many sorrows we find consolation only in your letters." There were also descriptions of mockery which fathers experienced. Father Vincenzo Berro writes that in Rome,

> those who went around the city heard a thousand outrages; the fathers who accompanied the students to their homes, according to custom, were offended and mortified, especially when they met other boys who came out of other schools saying out loud: "Look at the fathers of 'Discongregation'; look at the Flood Schools" [*Scuole Piene* (Flood Schools) instead of *Scuole Pie* (Pious Schools)]. "They are excommunicated, disobedient to the Supreme Pontiff, they give school against the will of the Pope" and other things I don't remember. So that they tried as

---

66   Original extended quote: "Ho ricevuto la lettera di V. R. de 21 del corrente e lodo la diligenza che V. R. dice haver fatto sin adesso e di voler far ancora per l'avvenire. E sebene li avversarii sono grandi e potenti havemo nondimeno noi da sperar nella divina bontà che non permetterà che si rovini affatto un Istituto come il nostro, approvato da tre Sommi Pontefici et applaudito e ricercato per tutta l'Europa et dagli eretici. Li quali Dio sa che cosa diranno quando vedranno il Breve stampato. Qui in Roma tutti ci hanno compassione, ma nissuno vuol esser il primo a trattarne con Nostro Signore. Preghiamo dunque tutti Dio benedetto che trovi il modo di conseguir questo nostro intento che è quanto per hora mi occorre. Roma adì 28 Aprile 1646." Archival reference: Archivio Generale delle Scuole Pie (AGSP), Epistola 4366, RC. n. 08, 206. The complete epistolary of Calasanz can be consulted on the website: http://scripta.scolopi.net.

much as possible not to leave the house so as not to be ashamed so much. And it was not only in Rome that this happened, but also in other cities where there were the Pious Schools.[67]

These statements are important not only because they articulate the feelings of the Piarists after the reduction, but also because they outline a social and physical geography of their roots in the Italian Peninsula. The places of origin of these quotations show us the variety of contexts in which the Piarists played an important educational role, from the small industrious centers of northern Italy to Rome, the capital of Catholicism, up to the most peripheral insular contexts, such as Sardinia.

But how did things really go? Was it the Jesuits who ordained a plot against their rival Piarists or did other factors intervene? At the time of the events, doubts were raised about a possible active involvement of the Society of Jesus. The fact that Pietrasanta was a Jesuit supported this conjecture. Suspicions were reinforced by an anonymous Jesuit who in 1645 wrote a letter to the Florentine ambassador in Rome. In the letter, the old Jesuit (he affirmed he was seventy-five) claimed that the Society of Jesus had consciously plotted against the Piarists to get rid of an ever-stronger rival in the educational market. Furthermore, the anonymous letter claimed that in central Europe the Jesuits were tired of being confused with Piarists, who were called "reformed Jesuits." Such confusion was dangerous since it implied that the Jesuits' customs were

---

67   Original quotes: From Pieve di Cento: 'Non può immaginare V.P. il grande dispiacere che hanno in generale questi paesani, sentendo in estremo la nostra contrarietà, e ancor più si dispiacerebbero se ce ne dovessimo andare via." From Cagliari: "Qui siamo stati screditati più di quanto si possa credere e non sappiamo cosa fare." From Rome "Quelli che andavano alla questua per la città udivano mille spropositi; i padri che accompagnavano gli alunni alle loro case, secondo la consuetudine, erano offesi e mortificati, soprattutto quando incontravano altri ragazzi che uscivano da altre scuole dicendo a voce alta: 'Guarda i padri della Discongregazione; guarda le Scuole dell'Alluvione ('Scuole delle Piene,' invece di Scuole Pie); sono scomunicati, disobbedienti al Sommo Pontefice, danno scuola contro la volontà del Papa e altre cose che non ricordo. Così che si cercava per quanto possibile di non uscire da casa per non vergognarsi così tanto. E non era solo a Roma che succedeva questo, ma anche in altre città dove c'erano le Scuole Pie." Quotes can be found in Lezàun, *Storia delle Scuole Pie*, 18–19. Vincenzo Berro (1603–1666), who joined the Piarists in 1623, was the first historian of the Pious Schools. He was appointed rector of many schools of the Order, becoming provincial of Tuscany in 1637. He was one of the most active promoters of the rehabilitation of the Order under the papacy of Alexander VII. After the death of the founder, he and Father Caputi promoted the cause of beatification of Calasanz in 1653. Berro later resigned from the Ligurian Province to be Postulator of the cause in Rome.

corrupt and, even worse, that the Piarists were their restorers.[68] Even the daily management of schools could apparently support this. Among the complaints received after the reduction, the remaining Piarists of Cagliari wrote in 1647 of the "amazing efforts made by Jesuits to take away our students."[69] Moreover, as we shall see in chapter 4, a real chess game was underway in the small Duchy of Modena for the division of the educational market.

In spite of all this, there is no certain evidence that the reduction of the Piarists was decided by the Jesuits. Contrasts at the local level, in fact, were never lacking, though at the top of the government of the two orders was fierce rivalry, but never true enmity.[70] Pietrasanta was now old, but he was also an intellectual and could not have any personal resentment against the order of the Pious Schools. The reduction is thus to be seen in the context of the Innocentian Inquiry into the small religious congregations, which also saw the creation of detailed reports on the internal state of other orders, such as Barnabites and Somascans. If we add to this the serious problems characterizing the rapid and impetuous but disorderly initial growth of the Piarists, it is easier to understand what moved Innocent X to the publication of the brief of 1646. We must also consider the connection between the Piarists and Galileo Galilei. It is true that the initial accusations of heresy linked to the teaching of heliocentric theories soon declined; nonetheless, we must not forget that Innocent X owed his nomination as cardinal to Urban VIII, under which the trial against the Piarists had begun. Maffeo Barberini had condemned Galileo to abjuration, and Galilei himself was still alive in 1641. If the Piarists had divulged theories in support of heliocentrism within their Florentine schools, it would have been enough to explain the hostility of the two popes towards them and why Innocent X wanted to end what his predecessor had begun.

The Piarists, however, survived. The crisis led to a reorganization of the congregation, which allowed a partial reconstitution in 1656 and a final

---

68 Grendler, *Did the Jesuits Cause the Reduction of the Piarists?* and Timon-David, *Une victime des Jésuites. Saint Joseph Calasanz.* See also: Giuseppe Boero, *Sentimenti e fatti del p. Silvestro Pietrasanta della Compagnia di Gesù in difesa di San Giuseppe Calasanzio e delle Scuole Pie* (Rome: Dalla Tipografia di Marini e Morini, 1847).
69 Original quote: "se V. P. sapesse delle diligenze che fanno i gesuiti per toglierci gli allievi, si stupirebbe." See Lezàun, *Storia delle Scuole Pie*, 23.
70 The situation was exacerbated by the publication of pamphlets in defence of the Piarists, such as that of the Capuchin friar Thomas of Viterbo, who in 1646 composed a two-page booklet entitled '*Amara passio Congregationis Matris Dei Scholarum Piarum, secundum Thomam,*' a sort of paraphrase of evangelical texts of the Passion of Christ applied to the Pious Schools in which the Jesuits are presented as the Sanhedrin who decides before Caiaphas to sacrifice the Pious Schools. Lezàun, *Storia delle Scuole Pie*, 26.

reconstitution in 1669, even if the trauma of the reduction would not be completely healed until the 1680s. Greater discipline and better education of its members, adaptation to the pedagogical forms of other religious orders, mainly the Jesuits, and the opening of new educational institutions such as seminaries, high schools and colleges for nobles re-launched the expansion of the Pious Schools and led to foundations being established in Italy, north-central and eastern Europe and Spain. Indeed, it was precisely after the reconstitution that competition with the Jesuits increased. During the generalate of Giovanni Carlo Pirroni (1677–1685), the expansion became more intense. In this period, the Jesuits in Poland and Sardinia worked, under various pretexts, to prevent, or at least to delay, the propagation of Pious Schools for fear of competition in teaching. A few decades later during the first half of the eighteenth century, contrasts with the Society of Jesus reached their peak. Pope Clement XII granted General Giuseppe Lalli the bull *Nobis quibus*, issued on May 1st, 1731, by which the dispute was resolved in favor of the Piarists, granting them freedom to teach at the Pious Schools. After some Jesuit protests, the Pious Schools quickly obtained the recognition and support of the civil authorities; moreover, the expulsion of the Society from Spain in 1767 and from Sicily in 1768, followed by the suppression of 1773, left an open space for Pious Schools which often took over institutions that had been abandoned by the Jesuits.[71]

From a pedagogical point of view, the reduction of Piarists also had positive effects, leading to a general reorganization of the studies that made their teaching more effective. The *Ratio Studiorum Pro Exteris*, issued in 1694, insisted on the uniformity of method to be maintained in all the Pious Schools. A second and more important document was produced in 1748 during the generalate of Agostino Delbecchi. This was the *Decreto per il buon regime delle Scuole Pie* (Decree for the Good Regulation of the Pious Schools). It stated that the secondary school was to be divided into three biennia for a total of six years. In the first two years, students were to study grammar, in the second year they would study rhetoric, and in the third philosophy, including mathematics, geometry, experimental physics, and theology. A decisive point in the policy of the Pious Schools remained the gratuitousness of the schools. A serious blow to the desire to maintain free access came in 1783 from Joseph II of Austria, who requisitioned most of the rents of the order and required students to pay the salary of the teachers. This change had significant repercussions on the Pious Schools in other parts of Europethat affected their identity; for instance,

---

71   Lezàun, *Storia delle Scuole Pie*, 73.

the Pious Schools in Spain, thanks to the gratuitous nature of their schools as compared to their Austrian counterparts, had almost become public schools.

Another area in which the educational activity of the Piarists was strengthened during the eighteenth century was colleges for nobles. During this period, they opened their own colleges and took charge of some of those which had been left by the Jesuits after the suppression. Among the most important were Parma and Ravenna as well as the College for Nobles in Warsaw, established in 1740. Other types of schools were colleges for non-nobles, diocesan seminaries, and professional schools, although these remained rare. Religious education and catechesis remained a cornerstone of Piarist pedagogy, although from the eighteenth century onwards it left more room for humanistic and scientific teaching.[72] A central aspect of the new pedagogical approach of the Piarist family concerned the scientific field, thanks to the enhancement of the Galilean heritage linked to the school of Florence in the first half of the seventeenth century. This intellectual heritage made it possible to link the Galilean experience of the order to Newtonian experimentalism. The mathematical interest of the Piarists until the time of reduction was but a simple practical interest linked to basic educational needs such as "doing the math." However, with the new cultural orientations that followed the reduction, the Piarists' scientific interests were able to arise and be placed among the religious orders most committed to sciences.[73]

1.5 *The Theatines and the Servites*

So far, we have seen three orders whose vocation became education, with full awareness and total dedication. Barnabites, Somascans and Piarists, after due gestation, opened public day and boarding schools, lay colleges and religious seminaries. These schools were intended for different categories of individuals, namely nobles and bourgeoisie, rich and poor, the religious and laypeople. The pedagogical commitment of religious orders, however, also passed through other channels, not necessarily through the systematic opening of their own educational institutions. We have seen how the members of some of these congregations could be hired by municipal councils to teach in public schools run by the community and not by the order to which they belonged. Sometimes this was the primary commitment of a religious order in the educational sphere. As we shall see later in this book, Servites and Theatines were called upon at various points to work in municipal schools. Although the

---

72 Lezàun, *Storia delle Scuole Pie*, 74–77.
73 Sangalli, *Le smanie per l'educazione*, 65–78.

Servites and the Theatines had not followed the same educational impetus of other orders in the foundations of colleges and schools, they still produced good teachers.

Let's start this analysis by examining the oldest of the two orders in terms of foundation, the *Ordo Servorum Beatae Mariae Virginis*, also known as Servants of Mary or, more simply, Servites. They were a mendicant order founded in Florence in 1233 due to the desire of the seven founders to create a group of pious people dedicated to prayers and a retired life. The group soon expanded, and new convents arose between Tuscany, Umbria and the Emilia-Romagna region. After an initial century of tormented life during which the order risked being dissolved, Pope Benedict XI approved the constitutions and the rule of the Servants of Mary in 1304 with the bull *Dum Levamus*. Although the Servites did not include education among their main charisms, they immediately took care of the theological education of their members.

A *Studium* was opened in Paris in the middle of the fourteenth century.[74] A 1328 decree demanded that four friars be sent to Paris from each province to reside and study there for three years. The chosen friars were to be provided with a Bible and the book of Sentences by Peter Lombard. In the second half of the fourteenth century other *Studia* were established, both in Italy and in other parts of Europe, particularly in Germany. The fifteenth century began, for the Servites, with the general chapter of Ferrara in 1404, which decided to work for a moral and spiritual recovery of the order, and it was from this chapter that the Congregation of the Observance was born in 1430. Among the Servites, however, there was no separation as had been the case with the Franciscan Observants.

During these decades, the regulation of internal studies of the Servites was better structured. In 1402, it was established that each province had to create its own *Studium* for grammar, arts, and theology, and that all provinces could send one or two students to the *Studium* in Bologna. In 1461, the reform of the *Studia* of Bologna, Pavia, Padua, Florence, and Perugia was ordered. It was decided that in each *Studium* only one master of theology or baccalaureate

---

74 *Regimini universalis Ecclesie edizione: Constitutiones recentiores fratrum Servorum s. Mariae 1503–1766*, ed. P. M. Soulier, in Monumenta OSM, VI, (Brussels: 1903–1904), 56–61; regesto: O. J. Dias, *I Servi nel Trecento (prima e dopo la grande peste del 1348)*, in *I Servi nel Trecento. Squarci di storia e documenti di spiritualità*. (3 settimana di Monte Senario, 8–13 settembre 1980), (Monte Senario 1980), 30–31; F. A. Dal Pino, *Tentativi di riforma e movimenti di osservanza presso i Servi di Maria nei secoli XIV-XV*, in *Reformbemuhngen und Observanzbestrebungen im spätmittelalterlichen Ordenwesen herausgegeben von K. Elm*, (Berlin: 1989), 358–59.

should teach theology, philosophy, and logic. It was also established that each province should have at least five students in all faculties. In 1473, it was determined that none of the friars could be promoted to an academic level except in a general chapter, and this had to be done with the consent of the friars of the convent and by the will of the prior general. In addition, none of the friars who received a doctoral degree at a university located in a city other than Rome, Padua, Pavia, Bologna, Florence, Ferrara, Perugia, Siena or Erfurt, or with an apostolic brief, could ask for any emoluments from their own convent.[75]

The Servites arrived on the eve of the Protestant Reformation with a very solid internal educational structure; however, they had to deal with a radical and violent change in the forms and aims of school and culture. While during the fourteenth and fifteenth centuries it was the increase in the number of friars choosing priesthood that required the development of a solid course of study, in the sixteenth century it was the challenge brought about by the break-up of Christian unity that demanded a better definition of internal education. Over the course of the century, this led to the formulation of three constitutions, those of Budrio in 1548, Bologna in 1556, and Parma in 1580. In each edition, a large part was dedicated to the definition of the course of studies. In the constitution of 1548, the threat felt within the order of the Protestant Reformation clearly emerged. The Servites' strong roots in Germany, together with their reforming and pauperistic charism and their adoption of Saint Augustin rule (the same as Martin Luther) exposed them to strong suspicion by Rome. During the sixteenth century, half of their priors were directly appointed by the pope and many convents in Germany were suppressed. Regarding studies, the Constitutions of Budrio forbade the interpretation and commentary of Sacred Scripture to all those who had not first received from the father general the faculty to exercise this task. Moreover, the *Baccelliere* and the master of study (*Maestro di Studio*) of each convent could only take lessons in arts and logic; however, in their disputes the students could support conclusions from Sacred Scripture, provided that it was previously examined and revised by their regent.[76]

The time devoted to the training of novices was also extended. It was established that no one could be promoted to the rank of baccalaureate without studying in the faculties for five continuous years. Likewise, the degree of *Magisterium* in theology could not be accessed earlier than three years after a baccalaureate was obtained. In addition, students, readers, and baccalaureates

---

[75] Monumenta OSM, vol. II, 51–53.
[76] Luigi M. De Candido and Pier Giorgio M. Di Domenico, eds., *Fonti Legislative*, Vol. III (Rome: Curia Generalizia OSM), XXII.

who had been absent from study for more than two months could no longer be admitted or promoted to these grades.[77]

A more explicit and dramatic reference to the current events was made in Article 27 in the Constitutions of 1548. It stated that

> No one should be allowed to carry out the task of preaching without an express letter from the Most Reverend Father General, without whose consent and signature the elections of preachers have no value. To eliminate from our Order the contagion of the Lutheran heresy and, if possible, to eradicate it, we order by virtue of salutary obedience and under sentence of excommunication, that after three canonical admonitions none of our friars dare to keep a book of Martin Luther, of any subject, either read his writings or defend and proclaim his doctrines, or discuss, speak or in any way compare about his opinions, conclusions, sentences. We want the same punishment to be imposed on those who have kept books of Philip Melanchthon, Brent, Calvin, Bullinger, Martin Butzer and other heretics, have read them or have declared and defended their sentences.[78]

Regarding the education of novices, it was established that each province should have a novitiate. The young men could be admitted after careful evaluation. The novices would have two teachers for their studies, one to give them a moral example according to the rule of Saint Augustine, the other to teach Latin and Greek. In addition, no friar could leave the novitiate before turning seventeen years of age.[79]

The Constitutions of Bologna of 1556 continued in this direction. They urged that novices should be rigorously trained. They insisted on the teaching

---

77 De Candido; Di Domenico, *Fonti Legislative*, art. XXV.
78 Original quote: "Nessuno si permetta di esercitare il compito della predicazione senza lettera espressa del Reverendissimo Padre Generale, senza il cui consenso e firma non hanno valore le elezioni dei predicatori. Per eliminare dal nostro Ordine il contagio dell'eresia luterana e, se possibile, per sradicarla, ordiniamo in virtù di salutare obbedienza e sotto sentenza di scomunica, che dopo tre ammonizioni canoniche comminiamo con questi nostri scritti, che nessuno dei nostri frati osi tenere presso di sé un libro di Martin Lutero, di qualsiasi lezione sia, o leggere suoi scritti o difendere e proclamare le sue dottrine, ovvero discutere, parlare o in qualsiasi modo confrontare circa le sue opinioni, conclusioni, sentenze. Della medesima pena vogliamo che siano colpiti chi abbia trattenuto presso di sé libri di Filippo Melantone, Brent, Calvino, Bullinger, Martin Butzer e di altri eretici, li abbia letti o abbia dichiarato e difeso le loro sentenze." *Fonti Legislative*, art. XXVII.
79 *Fonti Legislative*, art. XXXIII.

of natural philosophy, albeit in a completely Aristotelian way. The students best suited to philosophical speculation would complete it in six years and continue for another three years listening to more difficult teachers in some universities. They would later teach younger brethren. Students best suited to preaching, on the other hand, could devote themselves to morals and give sermons. The Constitutions of Parma of 1580 confirmed in substance what was established by the two previous versions. Minor changes were made only in the field of discipline and in the duration of studies. Overall, these reforms strengthened the Servites, but did not shelter them from further problems with Rome. It was Innocent X, with the reform imposed on the religious orders by the constitution *Instaurandae regularis disciplina* of 1652, who suppressed 102 Servite convents out of the 261 existing. Nevertheless, as we shall see, thanks to their rigorous humanistic and theological training, the Servites were in great demand as teachers by the municipal administrations of the seventeenth century. Though we cannot fully count the Servants of Mary among the religious teaching orders of the Counter-Reformation, it was precisely because of the challenges they had to face at that time that they became among the most theologically prepared.

Some similar aspects to the story of the Servites can be found in the historical path of the *Ordo clericorum regularium vulgo Theatinorum*, also known as Theatines. These clerics were an embodiment of the spiritual renewal of the pre-Tridentine Catholic Church. The purpose of these clerics was to restore original apostolic life. The Theatines were approved by Pope Clement VII on June 24th, 1524, even though the definitive confirmation of the establishment of the order came in 1533, with the brief *Dudum pro parte vestra*. Although the four founders, Gaetano da Thiene (1480–1547), Gian Pietro Carafa (1476–1559), Bonifacio de' Colli (?–1558) and Paolo Consiglieri (1499–1557), had no intention of establishing an actual teaching congregation, their educational commitment soon translated into a silent force of their life example and their attention to priestly ministry and preaching. All of these aspects required a solid theological education that made the Theatines esteemed teachers for the early modern Italian educational market.[80] As Elisa Novi Chavarria wrote, the "Theatines were real professionals in the practice of preaching. Experts in communication and the art of moving consciences, they gathered a large

---

80 Francesco Andreu, "I teatini dal 1524 al 1574. Sintesi storica," *Regnum Dei*, 30 (1974): 8–54; Id., "I chierici regolari," *Regnum Dei*, 30, (1974): 55–78; Id., "La regola dei Chierici Regolari nella lettera di Bonifacio de' Colli a Gian Matteo Giberti," Regnum Dei, 2, (1946): 38–53. See also Elisabetta Patrizi, *Pastoralità ed educazione. L'episcopato di Agostino Valier nella Verona post-tridentina, 1565–1606* (Milan: FrancoAngeli, 2015), 278.

number of acolytes and penitents, who chose them as their spiritual directors and to whom they will then direct their charity."[81]

In the first phase of Theatine life, the dominant orientation within the order was given by Gian Pietro Carafa, who became prefect for the Congregation of the Holy Office in 1542 and was elected pope in 1555. He had made the Theatines an instrument of Roman control, often with an inquisitorial function; however, after the death of Carafa in 1559, it became possible for the dominant orientation to be that of Gaetano da Thiene, meaning it was less hierarchical and more dedicated to works of assistance and charity.[82] By the time of Carafa's death, the Theatines had already experienced a first phase of expansion in Italy. Their primary headquarters was located in Rome on the Pincian Hill (*Colle Pincio*) but, like many intellectuals and artists of the time, the Theatines had to flee in 1527 because of the 1527 sacking of Rome brought about by the Landsknechten sent by Emperor Charles V. The first Theatines took refuge in Venice where they established a convent at the church of San Clemente, followed by another in Verona in 1528 and in Naples in 1533 and 1538. In this way, we see from the beginning the strong connection between the Theatine order and the large urban realities in which they were organically integrated. Like the other religious orders with a strong urban connotation, the Theatines also carried out their apostolate in response to the needs of metropolitan societies. As mentioned above, a central role was played by the preaching and fulfilment of all priestly ministries; however, despite the relatively low presence of direct sources, they also carried out didactic activities, as demonstrated by their presence in Messina. In this eastern Sicilian city, in fact, we know that in the middle of the seventeenth century the Theatines were paid by the municipality to publicly teach moral theology.[83] It is thus no surprise that quite often in the

---

81 Elisa Novi Chavarria, "I Teatini e 'il governo delle anime' (secoli XVI–XVII)," in *Sant'Andrea Avellino e i Teatini nella Napoli del Viceregno spagnolo. Arte religione società*, ed., D.A. D'Alessandro (Naples: D'Auria Editore, 2011), 273–86.

82 For a framework of the Theatine identity's evolution during the first decades of life of their existence, see Andrea Vanni, *"Fare diligente inquisitione." Gian Pietro Carafa e le origini dei chierici regolari teatini*, (Rome: Viella, 2010). See also: Roberto Tambelli, "Le missioni popolari dei teatini a Napoli," (MBA diss., Università degli Studi di Napoli "Ferderico II," 2011), 3–18.

83 Archivio Generale dei Teatini, folder 706. The source is reported also in Marcella, Campanelli, ed., *I Teatini* (Rome: Edizioni di storia e letteratura, 1987), 65–66. See also: Saverio Di Bella, *Caino Barocco. Messina e la Spagna 1672–1678* (Cosenza: Luigi Pellegrini editore, 2005), 217, 297.

historiography of religious teaching congregations we find Theatines side by side with Jesuits, Barnabites, Somascans and Piarists.[84]

Although the Theatines never opened their own schools to the lay population, we can find them engaged in teaching activities throughout the early modern age, from the sixteenth to the eighteenth centuries, at all educational levels from literacy to university. There is no lack of examples from northern to southern Italy; for instance, in 1616 the Theatines were called by the city council of the small town of Guastalla to teach the first rules of Latin in local municipal schools.[85] An instructive case is that of Paolo d'Alagona, who was born in Reggio Calabria at the end of the sixteenth century. He joined the Theatines in 1616, graduated in *utroque iure* and then undertook studies in theology. He was eventually hired by the University of Messina in 1637 to teach canon law.[86]

Another important example can be found in the biography of Michele Casati. He was born in Milan in 1699 and took the Theatine habit in 1716. He first publicly taught philosophy in Verona, and then returned to Milan to teach theology to the novices of his order. In the meantime, as a proof of how educational activity accompanied other apostolic commitments of Theatine life, he continued to preach in churches. In Milan, Casati continued to publicly teach geometry, experimental physics and Greek. Among his students was the famous scientist Maria Gaetana Agnesi (1718–1799), the first woman who obtained a university chair at the University of Bologna. Later, in 1739, he was called to Turin by Carlo Emanuele III to teach moral philosophy after the departure of the Jansenist Dominican Tommaso Crust. Casati's teaching was not original, but clear and moderated. His anti-Aristotelianism and anti-Cartesianism, and his polemical attitude against Thomas Hobbes and Samuel von Pufendorf on natural law, show a wide scholastic and Thomist substratum. In 1753, he was eventually appointed bishop of Mondovì.[87]

Another noteworthy example is that of Giovanni Girolamo Gradenigo. He was born in Venice in 1709, studied at the Jesuit College in Ferrara and entered

---

84   It happens mainly but not only with the erudite historiography of the 19th century. For example, see Claudio Bertolotto, *Il Real Collegio e i Barnabiti a Moncalieri: educazione e custodia delle memorie* (Torino: Celid, 1997), 19; and *Educazione cristiana ossia catechismo universale* (Venice: Eredi Curti, 1824).

85   Salomoni, *Scuola, maestri e scolari*, 397.

86   Antonio Francesco Vezzosi, *I Scrittori de' Chierici Regolari detti Teatini* (Rome: Nella stamperia della Sacra Congregazione di Propaganda Fide, 1780), 27–28.

87   On Michele Casati, see Pietro Stella, "Michele Casati," *Dizionario Biografico degli Italiani*, vol. 21 (1978) and Vezzosi, *I Scrittori de' Chierici Regolari detti Teatini*, 234–45. See also: Massimo Marcocchi, ed., *Il Concilio di Trento: istanze di riforma e aspetti dottrinali* (Milan: Vita e Pensiero, 1997), 13, 98–99.

the order of the Theatines in 1727. Gradenigo was sent to Milan to study theology and had Michele Casati as his professor. The bishop of Brescia wanted him to teach theology in his diocesan seminary in 1734. During his stay in Brescia, Gradenigo opened Schools of Christian Doctrine for the poor children of the city. He took up important positions, including Visitor of the Theatines for the Veneto part of the Republic of Venice (as a result of which he was later appointed ambassador to Paris while serving Pope Benedict XIV as consultant to the Index of Prohibited Books) and Examiner of the Clergy.[88]

So far, we have seen the widespread presence of Theatines committed to the world of education, so what was it that caused a lack of Theatine schools expressly for laypeople who were not members of the congregation? First, the early steps of the order were monopolized by the charism of Gian Pietro Carafa, who preferred to direct the activities of the Theatines towards doctrinal control rather than apostolate activities. The vocation of charitable works had been the starting ground for many congregations that later fully focused on education, such as Somascans and even Jesuits; however, the uncertain early stages of almost all the religious orders discussed so far show that there was no predetermined path to transform their members into teachers and educators.

A second reason is that the Theatines maintained their own original vocation, which was diversified by a series of activities. Education was included among these duties and, as we have seen, the Theatines produced excellent teachers who kept in mind the educational models of the other orders. The aforementioned Paolo d'Alagona lived in Messina during the years of the attempted Jesuit penetration and Michele Casati's successor to the chair of moral philosophy, after Casati's election as bishop, was the Barnabite Giacinto Sigismondo Gerdil, while Gradenigo studied at a Jesuit school. The Theatines, in some ways, completed the early modern landscape of the teaching congregations by representing a versatile instrument of education as an alternative to the traditional orders; however, they were also a male congregation whose teaching was mainly (though not exclusively, as in the case of Maria Gaetana Agnesi) addressed to males.

What happened, in the meantime, in the world of female education?

---

88 On Giovanni Girolamo Radenigo, see Paolo Tomea, *Tradizione apostolica e coscienza cittadina a Milano nel medioevo: la leggenda di San Barnaba* (Milan: Vita e Pensiero, 1993), 258; and Vezzosi, *I Scrittori de' Chierici Regolari detti Teatini*, 410–21.

2   Female Religious Orders

The educational world described so far has only been masculine. The problem of a female presence in early modern schools is articulated in and irreducible to predefined schemes. One feature certainly emerges, namely the scarcity of a female presence. For about fifty years now, however, the historiographic production concerning the participation of women in Renaissance and Reformation culture has aroused interest and participation.[89] We can observe that the scarce feminine presence in educational institutions is a widely shared theme in literature. As Grendler writes, "a limited number of girls [...] attended school. Female teachers, another minority, helped teach."[90] Other historians have confirmed Grendler's statement. To give a few examples, as Elisabetta Rasy said, during the Renaissance "we hear female voices either as background noise, behind and through men's speeches, or as songs, or isolated cries."[91] The hidden presence of women in early modernity has also had repercussions on this research. This chapter, therefore, cannot and does not want to exhaust an overly complex investigation, even for a limited territorial area such as the Italian Peninsula. The scarcity of documents on females' roles in schools is due to the fact that the production of texts, both literary and documentary, was largely a male prerogative. As Luisa Miglio observes, "writing is a male monopoly and in the male world it finds justification and legitimacy: to transmit, record, memorize, document; for women it is only an unproductive moment, for which it is not appropriate to spend even a few florins."[92]

It should not be taken for granted that the issue of women's education was not perceived as important, even during a period of substantial narrowing of women's margins of social activity, such as in sixteenth-century Europe. Though we find examples of charismatic women among the Barnabites, such as Paola Negri and Ludovica Torelli, who gave birth to the order of the Angeliche, it remains true that Rome quickly imposed limits on them. They were still moving in the socio-political spaces of the late Middle Ages that,

---

89   To cite few recent examples relating to other European contexts: Anne J. Cruz and Rosilie Hernández, ed., *Women's Literacy in Early Modern Spain and the New World* (New York: Routledge, 2011); Barbara J. Whitehead, ed., *Women's Education in Early Modern Europe. A History 1500–1800* (New York and London: Garland Publishing, 1999); Eve Rachele Sanders, *Gender and Literacy on Stage in Early Modern England* (Cambridge: Cambridge University Press, 1998).
90   Grendler, *Schooling in Renaissance Italy*, 87.
91   Luisa Miglio, *Governare l'alfabeto. Donne, scrittura e libri nel medioevo* (Rome: Viella, 2008), 7.
92   Elisabetta Rasy, *Le donne e la letteratura* (Rome: Editori Riuniti, 1984), 37.

between the end of the fifteenth and the beginning of the sixteenth centuries, had experienced in northern Italy a strong feminization of the territorial aristocracy in active government roles, but they clashed against the wall of a rapidly changing world.[93] The fact remains that they tried to give the religious changes taking place during that period an original imprint that, despite the obligation of claustration imposed by Rome in 1552, did not fail to bring future developments. The Italian cultural context, up until the end of the sixteenth century, was not totally and prejudicially closed to an active role of women in society.[94]

Nonetheless, even in the deeply confessionalized world of the post-Tridentine school, institutions specifically designed for girls' education were not lacking. As we have seen in the first chapter, in the "Rule of the Society of the Servants of Children in Charity" (*Regola de la Compagnia dei Servi di Puttini in Charità*), published in 1555, it was clearly stated that boys and girls should receive the same education.[95] Real religious orders were made specifically for the education of girls and the initiative was always taken by women.

2.1 The Ursulines

Among the most representative experience of this female phenomenon is the order of the Ursuline nuns. In the profile of their foundress, Angela Merici, we find similarities to the experiences of the male orders discussed above. It was the Lombard-Venetian context that gave great impetus to the educational religious renewal of the early sixteenth century. Angela Merici was born in 1474 in the village of Desenzano on the shores of Lake Garda in a territory that was culturally Lombard but under the political rule of Venice. The era in which Angela was born had not yet entered the militant Counter-Reformation and the fight against Protestantism, but was experiencing the late medieval eschatological anxieties and late humanism to which Battista Carioni himself belonged. This millenarianist atmosphere was the same that permitted and encouraged women, as we shall see in the case of Ludovica Torelli, to take important initiatives in the field of religion and education. Nonetheless, Angela Merici's

---

93 Serena Ferente, "Le donne e lo Stato," in *Lo Stato del Rinascimento in Italia*, ed. Andrea Gamberini and Isabella Lazzarini (Rome: Viella, 2014), 313–32; Letizia Arcangeli and Susanna Peyronel, eds., *Donne di potere nel Rinascimento* (Rome: Viella, 2008).

94 The Renaissance treatises of humanistic tradition on women's education demonstrate this. See David Salomoni, *Scuola, maestri e scolari negli stati Gonzagheschi e Estensi* (Rome: Anicia, 2017), 335–38.

95 *Regola della Compagnia delli Serui dei Puttini in Carità*, (In Ferrara: presso Francesco de' Rossi da Valenza, 1555), 1.

order clashed with the changes occurring during the mid-sixteenth century as a result of the resurgence of secular and ecclesiastical fears of non-cloistered female religious communities.[96] This, however, did not prevent the order from developing and spreading throughout Europe and other continents.

We know little about Angela Merici's early life. She belonged to a wealthy local family, from which came ecclesiastics and magistrates active in the region. The young Angela could not write, even though she might have been able to read. After the death of her parents, she became a Franciscan tertiary, a valid option for a life of devotion as an alternative to a life of seclusion. She took her religious commitments very seriously, attending them with rigor. Among the tasks assigned by her Franciscan superior was the task of going to Brescia in 1516 to console the widow Caterina Pantegola, who had lost her husband in the first phase of the Italian Wars. It is in this environment that we find the religious upheavals mentioned earlier. Lombardy, during the early sixteenth century, was devastated by wars and the passage of armies to the service of the Valois and the Habsburg families for the control of the region. Violence and corruption of religious and secular authorities were the norm. A strong sense of distrust pervaded both rural and urban societies. Fear, however, was counterbalanced by a strong desire for renewal. Congregations of laypeople often sprang up to take care of charitable works such as hospitals and orphanages. Young Angela was impressed by this world suspended between crisis and regeneration and wanted to take an active part in it.

The laypeople involved in the renewal were often from the nobility or the bourgeoisie of the city, such as the widow Caterina Pantegola. Through her contact with Pentegola, Merici met the Countesses Laura Gambara and Elisabetta Prato who, together with other noble widows, ran the Conservatory for the Converted of Charity (*Conservatorio delle Convertite della Carità*). It was an institution aimed at the recovery and education of young girls, often orphans or repentant prostitutes. The institute insisted on some characteristic elements of modern devotion, such as frequent confession and communion. We do not know if Angela took direct part in the activities of the *Conservatorio*,

---

96   For Angela Merici and the Ursulines' most recent bibliography, see Querciolo Mazzonis, "Angela Merici," in Oxford Bibliographies Online: Renaissance and Reformation, ed., Margaret King (New York: Oxford University Press, 2012); Id., "Ursulines," in Oxford Bibliographies Online: Renaissance and Reformation, ed., Margaret King (New York: Oxford University Press, 2013); Id., *Spirituality, Gender and the Self in Renaissance Italy: Angela Merici and the Company of St. Ursula, 1474–1540* (Washington DC: Catholic University of America Press, 2007) and Charmarie J. Blaisdell, "Angela Merici and the Ursulines," in *Religious Orders of the Catholic Reformation*, ed. Richard L. DeMolen (New York: Fordham University Press, 1994), 98–136.

but it is reasonable to imagine that for her such an institution could represent a model. Countess Prato herself later became a disciple of Angela and her successor as Mother General of the Ursulines. The late medieval nature of Angela Merici's profile is emphasized by her pilgrimage to the Holy Land. In 1532 a group of women from all social backgrounds had gathered around her, and in 1535 Angela and twenty-eight other virgins formally gathered in the church of Saint Afra in Brescia to create the Company of the Ursuline Sisters. Their rule was later approved in 1536 by Lorenzo Muzio, Vicar General of the Bishop of Brescia, Francesco Cornaro. On March 18th, 1537, Angela was elected "Superior and Mother General" for life. In 1539 she dictated the *Testamento* (Legacy) and the *Ricordi* (Memories) as a spiritual testament to the mothers and governors of the Company. By the time Angela died on January 27th, 1540, the Company had about 150 daughters; however, the order was still focused on charitable works. How did it progress to the world of education?

As Charmarie Blaisdell observed, the informal aggregation of women around Angela's charism resembled how, in the early stages of the Society of Jesus, men had congregated around Ignatius of Loyola in Montmartre. In addition to this, the first rule of the Ursulines was influenced by Franciscan simplicity.[97] The focus was placed on austerity of dress, representing the essential virginity of the sisters. Initially, the educational activity of the Ursulines was semi-formal, almost as if a minimum degree of literacy with religious purposes was implicit in their apostolic activity. In her *Testamento* and *Ricordi*, Merici was clear about the importance of education. She explained what methods to use to train the virgins in pedagogy, discipline, and love to apply when teaching their young students. In addition, Ursulines were widely present in the Schools of Christian Doctrine, although probably their teaching in Brescia began before the introduction of the schools created by Castellino da Castello. A 1566 source states that: "all the hospitals and all the schools of Christian doctrine for girls are staffed by the Ursulines."[98]

The death of the foundress was followed by a period of internal conflict in which various orientations within the order were competing for leadership. It was during this period that the Ursulines conformed more rigorously to the dictates of the Council of Trent and their educational activity became more institutionalized and widespread. In 1572, after the revision of the original

---

97 Blaisdell, *Angela Merici*, 107.
98 Historical Diocesan Archives of Milan (ASDM), Sezione XIII, Vol. 61, "Regola della Compagnia santa Orsola (Per Pacifico Ponte nel mese d'ottobre, 1569)"; Francesco Landini, Estratto, 27–32; Mariani et al., *Angela Merici*, 532. The source is reported in Blaisdell, *Angela Merici*, 111.

handwritten rule of 1569, Elisabetta Prato, the old friend of Angela Merici, was elected mother general of the order. This was a turning point. Under the Generalate of Prato, the Ursulines were noticed by the Archbishop of Milan, Carlo Borromeo, who recognized their potential to contribute to education. Borromeo proceeded in an authoritarian manner, partially overturning the balance just achieved. Within the diocese of Milan, Borromeo put the order under the control of Gaspare Belinzaghi, prior-general of the Schools of Christian Doctrine, effectively invalidating Prato's authority. It was with this overlap, or fusion, with the Schools of Christian Doctrine, that the educational identity of the Ursulines was definitively stabilized. Through a further modification of their rule, Carlo Borromeo established that their main charism should be directed towards the education of young women, then converted and regularized various charitable institutions run by the Ursulines for this purpose. In addition, in 1576 he declared it the duty of every bishop of the Archdiocese of Milan to create an Ursuline company in their dioceses for educational purposes.[99]

During the years of Borromeo's bishopric, the Ursulines experienced an impetuous spread both in Italy and abroad. Within Italy, the Ursulines settled in various cities and towns of Lombardy, like the male congregations whose expansion we will discuss in the next chapter. After Brescia and Milan, they settled in Cremona (1656/1616), Como (1570/1576), Busto Arsizio (1572), Lodi and Bergamo (1575), Legnano (1576), Desio (1577), and Novara (1593?/1625). After 1595, they settled in different territories of the pre-alpine belt, among which were Varese, including Arona, Angera, Arsago, Somma and Appiano, and Monza, including Vimercate and Cantù, and Lecco. Between the end of the sixteenth and the beginning of the seventeenth centuries, the Ursulines also settled in various towns on the plain, including Melegnano, Abbiategrasso, San Giuliano and San Donato. It is no coincidence that many of these villages were important manufacturing centers that experienced both rapid demographic growth and economic transformation during the second half of the sixteenth century.[100] In the mid-seventeenth century in Milan, the Ursulines were organized into congregations according to city gates, namely Santa Lucia in Porta Nuova, Santa Sofia in Porta Romana, Santa Cristina in Porta Comasina,

---

99   Acta ecclesiae Mediolanensis ab eius initiis usque ad nostram aetatem, 4 vols. (1892), (Acts of the Fourth Provincial Council, Milan, 1576), 2:493; Ledochowska, *Angela Merici*, 387–88; Massimo Marcocchi, "Le origini del Collegio della Beata Vergine di Cremona, istituzione della Riforma Cattolica (1610)," *Annali della Biblioteca statale e libreria civica di Cremona*, XXIV, (1974), 10; Blaisdell, *Angela Merici*, 112.

100 Luisa Chiappa Mauri, *Paesaggi rurali di Lombardia* (Rome-Bari: Laterza, 1990).

Santa Marcellina in Porta Tosa, and Santo Spirito in Porta Ticinese, but were absent from Porta Vercellina and Porta Orientale.[101] Outside of Lombardy they expanded first into the Venetian and the Emilia-Romagna regions. They established convents in Bologna (1565/1603), Venice (1571/1593–1642), Ferrara (1584–1587), Verona (1586/1594), Parma (1590/1623), Treviso (1590–1600/1603), Modena (1603), Reggio Emilia (1611), and Feltre (1600/1637). More modest during this initial phase was their spread in central and southern Italy. Ursuline convents were opened in Foligno (1570/1600), Naples (1609) and Pergola (1623).[102]

A peculiar aspect of the Ursulines was that often a community that settled in a town would establish itself as an autonomous congregation while remaining faithful to Augustinian rule and the charism of Angela Merici. Such was the case of the Ursulines of Arona. They arrived there in 1590 by the will of the Jesuit father Giovanni Mellino. In 1598, Margherita Trivulzio Borromeo, mother of Cardinal Federico Borromeo, asked for and obtained the establishment of a congregation of Ursulines in Arona in order to raise them spiritually.[103] The bishop of each diocese could approve new Ursuline congregations within their cities by approving a new rule that could be modified with respect to the original regulations of Angela Merici. New rules were approved in Brescia (1582), Ferrara (1587), Verona (1594) and Treviso (1603), drafted by the entourages of local bishops. The purpose of this flexibility was to have the activities of the Ursulines available within each diocese for the most urgent apostolate issues, even if education always remained central. The original hierarchical organization of the company was essentially feminine; at the top was the mother general, followed by the *Matrone* (aristocratic widows dealing with practical issues) and the *Colonnelle* (virgins who acted as spiritual guides). In the new

---

101　For the early expansion of the Ursulines, see Turichini, *Sotto l'occhio del padre*, 290–92. For their presence in the city of Milan, see Gualberto Vigotti, *S. Carlo Borromeo e la Compagnia di S. Orsola. Nel centenario della ricostituzione in Milano della Compagnia di S. Orsola figlie di S. Angela Merici, 1872–1972* (Milano: Scuola tipografica S. Benedetto Viboldone, 1972), 59; Querciolo Mazzonis, "The Company of St. Ursula in Counter-Reformation Italy," in *Devout Laywomen in the Early Modern World*, ed. Alison Weber, (London-New York: Routledge, 2016), 51. See also: Martine Sonnet, "L'educazione di una giovane," in *Storia delle donne in Occidente. Dal Rinascimento all'età moderna*, ed. Georges Duby and Michelle Perrot (Rome-Bari: Laterza, 1991), 135 and Danilo Zardin, "Confraternite e comunità nelle campagne milanesi fra Cinque e Seicento" *La scuola cattolica*, 112, (1984), 13.

102　Mazzonis, The Company of St. Ursula, 51.

103　Historical Diocesan Archives of Milan, Section X, Arona XII, papers 131–37, visit of 1602, folder containing the Statutes of the "Congregatione delle filiole della Madonna Santissima in Roma." Reported also in Turchini, *Sotto l'occhio del padre*, 295; Vigotti, *S. Carlo*, 72, Marcocchi, *Le origini*, 18.

congregations, however, the central role was played by a bishop granted the right to approve them.[104]

By the middle of the seventeenth century, there were two main types of schools run by the Ursulines. The first type was structured along the same lines as boarding schools for sons of the nobility; daughters of the aristocracy and rich bourgeoisie resided at the schools for a fee. Similarly to the *Educandato*, the girls were taught the vernacular curriculum in addition to arithmetic, domestic arts, music, dance, and painting. The second type of school was free, for poor young people. Young women could learn to read and write and cook, sew, and weave, useful skills for poor girls who would become working-class wives and mothers.[105] The Ursuline schools also provided some professional education. In this way the schools could earn extra money, as in the Lombard community of Besozzo, where the nuns earned money by selling the products woven by their students. Sometimes, according to the previous municipal tradition, Ursuline schools could be financed by the municipality in which they were located. Such was the case in Trezzo, located east of Monza, where in 1591 the Schools of Christian Doctrine were managed commonly by the local parish priest, the schoolteacher, and Ursuline nuns.[106] The education of each nun could vary greatly, however, at times preventing them from playing an active teaching role. Some Ursulines could not read or write, in which case they devoted themselves to manual work or craftsmanship.[107]

Overall, the origin and definition of the Ursuline's educational experiences followed the path of most of the male orders discussed; they began by responding to the spiritual and material needs of a rapidly (sometimes traumatically) changing society and arrived at a more institutional approach. However, this normalization, despite the profound transformations by Angela Merici, did not lose the originality of education for women promoted by other women. In addition to this, the influence of the territories is clear. It is not by chance that the vocation of Angela Merici originated in the fertile Lombard-Venetian territory, as in the case of the Barnabites and Somascans. Among other factors to be considered is the rapid economic and technological development, especially in the field of agriculture, which increased the demand for adequate education. These societal changes concerned women as well as men. The growth of an educated and literate female public was a characteristic of

---

104   Mazzonis, *The Company of St. Ursula*, 54.
105   Grendler, *Schooling in Renaissance Italy*, 392; Ledochowska, *Angela Merici*, 841–42.
106   Biblioteca Ambrosiana (Ambrosian Library), Manuscript C 321, page 314. Reported in Vigotti, 86 and Turchini, 296.
107   Turchini, 294–97, and Vigotti, 82.

Renaissance and Reformation Italy, and the Ursulines knew how to adapt to this social transformation.[108] This situation significantly contrasts with the idea that only in Protestant countries was female literacy considered important. The only possible difference was in the material being read, as Catholic countries were more oriented towards devotional books than direct reading of the Scriptures. This difference, however, did not affect the role of women in family and society, which remained essentially one of subordination in both the Catholic and Protestant worlds. What can be said, though, is that through religious orders and congregations, women in Catholic countries were able to find environments in which to assert themselves more autonomously. As Querciolo Mazzonis pointed out:

> The case of Italian Ursulines challenges the view that after Trent the church adopted a monolithic or repressive policy toward devout laywomen, forcing them to accept enclosure or otherwise restricting their ability to live a consecrated life. [...] Although Ursulines were more subjected to the church's control after Trent, they nevertheless retained the freedom to remain in the world and keep significant aspects of Merici's original spiritual model.[109]

2.2 The Angelic Sisters and the Guastalla College

Within the historical and geographical contexts in which the above-mentioned educational experiences originated, one of the most original and at the same time representative initiatives of this pedagogical renewal was that of the Angelic Sisters and the *Collegio della Guastalla* (Guastalla College).[110] This

---

108 Confirmation of this comes from sixteenth century writers themselves. Ludovico Ariosto, for example, in his *Orlando Furioso*, very often winks at the female audience, aware that women represented a considerable portion of his audience. See Ita Mac Carty, *Women and the Making of Poetry in Ariosto's Orlando Furioso* (Leicester: Troubador Publishing, 2007), 2.

109 Mazzonis, The Company of St. Ursula, 50. See also Id, "Donne devote nell'Italia post-tridentina: il caso delle compagnie di Sant'Orsola." *Rivista di Storia della Chiesa in Italia*, 2, (2014), 350.

110 On the Guastalla College: Attilio Toffolo, "Percorsi spirituali ed educativi nella Milano del XVI secolo. Ludovica Torelli tra chiostro e collegio," *Rivista della storia della Chiesa in Italia*, 2, (2012): 431–65. For further documentation, see also: *Il regio Collegio della Guastalla* (San Fruttuoso di Monza: Regio Collegio della Guastalla, 1938); *Regolamento interno del R. Collegio della Guastalla in Milano* (Milano: Artigianelli, 1932); *Statuto organico del R. Collegio della Guastalla in Milano* (Milan: F. Manini, 1883); *Raccolta di notizie e documenti sulla fondazione, sul patrimonio e sviluppo del r. Collegio della Guastalla in Milano* (Milan: F. Manini, 1881).

boarding school, established in 1557, did not take its name from the place where it was located but from its foundress' birthplace.

Ludovica Torelli, who we mentioned earlier while speaking of the Barnabites, was born in 1499 in Guastalla, a small, fortified town in the heart of the Po River Valley. Guastalla had been a small lordship with wide margins of political autonomy for more than a century. It was Ludovica's ancestor, Guido Torelli, who obtained the promotion of the fief to 'county' (*Contea*) in 1428 by the will of the Duke of Milan, Filippo Maria Visconti. Ludovica was the last descendant of this family to hold the government of the town and its territory. In 1539 she sold it to the imperial captain Ferrante Gonzaga who, in the framework of the Italian Wars, needed a fortified port on the river to oppose French troops. Gonzaga continued to consolidate the political autonomy of the small state. This small historical excursus is valuable, given the importance of the link between the place, foundress, and processes of identity-building related to the congregation and school that we will discuss.

Ludovica Torelli's youth and early adulthood were intense and tormented. As a mother, she lost her only child, a four-year-old, in 1521. As a woman, it was difficult to be accepted as the county's successor when her father died in 1522, leaving no male heirs. As a wife, she experienced two stormy marriages, both of which ended in the violent deaths of her husbands, the last in 1528. These events led Ludovica to develop profound spiritual growth.[111]

The turning point of her life arrived in 1527 when she met the Dominican preacher Battista Carioni. Ludovica was deeply influenced by Carioni's teaching and spirituality. He became Torelli's confessor and she invited him to live in her castle after due pontifical authorization. As mentioned, Carioni had been the spiritual guide of many prominent Italian religious characters of his time, and had led some of them to the founding of religious orders and congregations as a part of the overall process of the sixteenth century spiritual renewal movement. Torelli also participated in this movement. After the early 1530s, Ludovica started living mainly in Milan, returning to Guastalla only a few times a year. In 1535, one year after Carioni's death, she established the congregation of the Angelic Sisters (*Angeliche*) in Milan, together with Paola Antonia Negri. Pope Paul III, who formally approved this gathering of women, left the *Angeliche* free to come and go from their convent for apostolic purposes and he exempted them from the obligation of cloistering. Their main duties were

---

111   The most detailed picture of the religious and political context that served as a background to the life of Ludovica Torelli is in Elena Bonora, *I conflitti della Controriforma. Santità e obbedienza nell'esperienza religiosa dei primi barnabiti* (Florence: Le Lettere, 1998).

focused on activities such as the teaching of Christian doctrine to women and children and assisting the sick and prisoners.

Despite their intense charitable work in Milan, their activities were not always well regarded by the religious authorities due to the freedom of movement that characterized the Angelic Sisters.[112] In 1552, after an investigation into possible heresy in the works of their spiritual father, Battista Carioni, the Angeliche were forced to cloister. These traumatic events distanced Ludovica Torelli from the congregation, leading her to reconsider its spiritual commitment and apostolate. The outcome of her reflection led her to consider opening a school in line with what was by then becoming the central axis in the redefinition of Tridentine Catholic identity, namely education. In line with the religious-educational trends of the time, Torelli wanted the Jesuits to lead the new school, though they eventually declined the invitation.[113] The type of people that the new institution targeted was different from that of the Ursuline schools; Torelli wanted to respond to a deeply felt social issue in sixteenth and seventeenth century Spanish-ruled Lombardy, namely the impoverished nobility. Perhaps her personal experience as a noblewoman exacerbated her sensitivity to this problem. Even in the boarding school that Torelli wanted to establish, the gratuity for attendance remained a central feature, along with the provision of a dowry that left the young free to choose whether to opt for marriage or continue in religious life.

The school was officially opened in 1557, and the first official document on its activity dates back to 1559. The source is a notarial deed in which we read that the school was established in order to receive "thirteen young girls who will be educated, fed, clothed and then given to religion or married, according to what God will inspire in them."[114] Torelli invested a lot in the creation of the college. She signed her income over to the institution and donated all her possessions and the profits from the sale of her fief in 1539, thereby placing the existence and governance of the school completely in her hands, which gave the institution an utterly female leadership. Another central element in the creation

---

112   In addition, Ludovica Torelli was suspected of protecting spiritual and crypto-Protestant groups thanks to her powerful political support and her friendship with Ferrante Gonzaga, governor of Milan from 1546 to 1554.

113   Angelo Bianchi and Giancarlo Rocca, eds., "L'educazione femminile tra Cinque e Settecento," *Annali di storia dell'educazione e delle istituzioni scolastiche*, 14, (2007), 67.

114   The source is kept at the Guastalla College Historical Archives (Archivio Storico del Collegio Guastalla), *Istrumento di erezione fatto dalla contessa Paola Maria Torelli*, March 8th, 1559, f. 1r. "*tredici filine che dovranno essere educate, alimentate, vestite et poi dicate alla religione ovvero maritate, secondo saranno da Dio inspirate.*" The document is transcribed in: Toffolo, cit., 447.

of the new school is the fact that the foundress wanted to place it under the protection of secular rather than religious authorities. Authorizations and guarantees of protection were requested over the years from the Spanish King Philip II and the civil authorities of the Spanish governorate of Lombardy and the city of Milan. It is likely that this distrust of religious authorities could be traced back to her troubles with the Inquisition experienced by the Angelic Sisters. In 1565, Torelli had a series of educational orders drawn up for the college in addition to the existing economic orders in which she strengthened the link between the institution and local society. It was established that the girls should not be too young, a concern of the decayed and impoverished Milanese aristocracy. All girls not meeting these criteria could not be accepted.[115]

As Attilio Toffolo points out, such educational institutions filled a gap in Milan's pedagogical landscape. The Schools of Christian Doctrine, in fact, were for girls and boys of common families, to which were added, in a sort of merger, the Ursuline schools for girls. For boys of all social backgrounds, the schools of the male religious teaching orders examined so far in this chapter were gradually being structured. For impoverished noble girls, however, options were scarce unless they wanted to undertake a cloistered life. For this reason, in early records of the college we find the names of the oldest nobilities in Milan, such as Crivelli, Balbi, Ferrari, Giorgi, Casali, Biglia, Vimercati, Corti and Visconti.[116] The intended duration of the girls' stay in the institution was twelve years. In Ludovica Torelli's educational project, the aim of this long stay was to guarantee the human, emotional and spiritual maturity of the girls by keeping them away from possible sources of pressure to make life choices that were not theirs. In this sense we see a kind of education in support of female self-determination with proto-feminist traits, with all the necessary caution. In the ordinances of 1565, it was established that one year before the end of their stay the confessor should ask the girls "for the determination of their soul and that as a consequence they should be placed according to how their vocation will be shown, not straining their soul in any way."[117] To this end, the educational contents of the college were not of the highest level, being limited, as in the majority of contemporary female schools, to writing, reading, Catholic morals and domestic duties.[118] After all, if they did not become nuns, they

---

115   *Raccolta di notizie e documenti*, XXX.
116   *Ibidem*.
117   Original quote: "*la determinazione de l'animo loro et di poi si habbia a provedere siano allogate secondo che mostrarà essere la vocazione loro, non sforzando l'animo loro in alchun modo.*" *Ibidem*.
118   "In marriage and in conversation, they [the girls] should be a mirror of honesty, charity and patience, so that in the houses where they enter they may bring with them peace

would become wives, but they would at least be able to choose freely between these options.

However, we must not suspect Torelli of pedagogical myopia. In the context of the gender roles of her time, Torelli was convinced that women played a fundamental role in the moral reform of society; actions passed through the internal "reform" of every family thanks to the woman within it. The woman/wife, by means of her virtue, would make her family virtuous, and each family would likewise influence society. In this sense, a central pedagogical role was played by teachers in the education at Guastalla College. These teachers were chosen from within the Milanese aristocracy, and their moral example would instil in their pupils virtues of patience and charity.[119]

These were the years of Borromeo's Milan and of the great diffusion of the Ursuline congregation. During this time, the Jesuits also arrived in the Borromaic archdiocese, so a comparison with the Ursulines is essential. Both the Ursulines and the teachers of the Guastalla College were exempted from cloistering at a time when the issue was major; however, the Ursulines remained strictly under episcopal control while the Guastalla College, thanks to Torelli's powerful political support, managed to remain autonomous.[120] Despite the private vows of chastity made by the teachers of the Guastalla, they always remained a group of laywomen. The arrival of the Jesuits in Milan in 1563 provided Torelli's college with more support.

Since the birth of the Society of Jesus, in fact, the Ignatian charism and spirituality had quickly spread into the female religious sensibilities of the time. Women's communities and institutions in the field of education that were legally independent but inspired by the Society of Jesus quickly became rooted in various cities in the Italian Peninsula. The so-called 'Jesuitesses' (*Gesuitesse*) thus created structures for the education of the elite, relying on the Society of Jesus without ever formally merging with it. The Guastalla College was part of this phenomenon.[121] Ludovica Torelli took advantage of the arrival of the

---

        and good example." Translation: "*Nel matrimonio et conversando nel mondo siano specchio di honestà, charità e patientia, acioché nelle case dove intraranno portino seco la pace et il buon esempio*," in *Raccolta di notizie e documenti*, XXX. The quote is reported in Toffolo, cit., 452.

119   Elizabeth Rapley, *The Devotes: Women and Church in Seventeenth-Century France* (Montreal and Kingston: McGill-Queen's University Press, 1990), 157.

120   Bonora, *I conflitti della Controriforma*, 316–17.

121   Giancarlo Rocca, "Gesuiti, Gesuitesse e l'educazione femminile," in *L'educazione femminile tra Cinque e Settecento*, Annali di storia dell'educazione e delle istituzioni scolastiche, 14, (2007): 65–75. Although the term *Gesuitesse* had been initially used to define the communities created by Mary Ward during the 17th century, according to Rocca it may

Jesuits in Milan to further cut ties with the past and increase the autonomy of her educational institution; she removed the Barnabites from the role of confessors, replacing them with Jesuits.

During this brief exposition, we have observed all the evidence that justifies the definition given to the educational experience of the Guastalla College as both original and representative in respect to its time; in fact, this pedagogical experiment was placed in the most classical and tested fields of the Catholic Church. During those decades, the identities of many male and female religious teaching orders born at the beginning of the sixteenth century were structured around the educational apostolate. Ludovica Torelli was inspired by this atmosphere. Very often Jesuits served as an example for these congregations, Torelli's included; she called them to spiritually direct her college. Closeness to the Society of Jesus was also instrumental for the origins of the Guastalla College. Such a link served to consolidate the autonomy from episcopal authority, also demonstrated by the placement of the school under the secular authority of the King of Spain and the municipal authorities of Milan. Torelli, mindful of her experience with the Angelic Sisters and the Barnabites, wanted to keep interference by the religious authorities to a minimum and to protect the other original aspect of the institution, namely its female dimension. As we have seen, the school wanted to protect young nobility from the pressures of their families, giving them greater freedom of choice over their own destinies. Torelli was thus able to create an educational project, merging elements ranging from examples from Ursulines to Jesuits, animated by religious aims but protected by secular authorities.

2.3 *Rosa Venerini and Lucia Filippini: The Pious Teachers*

The educational experiences of women in post-Tridentine Italy were not limited to the north and the Po River Valley. We have seen that some Ursuline schools were also created in central and southern Italy, although to a lesser extent than in Lombardy. There was therefore an educational gap to fill. The initiative was taken in the city of Viterbo, in northern Lazio. In 1685, the bishop of the city allowed Rosa Venerini, a devout local woman, to open a school for the Christian education of girls. Rosa accepted, and with the help of two friends, Gerolama Coluzzelli and Porzia Bacci, she started the first school. Venerini was not just a pious woman; born in 1656, she was the daughter of Goffredo Venerini, an educated physician from Rome who moved to Viterbo

---

indicate other women's communities inspired by the Society of Jesus. See also: Toffolo, cit., 460.

to work in the city's largest hospital. Her mother was Marzia Zampichetti, the descendant of a local noble family. Rosa's origins give us a glimpse of a wealthy and cultivated background that no doubt informed her regarding the traditional forms expected for a girl.[122]

Rosa Venerini was not just an educated woman; as in the cases of Angela Merici and Ludovica Torelli, she was also devout. Part of her youth was devoted to determining whether to undertake a consecrated life or a married one. Finally, in 1676, she entered the local Dominican monastery where she remained only a few months due to the deaths, in rapid succession, of her father, brother, and mother. After leaving the monastery, she drew closer to Jesuit spirituality. After the death of her spiritual director, a Dominican friar, Rosa approached the Jesuit father Ignazio Martinelli, originally from Perugia, who was at that time teacher of philosophy in Viterbo.[123] Father Martinelli was a key figure in the creation of the Pious School of Rosa Venerini. She revealed to him that she already had an informal school of Christian doctrine for girls at her home. The Jesuit then asked the Bishop of Viterbo to institutionalize this work, and the school started in 1685.

The funding, in step with the widespread practice in early modern Italy, came from a rich noble lady of Viterbo. An initial question about the nature of the newly founded school concerned the audience to be admitted. There was no doubt that the institution was dedicated to girls, but Rosa Venerini only wanted to admit poor girls from the populace. Father Martinelli eventually convinced her to also accept impoverished young nobility. As in sixteenth century Lombardy, the impoverished aristocracy was also an important issue in central Italy. Ignatius Martinelli thus became the spiritual guide of Rosa Venerini and her school, which was fully incorporated into the Jesuit educational charism and spirituality. In this case, regarding the teachers of the Guastalla College, we can speak of true Jesuitesses. The first years of the school saw a slow but solid growth. The suspicions of the local society towards a group of women

---

122   About Rosa Venerini's life and pedagogical experience, see Pietro Zovatto, ed., Storia della spiritualità italiana (Rome: Città Nuova, 2001), 339; Maria Mascilongo, *Ho creduto nell'amore. Itinerario spirituale di Rosa Venerini* (Rome: Città Nuova, 2006); Luciana Bellatalla and Sira Sirenella Macchietti, *Questioni e esperienze di educazione femminile in Toscana: dalla Controriforma all'ultimo Ottocento* (Rome: Bulzoni, 1998): Sira Sirenella Macchietti, *Rosa Venerini all'origine della scuola popolare femminile: 'azione educativa del suo istituto dal 1685 ad oggi* (Brescia: La Scuola, 1986). See also: *Regole per maestre pie dell'istituto della serva di Dio Rosa Venerini ricavate dalla vita, dalla relazione e dai manoscritti della medesima* (Rome, coi tipi vaticani, 1837).

123   Giuseppe Antonio Patrignani, *Menologio di pie memorie d'alcuni religiosi della compagnia de Gesù*, Vol. 2, (Venice, presso Niccolò Pezzana, 1730), 177–80.

characterized by a wide margin of mobility and active life hindered the flow of girls to the new school in its early stages; within six years, however, the number of pupils grew and the number of teachers increased from three to five until the temporary removal of Father Martinelli from Viterbo in 1692.[124]

It was in that year that the real expansion of the Venerini Schools began. The bishop of Montefiascone, Cardinal Marcantonio Barbarigo, having heard of the activity of the Pious Venerini Schools, wanted to open another school in his diocese under Venerini's direction. Subsequently, the bishops of Civita Castellana, Sutri and Bagnoregio also wanted to establish Venerini Schools in their dioceses and in the regions of Marche and Umbria.[125] Between 1692 and 1694, Venerini established a total of ten new schools in the villages surrounding Lake Bolsena. It was not long before the fame of the Venerini Schools reached Rome. After a first disappointing attempt to open a school there in 1706, in 1713 Pope Clement XI invited the founder to open her own school in the capital of Catholicism. The foundation was made possible by the Abbot of Acts, and Rosa was able to open her school on the slopes of the Capitoline Hill, namely the *Campidoglio*.

During Rosa Venerini's stay in Rome, the Jesuit Ignazio Martinelli returned to Viterbo to take care of the spiritual direction of the teachers of the first school founded by Venerini. This direction corresponded to a real co-direction of the school with the foundress. The moment of ultimate success arrived on October 24th, 1716. On that day, Clement XI and eight cardinals went to the school to attend a lesson. The outcome was so positive that the Pope said to Rosa: "Signora Rosa, you are doing that which we cannot do. We thank you very much because with these schools you will sanctify Rome."[126] Consistency with the educational charism of the post-Tridentine militant church could not have been greater.

The charism of the Venerini Schools is summarized in their motto "educate to save" and was part of a non-intellectualistic educational concept. The main purpose of the schools was the moral education of the girls rather than academics. The aim was to make them good Christians and good wives if eventually they did not choose a religious life. Even the hierarchical structure remained quite simple. To the founding mother and the confessors, in addition to some charismatic figures of spiritual guidance such as the Jesuit Martinelli,

---

124 *Ibidem.*
125 *Regole per maestre pie*, IV.
126 http://www.vatican.va/news_services/liturgy/saints/ns_lit_doc_20061015_venerini_en.html.Original quote: "Signora, Rosa, voi fate quello che Noi non possiamo fare, Noi molto vi ringraziamo perché con queste scuole santificherete Roma."

were added directors of individual schools and teachers. These teachers, like those engaged in the Guastalla College, were not nuns, but laywomen who had taken a vow of poverty and chastity. They were soon called *Maestre Pie* (Pious Teachers). Both girls and mature women were admitted to the Venerini Schools. The emphasis was on teaching the catechism, the mysteries of the rosary, and reading and writing.

Despite the religious emphasis of the education given in Rosa Venerini's schools, however, there was no lack of willingness to provide the students with some concrete instruments of social emancipation and redemption, at least with respect to social conditions that, in some cases, were miserable. All this occurred, obviously, in a social context in which the women remained essentially subject to their husbands or fathers, yet, compared to an original condition of illiteracy and hard work in the fields, a girl able to manage domestic economy through reading and writing and eventually teaching her children, could legitimately aspire to a better life than the context into which she had been born. Venerini wanted to give women an experience that would allow them to "conquer the necessary education of all that they had to believe, hope, operate."[127] When Rosa Venerini died in 1728, forty of her schools had been opened in the small towns of central Italy.[128]

Lucia Filippini stood out among the teachers active in the Venerini Schools. She was born in 1672 in Tarquinia. Orphaned, she spent her childhood with an aristocratic aunt. Perhaps it is no coincidence that Lucia developed her spirituality at the local convent of Benedictine nuns. Although during the seventeenth century the female branch of the Benedictines were not particularly committed to education, written culture remained among the founding elements of the Benedictine charism. We cannot know to what extent, but it is reasonable to assume that the young Filippini was affected by these spiritual features of that monastery. Lucia met with Cardinal Marcantonio Barbarigo during a pastoral visit to Tarquinia. The bishop of Montefiascone, struck by Filippini's intelligence, thought that she could be useful in the school in his city that had been opened by Rosa Venerini in 1692. Initially brought to Montefiascone by Cardinal Barbarigo, Lucia was placed in the local convent of Santa Chiara, but she was not like the others, and received from the bishop the task of teaching the other girls in the monastery. Lucia thus became one of Rosa Venerini's closest collaborators in Montefiascone. The turning point in Lucia Filippini's apostolic activity was when Rosa Venerini returned first to Viterbo to take care

---

[127] Bellatalla; Macchietti, *Questioni e esperienze di educazione femminile*, 62; Macchietti, *Rosa Venerini*, 77, 83, 132; and Mascilongo, *Ho creduto all'amore*, 16.

[128] Grendler, *Schooling in Renaissance Italy*, 392.

of some problems that had arisen since her departure, and later to Rome, summoned by Clement XI. Filippini was to direct the school of Montefiascone and to continue opening new schools in the region. Cardinal Barbarigo supported Filippini in this task.[129] Lucia, assisted by some new carefully selected teachers including Chiara Candelari and Margherita Casali, continued opening schools in central Italy; by the end of her life, they totaled fifty-two. The educational and institutional model of the schools opened by Filippini was essentially the same as the Venerini Schools, the only significant change being the passage of spiritual direction from the Jesuits to the Congregation of the Pious Workers founded by Carlo Carafa in Naples in 1600, which helped Filippini to open a school in Rome in 1707.

How are we to evaluate the overall activity of these school founders? Two reasons explain the delay of these pedagogical occurrences compared to in northern Italy. The first is the economic stagnation of central Italian towns between the sixteenth and seventeenth centuries. While the hard-working cities of the Po River Valley, despite the devastation inflicted by the Italian Wars, underwent a profound transformation of agricultural structures that would lay the foundations for eighteenth century proto-industrialization, the inner cities of central and southern Italy, with their mountainous geography that made communication difficult, remained economically backward, resulting in a lower demand for literacy.[130] The second reason is the different conception of the feminine role in central-southern Italy as compared to the north, where women were granted greater social margins of activity. The freedom of movement enjoyed by Rosa Venerini and Lucia Filippini was viewed with suspicion and distrust by local societies, most of the religious authorities and the lower clergy. It is no coincidence that the bishop of Montefiascone, Cardinal Marcantonio Barbarigo, the "talent-scout" who discovered these two women and allowed them to make use of their educational genius, was originally from Venice.

The patronage of men was also a key factor. The position held by figures such as Barbarigo and the Jesuit Ignazio Martinelli was never intended to control the orientation and character of the pedagogical intuitions of Rosa

---

129   On the life and activity of Lucia Filippini, see Nicola D'Amico, *Un libro per Eva. Il difficile cammino dell'istruzione della donna in Italia: la storia, le protagoniste* (Milan: FrancoAngeli, 2016); Rita Pomponio, *Il tredicesimo apostolo. Santa Lucia Filippini* (Rome: San Paolo Edizioni, 2004); Francesco Di Simone, *Della vita della serva di Dio Lucia Filippini superiora delle scuole pie* (Rome: per l'Ansillioni al corallo vicino alla Chiesa Nova, 1732).

130   Carlo Maria Cipolla, *Istruzione e sviluppo: il declino dell'analfabetismo nel mondo occidentale* (Bologna: Il Mulino, 2002).

Venerini and Lucia Filippini; these men spontaneously opted for the forms and charisms offered by Venerini and Filippini without ever failing to bring their original idea to life. Venerini's story is exemplary. Her pedagogical method was certainly inspired by the programs and discipline of the Jesuit *Ratio Studiorum*; however, in actual practice she was able to adopt original solutions such as the use of several teachers for the same class. Overall, therefore, the Venerini and Filippini Pious Schools managed to create a synthesis of traditional and innovative educational elements led by female boldness yet following Tridentine dictates.

CHAPTER 3

Schools and Colleges

Processes of Settlement in Italy and Contiguous Areas

The bulk of the spread of religious orders throughout the Italian Peninsula occurred mainly between the last decades of the sixteenth and the first half of the eighteenth century. An investigation of the dynamics and causes of the settlement and foundation of convents and colleges highlights some differences in how the spread took place that we can identify as characteristic features of the various religious orders. In this chapter we will see the mechanisms of the displacement and arrival of religious teaching congregations in some areas of Italy, while in the next chapter we will focus on some case studies to better understand these processes.

There are three main factors that can be identified as engines of these movements. The first of these was the convergence of interests between religious orders and Italian aristocracies. On the one hand, as mentioned above, with the end of the Italian Wars and the affirmation in the Peninsula of a new political order, an alliance was established between the dynasties at the head of the Italian states and the new religious orders. Princes and regional monarchs wished to relieve public finances from the expense of schools and, eager to obtain stronger social control over their subjects, saw congregations devoted to education as instruments suited to their ends. Regular clerics who needed political protection to deploy their pedagogy found it useful to submit to these requests. However, there were not only ruling dynasties but also urban and provincial aristocracies which founded convents with adjoining schools and colleges by means of testaments, donations or legacies. In this practice we find the ancient medieval custom of nobles who, at the end of their earthly journey, bestowed donations on monasteries and churches to lighten their conscience and facilitate their entry into paradise. This custom was adapted to a new educational model, namely endowments for a community or village with a religious institution able to provide services to the population.[1]

---

1   An example of the new religious-educational adaptation of the ancient practice of endowing to or establishing religious institutions at the end of an aristocrat's public life is given in 1569–1570 by Camillo I Gonzaga of Novellara. He was an imperial captain at the service of Charles V and Ferdinand of Habsburg and had participated in several military campaigns conducted by the House of Austria in the mid sixteenth century. Having retired from military life in the

The second factor, as mentioned above, relates to the new educational needs of the two medieval and renaissance urban institutions *par excellence*: the episcopate and the municipality. Both these institutions, by the end of the Middle Ages, had lost their ability to respond to the educational, cultural and social needs of a rapidly changing era, but felt the need to keep up with their contemporaries. For this reason, bishops and municipal councils called members of religious orders, old and new, to serve in municipal and episcopal schools, or established new schools controlled by these congregations.

A third element that gave impetus to and partly determined the paths of school foundations by religious orders during the early modern age was the need to face the Protestant challenge. The struggle against Protestant doctrines led to the foundation of Catholic schools even in non-Italian contexts, particularly in the Kingdom of France through the Duchy of Savoy where the fight against the Huguenots and the proximity of Calvinist Geneva made the emergence particularly severe. We can find a similar situation in central and eastern Europe, where the competition for souls was not only with Protestants but also with the Orthodox Church. The campaigns to catholicize schools run by Jesuits (for example, Possevino in Savoy) were not the only such campaigns. Other congregations born during the sixteenth and seventeenth centuries were also deeply committed to this process, particularly the Barnabites and Piarists but also the Franciscans, as we shall see shortly. The reasons that led to new foundations, however, were not always external; in some circumstances the religious orders decided independently to move and to create schools in new cities, such as in the case of the Theatines and Somascans.

1   From Lombardy to the Kingdom of France

From the 1570s onward when the Barnabites were directly asked by the papacy for a greater commitment to the world of education, the expansion of the schools of this congregation was rapid and intense.[2] The first few years had been marked by a certain distrust of studies, as was quite often the case with many of the religious orders striving for spiritual renewal during the sixteenth

---

late 1560s, Camillo was moved by a sincere desire for spiritual redemption and he decided to establish an important Jesuit convent with an attached school and college to provide education to the youth of his dominion. For more information, refer to Salomoni, *Le scuole di una comunità emiliana*, 17–42.

2   For the history of the Barnabites in the sixteenth century, refer to: Orazio Maria Premoli, *Storia dei barnabiti nel Cinquecento* (Rome: Desclee editore, 1913).

century. However, the first steps taken by the Barnabites in the scholastic world were cautious; they preferred to opt for a gradual entry of lay students into the congregation's colleges. During the 1580s, the Barnabite Carlo Bascapé, future bishop of Novara and close collaborator of Carlo Borromeo as well as his imitator in the practices of pastoral government, decided to admit lay students into the Barnabite college of Cremona.[3] Later, in 1590, some young people from Milan were accepted into the Barnabite college of Pavia. The first Barnabite to be accepted by a diocesan seminary, that of Arona, was Father Timoteo Facciardi. In 1593 a first attempt to establish a new college for lay boys in Pisa failed, despite the support of the archbishop and the grand duke of Tuscany, Ferdinando de' Medici. Even the idea of Pope Clement VIII to open a college of Barnabites in Ragusa in 1603 was unsuccessful.

The turning point came in 1608, when, thanks to the legacy left by the noble Milanese cleric Giambattista Arcimboldi, the homonymous schools were opened in Milan. The Arcimboldi College was the first large college of Barnabites expressly designed for young laypeople. According to the legacy, the fathers had to oversee every pedagogical and organizational aspect of the new institution. From this moment on the road was open.[4] The opening of the school in Milan was quickly followed by the opening of schools in Vigevano (1609), Asti (1626), Arpino (1627), Lodi (1631 and 1662), Pisa (1632), Piacenza (in the 1640s), Casalmaggiore (1649), Livorno (1650), Alessandria (1660), Crema (1664), Fossombrone (1675), Genoa (1674), Udine (1679), Acqui (1682) and Cortona (1697). We note that the hard core of the Barnabite foundations has its roots in the northern Lombard-Piedmontese area, with some sporadic foundations in central and southern Italy. An interesting aspect, however, is that during the initial phase of this wave of foundations, the order immediately received great favor beyond the Alps. A few years after Milan and Vigevano, and throughout the entire first phase of the foundations listed here, Barnabite schools were opened in Savoy (Annecy, 1614; Thonon, 1616; Bonneville, 1659), Ile de France (Montargis, 1620; Étampes, 1644), Béarn (Lescar, 1624), the Landes (Dax, 1630; Mont-de-Marsan, 1657), the Pas De Calais (Loches, 1665) and Gironde (Bazas, 1695).

Although the foundations of Barnabite colleges in Italy knew some discontinuity between the seventeenth and eighteenth centuries, it is the French foundations that represent a watershed in the history of their schools.[5] Barnabite

---

3   Gentili, *Les Barnabites*, 92.
4   Angelo Bianchi, "Le scuole Arcimboldi a Milano nel XVII secolo: professori, studenti, cultura scolastica," *Barnabiti Studi* 19 (2002): 55–78.
5   For the history of the Barnabites in the seventeenth century, refer to Orazio Maria Premoli, *Storia dei barnabiti nel Seicento* (Rome: Industria tipografica romana, 1922).

foundations in France, in fact, stopped at the end of the seventeenth century, coinciding with the attenuation of religious conflict between Huguenots and Catholics. Barnabite schools in the French kingdom were opened as an educational answer to the challenge of Protestant ideas. During the eighteenth century, however, new Barnabite schools continued to spring up throughout Italy, firmly established in the Lombardy-Piedmont area by the foundations in Tortona (1700), Bergamo (1701), Finale Marina (1711), Milan (1723 and 1745), Chieri (1724), Casal Monferrato (1739), Aosta (1748), Porto Maurizio (1749), Bormio (1782), Cremona (1790) and Turin (1792). However, the new colleges were not limited to the northwest of Italy but also arose in other areas of the north such as Bologna (1737) and Vittorio Veneto (1738) and in the center of the Peninsula in places such as Foligno (1728), Florence (1735), Loreto (1794), San Severino (1798), and Macerata (1802). Virtually absent were Barnabite schools in southern Italy.

If we look at who was behind the newly established institutions, we find a balance between the nobility and municipal councils. Out of forty-two schools founded by the Barnabites between 1603 and 1792, fourteen were by the initiative of nobles and seventeen by communities. Among the aristocracy we find regional sovereigns, such as Cosimo III de' Medici, who in 1684 opened Barnabite public schools in Pescia, and Charles Emmanuel I, Duke of Savoy, who, in agreement with Saint Francis of Sales, called upon the Barnabites to establish grammar and philosophy schools in Annecy and Thonon. An even more important role was played by urban and provincial aristocracies. The new schools, according to the wishes of the donors, were to be created for young people from the city or from the country, for poor or noble boys, or for people of any social standing; the examples are many. One example shows the noblewoman Camilla Tavazzi Catenaga endowing in her will a school of grammar and rhetoric for the youth of the Lodi countryside in 1662.[6] In 1674, the noble Bartolomeo Gavanto established a school for young nobles with promising intellectual talents in Genoa.[7] The success of this college led the Genoese Guild of Notaries to donate a new section to the same school and dedicate it to the young bourgeoisie of the city in 1675. In 1735 the San Carlo College, which had been closed years before due to lack of funds, was reopened in Florence

---

6 Angelo Bianchi, *L'istruzione secondaria tra barocco ed età dei lumi. Il collegio di San Giovanni alle Vigne di Lodi e l'esperienza pedagogica dei Barnabiti* (Milan: Vita e pensiero, 1993), 38.
7 On Bartolomeo Gavanto, see Giuseppe Colombo, *Profili biografici di illustri barnabiti effigiati sotto i portici del Collegio S. Francesco in Lodi* (Crema: Tipografia Campanini, 1870), 74–76.

SCHOOLS AND COLLEGES 99

for students of any social background thanks to the endowment of the noble Francesco Boddi.[8]

The history of Barnabite institutions often intersected with that of the Jesuits, both in positive and negative ways. The Barnabite *Ratio Studiorum* was forged on that of the Jesuits and approved in 1666 during the general chapter of the order. From the beginning of their activity as educators, the comparison with the famous Society of Jesus was alive in the imagination of the Clerics Regular of Saint Paul. As early as 1616 the Barnabites had taken over the schools of Thonon in Savoy at the invitation of Saint Francis of Sales, from where the Jesuits had withdrawn. In 1631 a Milanese chronicler, in reference to the Arcimboldi College after the great plague of 1630, affirmed that the Barnabite schools were "so filled with pupils, that while those of the Jesuits had significantly decreased after the plague our families have grown so that the lower schools no longer contain the students."[9] However, it was with the suppression of the Society in 1773 that the taking over of Jesuit schools became more significant. In 1774, barely a year after the Jesuit suppression, the Barnabites took charge of the Bolognese college of San Luigi (Saint Louis), which was under the direction of Father Mariano Fontana, in addition to the college of nobles of Saint Francis Xavier and the schools of Santa Lucia together with the university library. In 1782, the Barnabites took charge of the schools of Bormio after the Jesuits had abandoned it, but in the same year they were expelled from the Grand Duchy of Tuscany because of their refusal to take over Jesuit schools within the borders of the state.[10] The same thing occurred with the college of nobles in Turin: in 1792 the Barnabites took charge of the direction of this institute from lazy diocesan priests who, in 1773, had taken over from the Jesuits. The Turin College thus experienced a new phase of flowering that raised the number of pupils to ninety in 1794, until the Napoleonic suppression of 1799.[11]

---

8   Licia Bertani, Giuseppe Cagni, Eugenio Castellani, Giampaolo Trotta, *San Carlo dei Barnabiti a Firenze: una chiesa ed un collegio all'ombra dei Granduchi e dell'Impero* (Florence: Comune di Firenze, 1995), and Giuseppe Richia S.J., *Notizie Istoriche delle Chiese Fiorentine Divise ne' suoi Quartieri* Tomo X, Parte II (Florence: Nella Stamperia di Pietri Gaetano Viviani, 1762), 373.
9   *I Barnabiti*, 245.
10 For an interesting case study concerning the Barnabite experience in Tuscany, see Angelo Gaudio, "I Barnabiti a Livorno: note da una ricerca in corso," *Rassegna Volterrana*, LXXXVII (2010): 591–97. See also Giovanni Battista Damioli, *Date e fatti degli Istituti di vita consacrata a Livorno*, (Livorno: Centro Diocesano Stampa, 1984), and Id., "Ordine dei Padri Barnabiti," in *I religiosi a Livorno. Fratelli e Padri* (Livorno, Centro Diocesano Stampa, 1984), 55–67.
11 Luigi Cibrario, *Origini e progresso delle istituzioni della Monarchia di Savoia*, parte seconda (Torino: Dalla Stamperia Reale, 1855), 449.

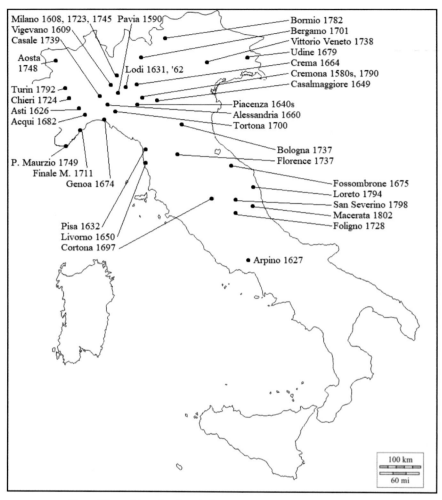

MAP 1   Map of Barnabite schools in Italy

2   Schools for Northern Italy and Small Towns

Another regular order in Lombardy, the Somascan fathers, was founded by the Venetian nobleman Girolamo Emiliani. Initially they addressed the care of orphans and abandoned children, but these activities were soon joined by teaching when they took charge of some schools and established others. The Somascan involvement in education, however, did not intensify with the pontifical approval granted by Pope Pius V in 1568 to raise the status of the secular priests and lay people gathered around Emiliani to a regular order. Before that date, only three schools had been opened by the congregation, one in Merone in the territory of Como in 1551, and two in Milan in 1557 and 1559. During this period, of the twenty-two existing institutes run by the fathers throughout Italy, nineteen were orphanages but only three were schools.[12]

It is probable that the difficulty in expanding beyond the management of orphanages to the creation of schools was due to the difficulty in defining the identity of the order.[13] Between 1546 and 1555, the fathers had been united with the Theatines and in 1566 they united with the reformed priests of Saint Mary the Little (*la Piccola*) of Tortona. This was still the case in 1612 when they united with the priests of the Good Jesus of Ravenna, while between 1616 and 1647 they united with the priests of the Christian doctrine of Avignon.[14] It was perhaps for this reason that between 1568 and the 1590s the Somascans did not open any schools except for the one in Novellara in 1569 where they remained for just a few months before being replaced by Jesuits.[15] However, starting in 1591 the Somascan pedagogical vocation reached its maturation and the spread of their schools began to be steady.

In regard to the geographical distribution of Somascan schools, their strong concentration in northern Italy is notable as they had even more than the Barnabites, particularly between Veneto, Lombardy and Piedmont. Out

---

12   ACTA CONGREGATIONIS (1528–1602), *Fonti per la storia dei Somaschi*, Vol. 1, ed. Maurizio Brioli C.R.S. (Rome: Curia generalizia dei padri Somaschi, 2006), 19, 26, 28. The orphanages were in Genoa, Savona, Triulzio, Reggio, Pavia, Rome, Vercelli, Naples, Siena, Milan, Tortona, Bergamo, Alessandria, Brescia, Verona, Venice, Somasca, Vicenza, and Ferrara. In this case we also note a concentration in the northern area, with a hard core in Lombardy, Piedmont and Veneto and only two institutions in the center (Rome and Siena) and one in the south (Naples).

13   It is true, however, that even in orphanages the children received basic grammatical education. See Marco Tentorio, "In merito alle istituzioni somasche 'Orfanotrofio-Collegio-Convitto,'" *Somascha* XXVI, (2001): 1–10.

14   The regular clerics of the Good Jesus were founded in Ravenna in 1526 by the priest Girolamo Muselli, approved by Pope Paul III in 1538 and recognized as a congregation by Julius III in 1551. In common with the Theatines and the Barnabites, they originated from an oratory and distinguished themselves by having unmasked Bernardino Ochino's heresy in 1535 while he was preaching in Ravenna. They were suppressed by Innocent X during the inquiry on religious orders of 1651. In general, see Pietro Zovatto, ed., *Storia della spiritualità italiana* (Rome: Città Nuova, 2001), 252. In particular, refer to: Michel Dortel-Cloudot, "Chierici Regolari del Buon Gesù," in *Dizionario degli Istituti di Perfezione*, vol II (Rome: Edizioni Paoline, 1974), 909. For the reformed priests of Santa Maria Piccola of Tortona, see Stefano Casati, "I preti riformati di Santa Maria Piccola e i Somaschi," *Somascha* XI, (1986): 55–72.

15   Refer to: Salomoni, "Le scuole di una comunità emiliana," 17–42 and Giovanni Alcaini, "Origini e progressi degli istituti diretti dai Padri Somaschi," *Somascha* IV, (1979): 70–175.

of thirty-eight schools established between 1591 and 1715, thirty-one were located in that area, while only four were located in central Italy (Amelia, 1601; Rome, 1604; Velletri, 1616; Macerata, 1689) and three in the south (Melfi, 1616; Naples, 1628; Caserta, 1696). Even among the northern regions, Emilia-Romagna, the southernmost, had only three schools, namely Ravenna (1646), Corte Maggiore (1662) and Cento (1690). A similar argument applies to the Liguria region, where schools were only built in Chiavari (1705) and Sarzana (1714). The three northernmost areas, on the other hand, were full of schools. In Lombardy, the Somascan cradle, twelve scholastic institutions were created, namely Lugano (1597), Rivolta d'Adda (1614), Paullo (1615), Orzinuovi (1626), Salò and Lodi (1627), Sabbioneta and Brescia (1628), Bergamo (1632), Soncino (1634), Treviglio (1641) and Voghera (1690). We observe a similar situation in Piedmont, where we find nine schools belonging to the congregatio, namely Tortona (1591), Novara and Fossano (1623), Albenga (1625), Casale Monferrato (1626), Biella (1632), Cavallermaggiore (1638), Alba (1662) and Novi (1649). Last but not least, in the Venetian area, including today's regions of Trentino and Friuli, five schools were present in Treviso (1597), Verona (1638), Rovereto (1655), Udine (1674) and Cividale (1705).[16]

The reason for such an unbalanced geographical distribution in favor of northern Italy can be related to the typology of the founders of such schools. For the Somascans, out of the forty-two schools founded or taken over between 1551 and 1715, only four had been at the initiative of the nobility, a number that increases to eleven if we include the list of prelates from the aristocracy. However, in relation to the diversified nature of early modern aristocracy, the reasons that led these nobles to found schools or colleges could differ greatly. A particular example is the Archimandrite of Messina, Felice Novello, who, beginning in 1601, donated 500 ducats annually to the Somascans to open a school in Amelia in the Umbria region. He was a native of Amelia, and therefore considered it worthwhile to have the Somascan fathers maintain the local schools.[17] In this way the prelate fulfilled both his religious duty and his role of benefactor of the community, maintaining his influence and relations with

---

16   All the data reported here are derived from the three volumes of the ACTA CONGREGATIONIS (1528–1737), *Fonti per la storia dei Somaschi* (Rome: Curia generalizia dei padri Somaschi, 2006).

17   ACTA CONGREGATIONIS, I, 150. The office of archimandrite was connected to the monastery of the Most Holy Savior of Messina, under whose jurisdiction fell all the Italian monasteries of the Greek-Byzantine rite. From 1635 the office was equated with that of a bishop. See Antonio De Lorenzo, *Memorie da servire alla storia sacra e civile di Reggio e delle Calabrie* (Reggio Calabria: Stamperia Siclari, 1873), 209, and Saverio Di Bella, *Caino Barocco. Messina e la Spagna 1672–1678* (Cosenza: Luigi Pellegrini editore, 2005), 99–101.

the local elites. Subsequently, the municipal authorities and the local bishop also contributed to the maintainance of the new schools, showing how a strict distinction between typologies of founders was often artificial and that the founding of new schools in a city or village was the result of collective efforts.

Another case is the Somascan school of Rivolta d'Adda in the Diocese of Cremona. In this case we also observe an alternation between religious orders, this time with a branch of the reformed Franciscans, the Capuchins. The college was created in 1614 by the counts of Maino, and initially donated to the Capuchin friars; however, these friars were soon declared incapable of maintaining the school because of their obstinacy in not wanting to have a regular income, but to live on charity. The Maino family, then, in agreement with public authorities and with the papal authorization of Paul V, replaced the Capuchins with Somascans, who were charged with teaching grammar and the humanities.[18]

Most of the schools founded by Somascan clerics were requested by twenty-three public authorities and city councils; however, it does not seem that that was the cause of the greater presence of the congregation in northern Italy, as the percentage of public and private foundations was more or less the same throughout the Peninsula. Such an investigative bias could be justified by the more urban-centric conception usually attributed by historiography to the north of Italy, but the data we possess does not support this. A more promising approach may be to consider the nature of the settlements that required the presence of Somascan schools. The regular clerics of Somascha, in fact, more markedly than the Barnabites and completely differently than the Theatines and Capuchins (as we will see shortly), preferred to build new schools in small and medium-sized settlements instead of in large urban centers, similarly to the Piarists, which can explain the greater diffusion of the religious order in northern Italy. Between the sixteenth and seventeenth centuries, the small and medium centers of the northern Italian regions saw an important demographic and economic expansion, making it necessary to have more schools to train more people for more tasks and professions.[19] These transformations

---

18   ACTA CONGREGATIONIS, II, 52.
19   On the relation between school and economy in early Modern Italy, see "Geografia, economia, politica e scuola. Determinismo o ipotesi plausibile?" in Salomoni, *Scuole, maestri e scolari*, 88–98. For demographic data, refer to: Maria Ginatempo and Lucia Sandri, *L'Italia delle città: il popolamento urbano tra Medioevo e Rinascimento (secoli XIII–XVI)* (Florence: Le Lettere, 1990), and Lorenzo Del Panta, "I processi demografici," in *Storia degli antichi stati italiani*, ed. Gaetano Greco and Mario Rosa, (Rome-Bari: Laterza, 2009), 215–48.

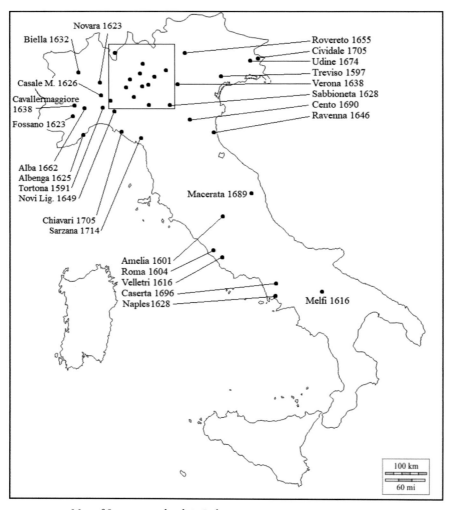

MAP 2   Map of Somascan schools in Italy

in non-urban centers were not as marked in the small cities of the south, thus leading to an increase in demand on the educational market of the north and a greater spread of Somascans into that area.[20]

---

20   Luigi Piccioni, "Città e reti insediative nel Mezzogiorno di età moderna," in *Scelte pubbliche, strategie private e sviluppo economico in Calabria*, ed., Giovanni Anania (Soveria Mannelli: Rubbettino, 2001), 217–35.

SCHOOLS AND COLLEGES

MAP 3   Map of Somascan schools in Lombardy

3   A Congregation for the Large Cities

Another religious order that played a key role in the early modern Italian educational scene was founded by Gaetano da Thiene and Gian Pietro Carafa (afterwards Pope Paul IV), and approved by Pope Clement VII on June 24th, 1524. The importance of the Congregation of the Clerics Regular of the Divine Providence was such that their contemporaries often confused them with the Jesuits. An important source which allows us to analyze the geography and the typology of Theanine scholastic foundations in Italy is the inquiry made by Pope Innocent X on regular orders in Italy in 1650.[21] The purpose of this survey was to systematically understand the economic, legal and demographic physiognomy of religious congregations in order to rationalize their presence in Italian territory.[22] The Innocentian inquiry was for many religious people a traumatic event that left painful wounds in the name of ruthless rationalization. When a convent was suppressed, the monks and friars were thrown out into the street if another convent would not accept them. Many were rendered homeless because other convents did not have the financial resources to support additional members.[23]

The inquiry took the Theatines by surprise, as it took place right after the time of their greatest expansion, which began in the first decades of the seventeenth century. As Marcella Campanelli points out, the Innocentian inquiry did not find great resistance from the Theatines. From a document dating to 1676 titled *Stato della religione teatina in Italia*, we know that only one house of the congregation was closed, the Genoese convent of San Pier d'Arena.[24] Unlike the orders previously considered, Theatine institutions spread more homogeneously across Italian territory, with rather marked regional characteristics. Among the aims of the order was the desire to restore the primitive rule of apostolic life. To religious vows of chastity, poverty and obedience they added direct subjection to the pope and the Holy See, like the Jesuits, and it is perhaps precisely for this reason that contemporaries tended to confuse the two congregations. The main functions of the Theatines were the administration of the sacraments, the care of souls, and preaching, yet at the time there still wasn't a wide and direct scholastic commitment towards laypeople, only a general religious pedagogy.[25] Although the order was founded in 1524, it, like other congregations, did not expand greatly until the 1600s. The founding of

---

21   Marcella Campanelli, ed., *L'inchiesta di Innocenzo X sui regolari in Italia. I teatini* (Rome: Edizioni di storia e letteratura, 1987).
22   Edoardo Barbieri and Danilo Zardin, ed., *Libri, biblioteche e cultura nell'Italia del Cinque e Seicento* (Milan: Vita e Pensiero, 2002), 78. The 1650 investigation also applied to the other religious orders considered here and allowed a closer comparison of the nature of convents and schools. However, as Sergio Pagano points out, for other orders, and particularly for the Barnabites, an "inorganic, sometimes summary and not always reliable" work was conducted. See Sergio Pagano, "Le biblioteche dei barnabiti italiani nel 1599. In margine ai loro più antichi cataloghi." *Barnabiti studi* 3, (1986): 26–39.
23   On the wounds left by the suppression of small convents in Italy, see Emanuele Boaga, *La soppressione innocenziana dei piccoli conventi in Italia* (Rome: Edizioni di storia e letteratura, 1971), 74.
24   Campanelli, ed., *L'inchiesta di Innocenzo X*, 88–90.
25   Francesco Andreu, "La regola dei Chierici Regolari nella lettera di Bonifacio de' Colli a Gian Matteo Giberti," *Regnum Dei* 2, (1946): 38–53.

each house was the result of a prudent choice, with respect to which the religious had to keep in mind the most important aspect of their vocation, namely the education of a reformed and renewed clergy. The Theatines aimed at creating a community of model priests to whom they could entrust urban parishes.[26] For these reasons, the education given by the Theatines was mainly, though not exclusively, addressed to their own members and religious people. For this purpose, all their houses were endowed with a novitiate and a *Studium* with its own teaching body.

Cities and large urban centers were the favorite places of the Theatines for carrying out their activities. The diocesan clergy were more abundant and the apostolate more challenging.[27] Between the year of the Theatine approval and 1650, forty-six convents were founded with adjoining internal schools. The Thetine Fathers were 1,111 in number and the order was divided into four provinces, namely the Roman with fourteen houses, the Neapolitan with thirteen, the Venetian with twelve and the Sicilian with seven. Among those listed, the Roman province was not only the one with the most houses but was also the broadest, including the current regions of Liguria, Emilia-Romagna, Tuscany and Lazio. What clearly emerges is the significant presence of convents in large urban centers, with the exceptions of Frascati (1608) and San Pier d'Arena (1597), about three miles from Genoa. Regarding the foundation of the houses, we note the strong rate of aristocratic establishments. Except for three cases in which the congregation itself created the houses in Modena (1615), Bologna (1599) and Rimini (1602), we always find aristocrats intervening.[28] In Genoa (1575), for example, Cardinal Giustiniani had donated the convent of San Siro, formerly owned by the Benedictines, while Duke Ottavio Farnese, together with Cardinal Alessandro, had called the Theatines to Piacenza (1571).[29] Cardinal Carlo Emanuele Pio of Savoy had purchased land for the Theatine foundation in Ferrara (1617) and for many years had paid their rent

---

26 Campanelli, ed., *L'inchiesta di Innocenzo X*, 6–7.
27 *Ibidem*. The same criterion was also adopted for choosing locations in other countries. The Theatines arrived in Spain in Madrid in 1622, expanding until 1650 in France and Portugal. From 1640, Theatine missionaries were sent to Georgia and the East Indies. For these foundations and missions, refer to: Giuseppe Silos, *Historiarum clericorum regularium a congregatione condita*, vol 2 (Rome: Typis Vitalis Mascardi, 1655), 452; Piero Chiminelli, *S. Gaetano da Thiene cuore della riforma cattolica* (Vicenza: Cattolici vicentini editrice, 1948), 964–65; Annibale Spalla, "Le Missioni teatine nelle Indie Orientali nel sec. XVIII e le cause della loro fine," *Regnum Dei* 27–28, (1971–1972): 1–76; 265–305.
28 For Rimini see Gian Ludovico Masetti-Zannini, "I teatini in Rimini," *Regnum Dei* 21–22, (1965–1966): 87–147; 58–102.
29 See Franco Molinari, "I teatini a Piacenza," *Regnum Dei* 35, (1979): 171–204.

in Borgonuovo, where they resided awaiting the end of the project. Cardinal Aldobrandini had introduced the Theatines to Ravenna (1608), securing their monthly income. The presence of lay nobles, however, was not inferior to that of the high clergy. The Farnese family proved to be particularly munificent towards the order by founding a second convent in Parma (1629) by the will of Margherita Aldobrandini-Farnese. The Farnese alliance with the Theatines is interesting when compared to the alliance that this family had had with the Jesuits, who had been called to collaborate in the University of Parma and to direct the College of the Nobles, as requested by Ranuccio I in 1601.[30]

A similar process of alliances between princely dynasties and religious orders, both Jesuits and Theatines, was under way in the Venetian province of the order. Venice hosted the first Theatine house in 1527, and the province included the current regions of Lombardy, Piedmont and Veneto. Its greatest development occurred between the 1570s and 1610s, followed by a sharp decline. After 1616, only two houses were created, in Turin (1634) and Como (1640). In this province, the fathers preferred large urban centers for their houses, often re-adapting existing buildings, as in the Roman province. Only in three cases were new buildings built, namely in Cremona (1579), Padua (1574) and Milan (1576). Moreover, in the Venetian province we can observe the process of expansion of one religious order to the detriment of another, such as the suppression of the Order of the Humiliati, decided by Pope Pius V in 1571.[31]

Immediately after the suppression of the Humiliati, the Theatines became the owners of the convents of Padua, Milan, Cremona, and Verona (1591). In some cases, before passing to the Theatines, the monasteries of the suppressed Humiliati congregation had been transferred by commendation to other institutions or persons and only later passed to the regular clerics of the Divine Providence. For example, the convent of Padua had passed to the diocesan seminary whose deputies, after an apostolic license, had sold it to Domenico Suriano, who in turn gave it to the Theatines. In Milan, the former convent of the Humiliati passed to the nobleman Marsilio Landriani who later ceded it to the Theatines. In Cremona, Pope Gregory XIII assigned the complex to

---

30   Cristiano Casalini, "Building a Duchy to the Greater Glory of God. The Jesuits and the Farnesian Educational Policy in Parma (1539–1604)," *Educazione. Giornale di pedagogia critica* IV, 1 (2015): 29–48.

31   Pius V suppressed the Order of the Humiliati after many acts of insubordination by the religious, culminating in a failed attempt to kill Cardinal Borromeo. In general, see "Humiliati," *Encyclopædia Britannica*, 11th ed., Vol. 12 (Cambridge: Cambridge University Press, 1910), 884. For a more recent work refer to: Maria Pia Alberzoni, Annamaria Ambrosioni, Alfredo Lucioni, eds., *Sulle tracce degli Umiliati* (Milan: Vita e Pensiero, 1997).

SCHOOLS AND COLLEGES

clerics.[32] In the cases of Vicenza (1595) and Bergamo (1608), the parish priests of Saint Agata and Saint Stefano had renounced the rights on their churches in favor of the Theatines, but in the Venetian province there was no lack of alliance with the high ranks of aristocracy.[33] The most notable cases are those of the Convents of Mantua (1604), requested by Margherita Gonzaga, Guastalla (1616), requested by Ferrante II Gonzaga, and Turin (1634), created by the Duke of Savoy Victor Amadeus.[34]

The third Theatine province, the Neapolitan one, was extended into the regions now known as Campania and Puglia that in 1650 included thirteen houses and 341 religious people. The first house of the circumscription was that of Saint Paul the Major in Naples, founded in 1538, after which almost forty years passed before a second was opened in 1574, in Capua. After that, the expansion in southern Italy was continuous, leading to a period of greater intensity in the 1620s.[35] As in the rest of Italy, the Theatine foundations were located in the centers of the major cities of the kingdom, such as Foggia (1625) where the house was located "in the largest site of the public," and Lecce (1584) where the church of Saint Irene was "in the belly button of the city."[36]

The heterogeneity of the founders (nobles, communities, bourgeoisie) testifies that the proselytism of the Theatine fathers at different social levels exerted a great influence on the whole of society. In four cases it was the fathers who promoted new foundations, the aforementioned houses of Saint Paul the Major and Saint Irene, in Lecce, the house of Saint Mary of Loreto (1629), in Naples, and the house of Bitonto (1603).[37] Only in three cases in southern Italy did members of the aristocracy directly establish houses for the clerics, again all in

---

32 Theatines General Archives, Envelope 704. In general, see Campanelli, ed., *L'inchiesta di Innocenzo X*, 27.

33 On the convents of Vicenza and Bergamo, see respectively: Vincenzo Porta, "I teatini a Vicenza," *Regnum Dei* 16, (1960): 85–43, S. Ferrari, E. Frecassetti, O. Galli, R. Gilardi, "La chiesa e la casa teatina di Sant'Agata in Bergamo alta," *Regnum Dei* 46, (1990): 81–06, and Giambattista Del Tufo, *Historia della Religione de' Padri Chierici Regolari* (Rome: Presso Girolamo Facciotto e Stefano Paolini, 1609), 291–92.

34 Although we find many nobles among the founders of convents in the Venetian province, very often these convents flourished thanks to legacies of the bourgeoisie, see Campanelli, *L'inchiesta di Innocenzo X*, 28–29.

35 On Theatines convents of Naples, see Franco Strazzullo, *Edilizia e urbanistica a Napoli dal '500 al '700* (Napoli: Berisio Arturo Editore, 1958), 178–79; Cesare De Seta, *Storia della città di Napoli dalle origini al Settecento* (Rome-Bari: Laterza, 1973), 250.

36 In general see Campanelli, *L'inchiesta di Innocenzo X*, 37. For Lecce, refer to: Michele Paone, "I teatini in Lecce," *Regnum Dei* 21, (1965): 148–72.

37 For the convent of Bitonto, see Donato De Capua, "I Teatini a Bitonto," *Regnum Dei* 25, (1969): 3–143.

Naples. These nobles were Filippo Caracciolo, Marquis of Vico, who founded the convent of the Holy Apostles (1575), Donna Costanza del Carretto, who opened the house of Saint Mary of the Angels (1587), and John of Austria, who established the house of Saint Mary the Advocate (1630). As far as the bourgeois element is concerned, there are the cases of Cesare Anfora, Alessandro Visco and Giuseppe Antonio Blanco who endowed Sorrento (1608), Barletta (1624) and Foggia with Theatine houses.[38]

The fourth and smallest province, the Sicilian one, included what we now know as Sicily and Calabria. In this province we find only one case of a noble family founding a Theatine house in Palermo in 1602, namely the dukes of Terranova. The second house of Palermo was created by the Theatines themselves in 1603. The same dynamic occurred in the case of Messina, where a Theatine house was opened in 1607 at the behest of the congregation. The Theatines also took the initiative in the city of Piazza Armerina, while it was the city council that promoted the founding of new houses in the cities of Syracuse (1611), Cosenza (1624) and Catanzaro (1632). The poor presence of the Theatines in Calabria seemed to be due to the difficulty in obtaining financing in that territory, considering that Cosenza and Catanzaro were at the time the only important centers, according to the criteria of the Order in the choice of their offices. In Sicily, the situation was different. The Theatines always maintained strong relations with local society and the economic fabric, namely confraternities, both lay and ecclesiastical, and corporations. The pedagogical role of regular clerics was therefore defined in response to the needs of the categories that supported their work in various areas.

What was the cultural level of the Theatine houses and schools in Calabria and Sicily? Within the Calabrian houses, there were no significant cultural expenses. In Cosenza, ten ducats were spent every year on books; no money was spent on the library in the city of Piazza Armerina.[39] In Palermo, in the house of Saint Joseph, there were two large classrooms used as a *Studium*. Worthy of attention, however, is the case of Messina where the Theatines of the Annunciation received an annual fee from the city for public teaching of moral theology. This gave them an important pedagogical role in Messina; in addition, the presence of the important Jesuit college stimulated Theatine

---

38 Campanelli, *Ibid.*, 39. For Barletta and Foggia, see respectively: Vincenzo Maulucci, "I teatini a Barletta," *Regnum Dei* 49, (1993): 3–58, and Id., "I teatini a Foggia," *Regnum Dei* 51, (1995): 57–172.

39 See Litterio Villari, "I Padri teatini nella città di Piazza Armerina," *Regnum Dei* 40, (1984): 91–146. Further information on the Theatine convent of Piazza can be found in: Enna State Archives (Sicily), Section: Piazza Armerina, *Padri Teatini* fund, 1574–1866 vol.4.

educational activity. We know, in fact, that the Theatines of Messina claimed the privilege which had already been granted to the Jesuits to confer degrees and to promote doctoral students because they taught in public schools.[40] In conclusion, we observe that the Theatine congregation favored the great urban centers of the Italian territories for their activities, continuing the traditions of the medieval Mendicant orders; however, the 1650 Innocentian survey shows marked regional differences. In northern Italy, the Theatines appear to have been more attached to nobility and high prelates, while in the southern part of the Peninsula they were more likely to interact with the bourgeoisie and civil authorities. In Sicily there was also a particular form of collaboration between the Theatines and the confraternities aimed at monopolizing city religious life, including education.

4   Between Central, Southern and Eastern Europe

In chronological terms, the last congregation to arrive on the Italian educational scene was the Order of Poor Clerics Regular of the Mother of God of the Pious Schools, also known as the Piarists, officially recognized by Pope Gregory XV in November 1621.[41] Among the religious orders listed here, the followers of José de Calasanz (1557–1648) were probably those whose vocation was more clearly and consciously focused on education.[42] This precocity was the result of a belated historical genesis when the processes of redefinition of a Catholic identity centered on the educational sphere had already been accomplished and the early sixteenth-century yearning for spiritual renewal had already been sublimated and tamed. In other words, the Piarists did not pass from an initial phase of uncertainty due to the fear that love for studies represented a road to pride and perdition.

The first years of the life of the order saw a great success of adhesions that spread rapidly first in the regions under the Papal State, and then in the

---

40   For obtaining such privilege, the Theatines in Messina were ready to pay the municipality the sum of 30,000 *scudi*. On the Theatine college of Messina, refer to Antonio Francesco Vezzosi, *I Scrittori de' Chierici Regolari detti Teatini* Vol. 2 (Rome: Nella stamperia della Sacra Congregazione di Propaganda Fide, 1780), 36.

41   An accurate and recent chronological description of the opening process of the Piarists' schools in Italy is contained in Sabina Pavone, "I Gesuiti in Italia 1548–1773," in *Atlante della letteratura italiana*. Vol. 2: *Dalla Controriforma alla Restaurazione*, ed. Sergio Luzzatto, Gabriele Pedullà, Eriminia Irace, (Torino: Einaudi, 2011), 364–68.

42   Maurizio Sangalli, *Le smanie per l'educazione. Gli scolopi a Venezia tra Sei e Settecento* (Rome: Viella, 2012), 35.

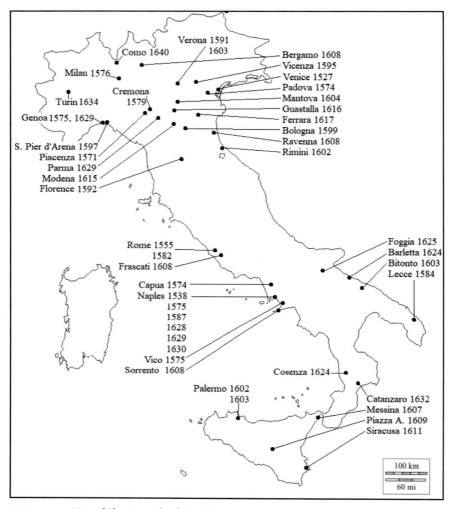

MAP 4   Map of Theatine schools in Italy

Republic of Genoa. After the establishment of a school in Rome, more schools were opened in Frascati (1616), Mentana, Narni (1618), Moricone (1619), Magliano (1620), Norcia (1621), the Genoese territory of Carcare (1621), Savona (1622) and two in the city Genoa (1624, 1625).[43] In the first phase of expansion a school was established in the mountain village of Fanano (1621) within the

---

43   The house established in 1624, in the former autonomous suburb of Oregina, was a probation house, while the one founded in 1625 in the proper city of Genoa was an actual school. Pavone, *I gesuiti in Italia*, 366.

Duchy of Modena, and the founding of schools continued in the Papal territory of Poli (1629), Ancona (1631) and in the northernmost part of the State in Pieve di Cento (1641), a small town between Ferrara and Bologna. The southern part of the Peninsula, even more than the north, also saw Piarist expansion. The Pious Schools were opened in Messina (1625), Posillipo (1625), Bisignano (1627), Campi Salentina (1628), Chieti (1630), Cosenza (1631), and Manduria (1688).[44] Capital cities of late Renaissance Italy were also included: Naples (1626), Florence (1630), Venice (1632) and Palermo (1634) also had Pious Schools. At the time of the general chapter of 1637, nine years before the reduction of the Piarists to a congregation of secular priests subject to the jurisdiction of the local bishops, the Order had twenty-four houses scattered between northern and southern Italy (with a greater presence in the south of the Peninsula) and six provinces, namely Rome, Liguria, Naples, Tuscany, Sicily and Germany. In 1646, on the eve of their reduction, the Piarists had thirty-seven houses and 500 members throughout Italy and Europe.[45]

As we saw in the previous chapter, it was precisely the impetuous growth of the Piarist's first period that determined their reduction. The frequent demand for schools and the great distances between areas in which some of the schools were founded made the governing of new institutes exceedingly difficult. Even harder was supplying the schools with appropriately trained and educated teachers. An inadequate theological formation, together with the presence of members of the order in central Europe where Protestant ideas were strong, represented a risk that in the early decades of the 1600s the fathers could not take. In addition, the strong pauperistic rigor observed by the Piarists aroused suspicions of crypto-Protestantism in Catholic hierarchies. These were the perplexities emerging from reports made by the Jesuit father Silvestro Pietrasanta,

---

44 On the first phase of the foundation of the Pious Schools, refer to: Paul Grendler, "The Piarist of the Pious Schools," in *Religious Orders of the Catholic Reformation: In honor of John C. Olin on his Seventy-Fifth Birthday*, ed. Richard DeMolen, (New York: Fordham University Press, 1994): 252–78. For the Sicilian foundations, see Angelo Sindoni, "Le Scuole pie in Sicilia. Note sulla storia dell'ordine scolopico dalle origini al secolo XIX," *Rivista di storia della Chiesa in Italia* XXV, (1971): 375–421, while for the Duchy of Modena, see Giuseppe Bedoni, "Il pedagogista Bruno Bruni docente nelle Scuole Pie correggesi," *Bollettino storico reggiano* III, (1970): 1–15 and Francesco Ferrari, *Il collegio delle Scuole Pie di Fanano* (Modena: Società Tipografica Modenese, 1917). For other centers mentioned here: Alberto Tanturri, "Il collegio degli scolopi a Posillipo. Metamorfosi di una struttura educativa," *Campania Sacra* 31, (2000): 5–28.

45 Data reported in: Sangalli, *Le smanie*, 37, and Grendler, "The Piarist of the Pious School," 264. To deepen the topic, see "Numero delle provincie, luoghi e padri, dei Poveri della Madre di Dio delle Scuole Pie, raccolto con l'occasione del capitolo generale celebrato in Roma a 15 d'ottobre 1637," *Archivum Scholarum Piarum*, XIII, (1954): 31–79.

who was in charge of carrying out an inquiry into the situation of the Pious Schools by the will of Pope Urban VIII during the early 1640s.[46] Moreover, contact with Tommaso Campanella, who had been teaching in the Pious School of Frascati in 1631, and with Galileo Galilei, helped ruin the image of the Piarist congregation in the eyes of the popes, eventually leading to the downgrading of the congregation by the will of Innocent X, in 1646.[47]

The result of the downgrading was the reduction of the order to a simple congregation of secular priests subject to obedience to the bishops of their respective dioceses without the possibility of professing vows and welcoming new members. The decision was made by Innocent X in March 1646 in the papal brief *Ea Quae*, almost an anticipation of the inquiry on the regular orders that he would promote in 1650; however, the order survived and was gradually reconstituted during the seventeenth century. In the meantime, the expansion of the Piarists in Italy and Europe continued.

Even before the reduction, houses had been opened in Nikolsburg in Moravia (1631) and Warsaw (1642). After reconstruction, new houses were opened in Koper (1708), Rastatt (1715), Budapest (1717), Vilnius (1720), Madrid, Zaragoza, Valencia (1728), Prague (1752) and Milan (1759). To better understand the success experienced by the Piarists during the eighteenth century, we can examine the well-documented case study represented by the Republic of Venice.[48] Among the authorities most often applying for a new school were communities. These did not always require the opening of public schools only, as in the cases of Conegliano (1708), Feltre (1712), Bassano (1722, 1754), Adria (1739), Chiari (1754), Pinguente (1759), Dubrovnik-*Ragusa* (1776), Gemona (1786) and Piran-*Pirano* (1801), but also of boarding schools and colleges for the nobility, as in the cases of Treviso (1677), Koper-*Capodistria* (1699), Serravalle (1731), Tolmezzo (1738) and Rovinj-*Rovigno* (1767). Five schools were opened by bishops. The Piarist Fathers directed these schools to add seminaries where priests were trained, as in the cases of Krk-*Veglia* (1689), Ceneda (1710), Poreč-*Parenzo* (1713), Murano (1721)

---

46 On the reports by Silvestro Pietrasanta, see Sangalli, *Le smanie per l'educazione*, 46–50; Georgio Sàntha, "L'opera delle Scuole Pie e le cause della loro riduzione sotto Innocenzo X," in *Monumenta Historica Scholarum Piarum*, (Rome: Apud Curiam Generalitiam, 1989), 95–115; and Joseph-Marie Timon-David, *Une victime des Jésuites. Saint Joseph Calasanz. Le P. Pietrasanta*, S.J. contre les écoles pies (Paris: Librairie Moderne, 1922).

47 Grendler, "The Piarist of the Pious Schools," 268.

48 Until 1796, the territory of the Venetian Republic extended from eastern Lombardy to the present Italian regions of Veneto, Trentino, Friuli Venezia-Giulia and to Istria and Dalmatia corresponding to parts of present-day Slovenia and almost the entire coast of Croatia. The data shown in the following paragraph are based on Sangalli, *Le smanie per l'educazione*, 351–52.

and Split-*Spalato* (1758). Greater heterogeneity can be observed among Pious Schools promoted by private individuals, nobles, and the bourgeoisie: colleges (Piran-*Pirano*, 1704; Rovereto, 1737), seminaries (Gradisca d'Isonzo, 1709) and public schools (Piran, 1752; Venice; 1779). Finally, in Gorizia in 1780, the Holy Roman Emperor Joseph II called the Piarists to teach philosophy.

Within this dense list of new institutions, we can find different ways of understanding them. In addition to the Italian Peninsula, the picture is enriched by the border area of the Venetian state straddling the Italic, Germanic, and Slavic world between northern, southern, and eastern Europe. It is worth noting how the eighteenth century was peppered by new and strong tensions reflected by the Piarist expansionist strategy. Dalmatia, for example, represented a fundamental bridgehead for expansion into the Balkans. The religious heterogeneity of this area inhabited by Orthodox Christians, Catholics and Muslims made it an ideal place for a mission and a religious order. Jesuits and Capuchins had already arrived at that conclusion, and Piarist interests in central Europe made the Balkans a natural location for their educational mission.[49] When observing the typology of the centers where the Piarists settled, we find them mainly in medium-sized towns. These were often coastal towns with a port, economic activity and mercantile traffic. Similar to the Lombard towns of the sixteenth century, the economic and demographic expansion in these towns opened up margins of activity to a group of religious people who were intent on exploiting the growing anti-Jesuit distrust. The Piarists were forging alliances with the local ruling classes who were eager to find trained teachers to form their economic and political executives. All this, of course, included religious and spiritual care. Similarities to the educational activities of the Barnabites in Lombardy, Piedmont, and the transalpine regions of Savoy and southern France through the Savoyard influence appear pertinent. It is possible to state that similar dynamics, in different geographical and chronological contexts, partly determined the directions for the expansion of these two orders, the Barnabites towards the west and the Piarists towards the east.

In 1784, at the height of their flourishing, the Piarists counted 218 Pious Schools in sixteen provinces with about 3,000 members throughout Europe. From then on a new phase of decline began due to the religious reforms promoted by absolutist states and the upheavals triggered by the French Revolution and Napoleonic ascent, followed by a new rebirth in the nineteenth century.

---

49   Sangalli, *ibid.*, 330. See also: Dario Pasero, "Per la storia delle Scuole Pie in Dalmazia. Documenti (1776–1854)," *Archivum Scholarum Piarum* XVIII, 36 (1994): 1–127, and Osvaldo Tosti, "Ancora sulle Scuole Pie in Dalmazia," *Archivum Scholarum Piarum* XX, 31 (1996): 121–92.

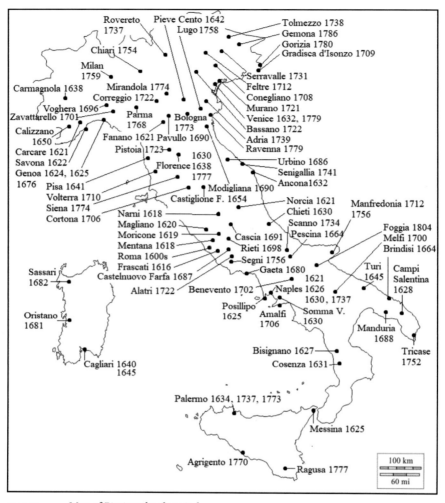

MAP 5   Map of Piarist schools in Italy

5 The Franciscans between Continuity and Rupture

The Franciscans and Dominicans were the two most important medieval religious orders for whom education was a major activity, but it was the Franciscans who, in the course of their own history, anticipated and in a certain sense brought to light the eschatological anxieties that characterized the end of the Middle Ages and the beginning of the Renaissance. The need for moral reform of Christianity was at the very base of the Franciscan order and part of its DNA, and it conditioned its development through the centuries. This resulted in several acts of internal reform that took place between the fifteenth and sixteenth centuries, such as the birth of the branches of the Observants and Capuchins, who were not immune to the religious tensions of their times.

The Franciscan Order was officially born in 1223 after the final approval of the rule by Pope Honorius III.[50] The rapid growth of the order, together with the accumulation of great wealth, created discontent amongst the Franciscans, which led to internal currents of unrest wishing for greater adherence to the example of poverty of the founder. On the one hand, there were friars dedicated to pastoral activity inserted into urban life and, as we will see, increasingly involved in education, both in universities and lower schools. On the other hand, there were the so-called Spirituals, oriented towards a life of asceticism and contemplation. In the fourteenth century, the Observants emerged from the Spirituals, eager to return to the primitive example of poverty set by Saint Francis. The friars who remained in the group that did not adhere to the Observance were named Conventuals. Despite the formal unity of the two groups throughout the fifteenth century, in 1517 the impossibility of having a single internal policy led Leo X to sanction the formal detachment of the Observants as an autonomous family with the right to elect their own general. A similar dynamic took place amongst the Capuchin friars. The order was born when the Franciscan Observant Matteo da Bascio (1495–1557) decided that the lifestyle of his brethren was not the one imagined by Saint Francis. Bascio and his first followers, eager to be hermits, were initially forced to flee arrest on charges of shirking their religious duties; however, Clement VII gave them permission to live as hermits and to preach. In 1529 the Capuchins held their first general chapter and in 1535 they composed their own constitution. These phenomena had deep repercussions on the educational activity carried out by the various branches of the order which, in different times and ways, never ceased to struggle amongst themselves to obtain hegemony for their prestigious colleges, especially in Paris. These dynamics also influenced the geography of where Franciscan schools were established; in fact, while it may seem improper to talk about settlement processes for a religious order that for

---

50 For a recent general history of the Franciscan families from birth until the late sixteenth century, refer to Steven McMichael, ed., *The Medieval Franciscans* (Leiden-Boston: Brill, 2019).

centuries had created a dense network of schools, the contrasts and innovations during the first half of the sixteenth century triggered a redefinition of school geography and a new wave of founding new institutions.

At the time of its birth in the fourteenth century, the attitude of the observant branch of the Franciscans towards studies was very similar to the distrust that characterized other orders born at the beginning of the sixteenth century, such as the Barnabites and Capuchins. The fear was that the pursuit of knowledge and academic degrees, a path of earthly glory, could divert the friars from spiritual perfection by tempting them with pride. However, after the opening of the first observant *studium* in Perugia in 1440 by Bernardino of Siena (1380–1444), the establishment of other *studia* followed quickly, especially in Italy. In the second half of the fifteenth century, new houses of study were opened in Bologna, Ferrara, Mantua, Fabriano, Florence, Pavia, Milan and Venice, and from the beginning of the 1500s others were opened in Brescia, Lucca, Naples, Rome, Siena and Vercelli. In 1529 the decrees issued in the general chapter held in Parma mention a series of *Studia Generalia* already existing or to be erected in Naples, Siena, Pisa and Calabria. By 1532, the number had risen to at least twelve, while during the 1618 general chapter of Salamanca and the 1654 *congregatione generalis* of Rome, the listed Observant *Studia Generalia* rose to twenty-three within the Italian Peninsula alone.[51] In the period between the fifteenth and the sixteenth-seventeenth centuries we therefore note a continuity in the predilection of the Franciscans for urban centers over villages.

The papal bull of 1517, *Ite et vos* by Leo X, granted the Observants the election of the entire Franciscan family general minister, sanctioning their primacy and removing the control of several *Studia* from the Conventual branch. This action prevented many Conventuals from accessing higher levels of education. After a few decades of reorganization during which Conventuals had been granted access to external theological faculties, a new papal bull enacted by Sixtus V in 1587, *Ineffabilis divinae Providenziae*, established a new Conventual educational institution in Rome, known as *Collegium Sancti Bonaventurae* or Pontifical Sistine and Seraphic College. This college was based on the model of the Jesuit Roman College and the Dominican College of San Tommaso.[52]

---

51   The data shown in the following paragraph are based on "Franciscan School Networks, c. 1450–1650," in Roest, *Franciscan Learning*, 132–95. In particular, data reported by Roest on the intensification of the observant *Studia* network are drawn from: *Chronologia Historico-Legalis Seraphici Ordinis Minorum Sancti Patris Francisci*, Vol. I–II, (Neapoli: ex Typographia Camilli Cavalli, 1650), I, 551–52; II, 77.

52   *Collectio bullarum, constitutionum, brevium, ac decretorum omnium ad Seraphicum Sancti Bonaventurae collegium* (Romae: ex typographia Pauli Junchii, 1780), 37–50. On the Conventual branch of the Franciscan order refer to: Lorenzo di Fonzo, Giovanni Odoardi,

Between 1580 and 1630, the founding of new Conventual schools began in Assisi, Bologna and Naples in Italy and beyond the Alps in Prague, Cologne and Krakow. Another college was opened in Urbino in 1701.

The 1625 Conventual constitutions, the so-called *Constitutiones Urbanae*, approved in 1628 by Urban VIII, contained important educational reforms based on the *Reformatio Studiorum* proposals of 1620; thus, two types of seminaries were created. The first type was for young lay boys willing to enter the order at as young as twelve years of age. As Bert Roest explains, the boys who entered this first type of school were especially gifted in choral singing.[53] Nevertheless, it was rare for a boy to enter the novitiate before the age of fifteen or sixteen. At this stage, however, the foundations were laid for future entries. The second type was for newly professed friars who were given grammatical and theological lessons. After attaining twenty-one years of age, the friars could access a third, second or first-class gymnasia, based on the previous scholastic model of logic, philosophy, and theology. The 1628 Constitutions name forty-three third-class schools,[54] twenty second-class schools in Messina, Treviso, Rimini, Avignon, Cesena, Ravenna, Urbino, Fano, Osimo, Salerno, Monteleone (today Vibo Valentia), Pisa, Siena, Brescia, Pavia, Turin, L'Aquila and Cagliari, and ten first-class schools in Padua, Venice, Palermo, Milan, Ferrara, Perugia, Florence, Genoa, in Italy and Vienna and Lviv outside the Peninsula.[55] Even the Conventual Franciscans, according to their response during the seventeenth century to the hegemony reached by the Observants, continued the medieval

---

Alfonso Pompei, eds., *I frati minori conventuali. Storia e vita 1209–1976* (Rome: Curia generalizia O.F.M. Conv., 1978).

53   Roest, *Franciscan Learning*, 157–58.

54   *Constitutiones urbanae* (ed. 1628), 176–77, 'IN PROVINCIA S. FRANCISCI: Montis Falchij, Interamnae, Thiferni. IN PROVINCIA ROMANA: Ferentini, Urbis Veteris. IN PROVINCIA S. ANTONII: Veronae. IN PROVINCIA BONONIAE: Parmae, Cremonae, Placentiae. IN PROVINCIA MARCHIAE: Asculi, Aesij, Pisauri. IN PROVINCIA NEAPOLIS: Mirabellaes, Montis Herculei. IN PROVINCIA S. NICOLAI: Licij, Monopoli, Barij. IN PROVINCIA CALABRIAE: Castro Villari. IN PROVINCIA HETRURIAE: S. Miniati. IN PROVINCIA MEDIOLANI: Bergomi. IN PROVINCIA IANUAE: Casalis. IN PROVINCIA S. BERNARDINI: Sulmonae, Taliacotij. IN PROVINCIA SICILIAE: Drepani, Agrigenti, Catanae. IN PROVINCIA S. ANGELI: Venafri, Buiani. IN PROVINCIA POLONIAE: Caliscij. IN PROVINCIA STYRIAE: Petoviae. IN PROVINCIA BOEMIAE: Cromovij. IN PROVINCIA COLONIAE: Monasterij, Trevirorum. IN PROVINCIA ARGENTINAE: Herbipolis, Maingae, Lucernae. IN PROVINCIA S. BONAVENTURAE: Podij, Salinis. IN PROVINCIA S. LUDOVICI: Arelatae, Mentes, Bocchariae, Ambrum. IN PROVINCIA RUSCIAE: Zamoscij, Moderetij.'

55   The lists of first, second, and third-class schools can be found in: *Constitutiones urbanae fratrum ord. Min. conv. S. Francisci* (Romae: apud impressore camerale, 1628), 175–78. The lists of second and first-class schools are also reported and transcribed in: Roest, *Franciscan Learning*, 160–61.

tradition of preferring main urban centers for their most important schools. A partial exception can be found within third-class schools. These, being the least prestigious, sometimes had their headquarters in smaller towns, namely San Miniato (Tuscany), Iesi (Marche region), Tagliacozzo (Abruzzo region) and Venafro (between Campania and Lazio), to name a few.

The third branch of the Franciscan family, the Capuchins, arose in 1525 and was officially approved in 1528 by Pope Clement VII with the bull *Religionis Zelus*. After a period of distrust towards education, which was not considered very useful because the first Capuchins were essentially Observants and Conventuals already endowed with a solid theological base, the order began to develop their own places of study. The need was felt especially after the adhesion to Protestant doctrines by the two-time Capuchin general Bernardino Ochino and in relation to the many young postulants who wanted to join the congregation without a solid theological education in order to structure their intellects and faith so as not to fall into Protestant temptation. Thus, by 1560, inspired by the Tridentine decree *Super lectione et praedicatione*, the Capuchins began to create a series of *Studia Generalia* first in Naples, then in Rome and later in Brescia, Bologna, Milan, Genoa, and Perugia.[56]

From that time forward, the Capuchin school network experienced intense development, as we can see in two different editions of the *Chorographica descriptio provinciarum et conventuum fratrum minorum S. Francisci capucinorum*, published in 1654 and 1712.[57] In the 1654 edition, twenty-three Italian provinces are listed, each with two places of study, for a total of forty-two schools, the only exceptions being the provinces of Corsica and Sardinia, where there were no schools.[58] In the 1712 edition, though, we witness a real surge in the

---

56 Roest, *ibid.*, 190.
57 The atlas is designed as a geographical tool for pastoral visits, useful for calculating the distances between various settlements and to allow viewers to look in detail at each province of the Order in regard to member consistency, places of study, number and hierarchical typology of religious centers, and their location and spread throughout the territory. The 1654 *Chorographia* was the third edition of the one published in 1646, commissioned by the 24th Capuchin general Giovanni da Moncalieri, while the 1712 edition represented a complete revision of the previous one and was commissioned by the 34th Capuchin general, Agostino de Tisana. Giovanni Moncalieri, *Chorographica descriptio provinciarum et conventuum fratrum minorum S. Francisci capucinorum Praedicatorum, Sacerdotum, Clericorum, et Lacos universorum eiusdem ordinis collection* (Augustae Taurinorum: 1654), and Agostino de Tisana, *Chorographica descriptio Provinciarum et Conventuum Fratrum Minorum Sancti Francisci Capocinorum* (Mediolanum: Giuseppe Pandolfo Malatesta, 1712).
58 *Chorographica descriptio* (ed. 1654). The listed provinces are, in order: Piedmont, Genoa, Milan, Brescia, Venice, Bologna, Tuscany, Marca, San Francesco (Umbria), Rome, Naples, Abruzzo, Sant'Angelo (northern Puglia and Molise), Bari, Land of Otranto, Basilicata, Cosenza, Reggio Calabria, Messina, Palermo, Syracuse, Corsica and Sardinia.

number of places of study, which increased to 111. The provinces of Basilicata and Cosenza retained two schools, while the Land of Otranto (*Terra d'Otranto*) expanded from two to nine schools, the province of Corsica increased from zero to three, and the province of Sardinia, divided into two distinct provinces, namely those of Cagliari and Torres, both had two places of study. The province of Bologna was divided into two parts, giving birth to the new province of Lombardy, corresponding to the current western Emilia region, and was endowed with three places of study.[59]

The generic term "place of study" does not specify hierarchies and typologies, but it is reasonable to think that it included all the *Studia Generalia* and *Provincialia*, and other places where the friars were school teachers, including the municipal schools where it was not unusual for them to be called and hired. As for the other branches of the Franciscan family, the Capuchins were present in urban centers, but, in line with their origins, they were more adherent to the new spiritual climate of the sixteenth century. This meant that the Capuchins were particularly attentive to the pastoral ideal of 'capillaryizing' their presence in smaller and less important settlements. As noted for the other religious orders, the Capuchins experienced an expansive phase between the mid-1500s and the early 1700s.

Overall, therefore, the settlement processes familiar to religious orders in early modern Italy, particularly in relation to school networks, had common dynamics with different characters based on vocational, charismatic, relational, and political specificities. All religious orders expanded their number of schools over the course of these three centuries, though this sometimes occurred at the expense of other groups of friars or clerics, as in the case of the Theatines, who had their surge in northern Italy thanks to the suppression of the Humiliati congregation, whose convents came into Theatine possession. On the other hand, for many of the religious the path was not immune to danger and reflux. Within this dynamic, the shadow of conflict and competition with other congregations was not absent, as in the case of the Piarists, even if there is no evidence of a Jesuit plot against them. The Jesuits, in turn, at the time of their suppression in 1773, were supplanted in many of their schools by Piarists.

---

59 *Chorographica descriptio* (ed. 1712). Number of places of study for each province: Piedmont 4, Genoa 5, Milan 6, Brescia 3, Venice 4, Bologna 4, Lombardy 3, Tuscany 5, Marca 6, San Francesco (Umbria) 5, Rome 6, Naples 6, Abruzzo 4, Sant'Angelo (northern Puglia and Molise) 5, Bari 5, Land of Otranto 9, Basilicata 2, Cosenza 2, Reggio Calabria 6, Messina 6, Palermo 5, Syracuse 3, Corsica 3, Cagliari 2, Torres 2.

It is possible to find preferences for certain places, namely cities or villages, and regions, such as northern, central or southern Italy, linked to specific features of each congregation. We can find the schools of the biggest and oldest orders (Franciscan Conventuals and Observants, Theatines, Barnabites and, of course, Jesuits) in the main urban centers, while those that arose later or that matured later in their educational vocation (Capuchins, Somascans, Piarists) were more common in villages and small towns, due to an already saturated urban educational market. Another key role in this partition was played by the greater adherence to a pastoral ideal in which the rural areas were considered a mission land for education and catechism. We can observe a greater dynamism and an educational competition in northern Italy, where demographic growth and economic transformations were more intense. Even the greater bond of some religious orders with the nobility of northern Italy (Theatines, Barnabites) can be read in this sense, since the aristocracy of the northern regions invested capital in the economic transformation of the territory compared to the southern nobility, which was more attached to old landowner economic models. Of course, these distinctions are mere heuristic tools and not exhaustive. The exceptions are widespread and important, useful tools to orientate within the macro-elements of Early Modern Italian religious scholastic physiognomy.

CHAPTER 4

Different Types of Schools Operated by Religious Orders

1 Public Education Entrusted to Religious Orders and Secular Priests

Chapter three examined the dynamics of expansion and settlement of religious teaching orders in the Italian Peninsula and in some contiguous areas. We have seen the forces and the needs that determined the differences in the dynamics of the spread of schools run by the fathers; however, some meaningful case studies have not been thoroughly investigated, which allow us to know in detail the terms and peculiarities of the arrival and integration within different contexts of religious orders wishing to open a new school or manage an already existing one. As we have seen, one of the main engines of this expansion was the need of municipal councils to recruit new teachers for the new religious, political, and economic contexts that had come into existence since the early sixteenth century. Within this framework, the most frequent cases of collaboration between religious orders and municipal councils emerged for essentially two reasons: the fathers established a new schoolhouse or college to oversee public education and make up for the lack of schools in one center, or the religious arrived individually and became teachers within an existing scholastic institution. The complexity of these relationships, however, is irreducible to abstract unity, and requires concrete and well documented examples.

1.1 *Udine and the Barnabites: On the Outskirts of the Peninsula*
As mentioned, when talking about the expansion of schools operated by religious orders, a large number of educational initiatives saw the establishment of new institutions. Among the characteristic elements common to all congregations was the gratuitousness and openness to the public and the partial substitution of previous public schools governed and financed by the municipalities.

One significant case is that of the Barnabites. In 1679 the municipal council of Udine obtained permission from the Republic of Venice,[1] of which it was a

---

1 The educational history of norteastern Italy between the sixteenth and the eighteenth century, especially the Friulian region, due to its position at the crossroad between different cultures, is particularly rich. Among the main works are: Giuseppe Dabalà, "Le scuole pubbliche di Udine dal 1297 al 1851," *Annuario del R. Liceo Ginnasio 'Iacopo Stellini,'* (1925–'26): 13–70;

part, to establish a Barnabite college in the city. The discussion of the counsellors was animated, but eventually the new foundation obtained an almost unanimous consensus, with only one vote against. The *Gymnasium Civitatis Utini* was then created in direct continuity of the city schools, whose activity had been attested since 1297. It is important to underline that the school activity of the Udine Barnabites was grafted onto an uninterrupted centuries-long municipal school tradition. The new college would last for 130 years, until 1810.[2]

Regular Clerics of Saint Paul arrived in the Friulian city because of a precise balance of strength among religious educational orders within the region. The religious and educational panorama of the northeastern Veneto area was overly complex. The northwestern area of the Republic of Venice was particularly vulnerable to the Protestant threat because of its proximity to the Germanic world. The situation was not very different from what was happening in Piedmont close to Calvinist Geneva. In particular, the Friulian, Julian, and Istrian regions bordering the Princely County of Gorizia and Gradisca,

---

Mario Brancati, *L'organizzazione scolastica nella Contea principesca di Gorizia e Gradisca dal 1615 al 1874*, (Udine: Grillo, 1978); Manlio Michelutti, "Scuola e istruzione in Friuli," in *Enciclopedia monografica del Friuli-Venezia Giulia*, vol. 4, (Udine: Istituto per l'enciclopedia del Friuli Venezia-Giulia, 1983), 119–60; Diana De Rosa, *Libro di scorno, libro d'onore: la scuola elementare triestina durante l'amministrazione austriaca, 1761–1918* (Udine: Del Bianco, 1991); Franco Cecotti; Giulio Mellinato, eds., *Archivi e fonti per la storia delle istituzioni educative giuliane*, Vol. 1/XXIX, *Qualestoria: Bollettino dell'Istituto regionale per la storia del movimento di liberazione nel Friuli Venezia-Giulia* (Trieste: Istituto regionale per la storia del movimento di liberazione nel Friuli Venice-Giulia, 2001); Maria Renata Sasso, "Dal leone marciano all'aquila bicipite. Il caso della scuola elementare di Palmanova," *Annali di storia dell'educazione e delle istituzioni scolastiche*, 15, (2008): 193–201; Maurizio Sangalli, "Da Bergamo a Capodistria. Scuole, collegi, clero tra Sette e Ottocento," in *L'istruzione in Italia tra Sette e Ottocento. Lombardia-Veneto-Umbria*. 1: Studi, atti del convegno nazionale di studi, Milan-Pavia 28–30 October 2004, ed. Angelo Bianchi, (Brescia: La Scuola, 2007), 235–68; Sangalli, "The Piarist in a Frontier Region between the Republic of Venice and the Empire of the Habsburg: Economic and Educational Strategies of a Teaching Religious Congregation in the Eighteenth Century" in *Growing in the Shadow of an Empire: How Spanish Colonialism Affected Economic Development in Europe and in the World (XVI–XVIII cc.)*, ed. Giuseppe De Luca and Gaetano Sabatini (Milan: FrancoAngeli, 2012), 377–92.

2 On the Barnabite College in Udine, the most recent works are by Maria Caterina Diemoz, "L'istruzione a Udine tra Repubblica Veneta e Regno Italico. L'impatto di un modello accentrato," (PhD diss., University of Udine, 2012), 58–65; and Id. "L'istruzione di base maschile a Udine tra la Repubblica di Venezia e il Regno d'Italia (1798–1813)," *Annali di storia dell'educazione e delle istituzioni scolastiche* 21, (2014): 161–92; Filippo M. Lovison, "Le scuole dei barnabiti a Udine (1679–1810)," *Barnabiti Studi*, 15, (1998): 91–211. See also Raffaele Gianesini, "Istituti di istruzione a Udine nell'età moderna," in *La lavagna nera. Le fonti per la storia dell'istruzione nel Friuli-Venezia-Giulia*, ed., Grazia Tatò, (Trieste: Associazione nazionale archivistica italiana. Sez. Friuli-Venezia-Giulia, 1995), 123–40.

and present-day Slovenia had a large population of German culture and language.[3] The complexity of this situation called for the arrival of the Jesuits, the breaking rams of the Church for preaching and education. (Just think of the missions of Possevino in Piedmont!) The first step taken by the Society of Jesus was to establish a college in Gorizia, a city considered to be particularly exposed to the Protestant risk.[4] The first projects for a Jesuit boarding school in Gorizia dated back to the late 1550s, but the erection of a school was complicated and took a long time. A complex game of contacts between the Austrian Jesuit authorities and the Venetian religious hierarchies was triggered. As Claudio Ferlan explains, there were several issues obstructing a Jesuit college in Gorizia; "from the German-speaking countries came the request to favor the establishment of new professed houses over colleges, since the number of teachers available could not keep up with the rapid increase in the number of schools."[5] However, the problem of educating the clergy and the nobility,

---

3 On the religious situation between northeastern Italy and the German world during the sixteenth century, refer to Pio Paschini, *Eresia e Riforma cattolica al confine orientale d'Italia* (Rome: Lateranum, 1956) and to the most recent article of Silvano Cavazza, "Un'eresia di frontiera. Propaganda luterana e dissenso religioso sul confine austro-veneto nel Cinquecento," *Annali di storia isontina*, 4 (1991): 7–33. See also Robert Bireley, *Religion and Politics in the Age of the Counterreformation: Emperor Ferdinand II, William Lamormaini, S.J., and the Formation of Imperial Policy* (Chapel Hill NC: University of North Carolina Press, 1981); Id., *The Jesuits and the Thirty Years War. Kings, Courts and Confessors* (New York: Cambridge University Press, 2003). On the spread of Protestant ideas in the northwestern Slavic world, refer to Valdo Vinay, "La Riforma in Croazia e Slovenia e il 'Beneficio di Cristo,'" *Bollettino della società di studi valdesi*, 116, (1964): 19–32 and more recently Regina Pörtner, *The Counter-Reformation in Central Europe: Styria 1580–1630* (Oxford, Oxford University Press, 2008).
4 On the Jesuit presence in northeastern Italy, particularly in Gorizia, the main reference is Claudio Ferlan, *Dentro e fuori le aule. La Compagnia di Gesù a Gorizia e nell'Austria interna, secoli XVI–XVII*, (Bologna: Il Mulino, 2012) and Id., "La fondazione del collegio dei Gesuiti di Gorizia. Progetti e realizzazione," *Quaderni giuliani di storia*, 2/XXVII, (2006): 435–62. See also Francesco Spessot, "Primordi, incremento e sviluppo delle istituzioni gesuitiche di Gorizia (1615–1773)," *Studi Goriziani*, 3, (1925): 83–142; and Maria Walcher Casotti, "Il collegio e la chiesa dei gesuiti a Gorizia," *Studi Goriziani*, 71, (1990): 113–70. For the Jesuits in Venice, see Mario Zanardi, ed., *I gesuiti a Venezia: Momenti e problemi di storia veneziana della Compagnia di Gesù* (Padova: Gregoriana Libreria Editrice, 1994). For the Jesuit relation with other religious orders, see Maurizio Sangalli, *Cultura, politica e religione nella Repubblica di Venezia tra Cinque e Seicento. Gesuiti e Somaschi a Venezia* (Venice: Istituto veneto di scienze morali, lettere ed arti, 1999). See also Riccardo Caimmi, *La guerra del Friuli 1615–'17 altrimenti nota come Guerra di Gradisca o degli Uscocchi* (Gorizia: Confine Orientale, 2007). For Possevino see Domenico Caccamo, "La diplomazia della Controriforma e la crociata: dai piani del Possevino alla 'lunga guerra' di Clemente VIII," *Archivio Storico Italiano*, 2/128 (1979): 255–81.
5 Original quote: "dai paesi di lingua tedesca proveniva la richiesta di privilegiare rispetto ai collegi la costituzione di nuove case professe, dal momento che la quantità degli insegnanti

among whom Protestant doctrines were widespread, was perceived as central by the Jesuit and Venetian religious authorities. The response to the risk was to make Gorizia the new Geneva on the eastern Italian border. At first, establishing more schools for the nobility, as in the case of Studenz in Styria, or Udine in the Friulian territory, was considered; however, the erection of colleges for the nobility, as Ferlan explains, was feared to be to the detriment of diocesan seminaries for the clergy, whose religious education was perhaps more urgent than that of the nobles.[6] Despite the persisting perception of boarding schools and seminaries for priests as alternative options, the belief that a Jesuit college in Gorizia, now given priority over other cities in the area, could meet both needs, increased significantly. After some quarrels about the usefulness of creating a Jesuit school for nobles in Gorizia, an adequate patrimonial income for the foundation of the college was found. Eventually the Jesuits officially settled in Gorizia in 1615.[7]

For a few decades, the Jesuit college of Gorizia had attracted the backbone of the local aristocracy eager to secure high-level education, as was the case in many other Italian centers. However, in its first decades of life, the dependence of the college on the Austrian college located in Graz created many problems for the Italian speaking aristocracy coming as much from Gorizia itself as from the other Friulian territories, including Udine.[8] Among the Jesuits present in the college in the first half of the seventeenth century were Kettner, Kelbel, Klingenstein, Roththaller, Phuster, Zehentgraf, Hamerlen and Scherer; as Prospero Antonini wrote, Bishop Giusto Fontanini remarked that "while narrating that in his early years he attended the Jesuit college in Gorizia, he confessed that little profit stemmed from the teaching of certain teachers from Styria and Carinthia to Italian disciples with barbaric pronouncements of the Italian letters" and added that "the youth of the neighboring Venetian territories, who came in large numbers to the schools of Gorizia, preferred those of the Barnabites of Udine and of the Somascans of Cividale."[9]

---

disponibili non riusciva a tenere dietro al rapido aumento del numero delle scuole." Ferlan, *La fondazione del collegio dei Gesuiti di Gorizia*, 435.
6 Ferlan, *La fondazione del collegio dei Gesuiti di Gorizia*, 439.
7 Ferlan, *La fondazione del collegio dei Gesuiti di Gorizia*, 443.
8 About Graz' Jesuit college, see Paul Grendler, *The Jesuits and Italian Universities 1548–1773* (Washington: The Catholic University of America Press, 2017), 325; and Oskar Garstein, *Rome and the Counter-Reformation in Scandinavia. Jesuit Educational Strategy 1553–1622* (Leiden-New York-Copenhagen-Cologne: Brill, 1992). See chapter seven: "The Ferdinandeum at Graz," 156–74.
9 Prospero Antonini, *Il Friuli orientale. Studi* (Milan: Francesco Vallardi Tipografo Editore, 1865), 355. The quote is also reported in Diemoz, *L'istruzione a Udine*, 59.

Despite Jesuit efforts towards the Italianization of their college in Gorizia during the second half of the century as a response to this issue, the problem favored the emergence of other religious orders previously relegated to more peripheral centers, but now pushed by this conjuncture into major cities. It was in this context that the Barnabites arrived in Udine. The preference for clerics of Saint Paul, it must be said, was not obvious. Negotiations were held between Jesuits and Somascans. The following story shows how difficult and troubled the foundation of an early modern religious college, functioning as a public school, could be, even in an apparently favorable situation.[10]

The fathers were not immediately allowed to arrive in the city as a congregation to open a convent with an attached college. The city council only approved the arrival of five religious people to work in public schools, albeit with an exclusive concession. In this prohibition we find, on one hand, the distrust of Venice towards possible interference by religious orders, especially after the events of the so-called Venetian Interdict War of 1606, which led to the expulsion of Jesuits from the territories of the Republic.[11] On the other hand, we find the ancient medieval civic attachment to the self-government of schools. Education, indeed, was one of the areas in which medieval and early modern-age cities proved to be more recalcitrant to give up their privileges during the modern state building process.[12]

Nonetheless, the experiment worked. As early as 1680, a year after the start of school activity, there were 400 students, a number that would remain stable until the early decades of the eighteenth century. So far, so good. Yet the conflict between the fathers and the city council was not dormant and was waiting for an opportunity to re-emerge from under the embers. The gears of integration between the religious and the community were still struggling. In order to keep the schools independent from the Barnabites (and to keep the Barnabites

---

10   On the political periphery of the Friulian area during the late middle-ages and the early modern time, see Marco Bellabarba, "The feudal principalities: the east (Trent, Bressanone/Brixen, Aquileia, Tyrol and Gorizia)," in *The Italian Renaissance State*, ed. Andrea Gamberini and Isabella Lazzarini (Cambridge: Cambridge University Press, 2012), 197–219.

11   For the Venetian Interdict War, refer to William J. Bouwsma, *Venice and the Defense of Republican Liberty. Renaissance Values in the Age of the Counter Reformation* (Berkeley: University of California Press, 1968), and Federico Seneca, *La politica veneziana dopo l'interdetto* (Padova: Liviana, 1957). The so-called Interdict war was not an actual war; it was an acrimonious jurisdictional-political-religious dispute carried on by excommunication, words, and expulsions.

12   Ravaglioli, "L'educazione umanistica nel passaggio dalla città-stato tardomedievale alla città capitale," 95–108.

under its control), the municipality continued to bear most of the educational expenses.[13] This heavy budget could not be sustained forever, and the increase in taxes to be paid to Venice for the Morean War in 1695 obliged the council to impose the payment of a school fee by the pupils. At the beginning it was ten *lire* to be paid by each student, but later the amount increased to fifteen *lire*. The decision, as is easily understood, provoked discontent that the Barnabites instrumentally used to obtain their official admission as a regular order for the school of the city. The controversy was no longer delayable and in 1730 the fathers used blackmail, threatening to leave the city. The official reason given was that they no longer intended to serve as "mercenaries."[14]

Despite the official admission into Udine of the Regular Clerics of Saint Paul, obtained with the permission of the Venetian Senate on April 20th, 1730, the opening of a real college was neither obvious nor immediate, although a construction project had already been in circulation since 1710. The decisive impulse for the construction of a building to be used definitively for this function arrived due to a deep crisis in which the schools of Udine inherited by Barnabites had fallen in the last few years. In addition to the diminished number of young people present in the territory until the suppression of the Patriarchate of Aquileia in 1751, the schools of Udine experienced a real haemorrhage of students, diverted into recently opened competing schools, free schools with private teachers opened by the diocesan seminary.[15] This led to the establishment of a first college for local and foreign nobles, opened in 1750 and dedicated to Saint Paul, followed by a college for non-nobles wishing to receive a high-profile education, completed in 1765 and dedicated to Saint Lorenzo Giustiniani.[16] The Giustiniani college, however, did not end the problem of the decline in the student population, and was closed a few years later, in 1780.

---

13   In 1726 the municipality spent 850 ducats for teachers, 60 for the cited preceptor, and 150 for the maintenance of buildings. Cfr. Diemoz, *L'istruzione a Udine*, 60.

14   The quote from the source dates to April 20th, 1730 and can be found in the Udine Communal Library (BCU), Ancient Communal Archives section (ACA), Ann., 106; *Fondo Joppi* b. 195 and *Fondo Principale* 860/A. Reported in Diemoz, *L'istruzione a Udine*, 61.

15   The previous 15 *lire* tax to be paid by the students to the municipality, in fact, had been assigned to the Barnabites for the next 40 years and for the 25 years following to be divided between the fathers and the communal pawnshop (*monte di pietà*). This explains how schools with a lower cost, or even no cost, such as those of the diocesan seminary, represented a strong competition for the congregation.

16   *I barnabiti nel IV centenario dalla fondazione 1533–1933* (Genoa: Tipografia Artigianelli, 1933), 253.

The French occupation between 1796 and 1797 did not improve the situation for the surviving college of Saint Paul. With the transfer of the Republic of Venice to Austria following the Treaty of Campoformio, the city authorities requested that the Emperor Francis II of Habsburg take an interest in the institute, since it had received the title of "imperial" with the same privileges as the Imperial College of Milan.

How to evaluate, then, in light of what has been said, the historical experience of the Barnabites in Udine? We briefly mentioned various factors that led to the entry of the Barnabites into Udine and the subsequent opening of the colleges. The congregation was historically reluctant to open colleges, preferring, as was initially the case, simple employment, albeit exclusively, in public schools. The opening of the boarding school of Udine was the last of a series of positive experiences within the regular Congregation of Saint Paul that paved the way for the adoption of this educational system, despite initial suspicions and difficulties.[17]

To better understand the dynamics of settlement of the Barnabites in Udine, it is also necessary to look at the other teaching congregations present in the area. Upon the arrival of the Barnabites in Udine in the mid-1600s, the Somascans managed colleges, seminaries and other houses in Brescia, Salò, Verona, Vicenza, Feltre, Belluno, Padua, Treviso, Venice and Cividale. The Jesuits, welcomed back to the Republic in 1657, were again active in Brescia (with two colleges), Verona, Vicenza, Belluno, Padua and Venice. The Piarists, between the seventeenth and eighteenth centuries, were operating only in Koper (*Capodistria*) and Murano. In addition to Udine, the Barnabites also taught in Bergamo and Crema in 1699.[18] As pointed out by Maurizio Sangalli, this more decentralized location of some orders, such as Barnabites and Piarists, and the control of smaller educational centers could be interpreted as a lower penetrative force within a complex political entity like the Republic of Venice. After all, the Jesuits, although driven out, had been able within a few decades to re-establish themselves in important centers, especially near to universities.[19] Yet, this peripherality could be exploited as opportunity. The

---

17   Filippo M. Lovison, "Le scuole dei barnabiti. Pietà e scienza nell'età dei lumi," *Barnabiti Studi* 26 (2009): 135–38. In particular, what opened the road in the Barnabite congregation to the development of boarding schools were the experiments conducted in this direction in the French provinces, especially in Montargis, where in 1680 the fathers requested that a section of boarders join the college.
18   The data shown are taken from: Sangalli, *Le smanie per l'educazione*, 15.
19   Ibidem.

schools in more decentralized areas had, in fact, lower fees than those located in the busiest cities and could thus intercept large segments of local companies.

In this light, it becomes clearer how the institutional typology of the college boarding school met with success in Udine despite the aforementioned Barnabite diffidence towards this type of foundation. The Venetian Piarists opted for the model of colleges for nobles in order to intercept the desire of provincial aristocracies, who were not always economically able to send their offspring to school in major cities, to give them an education in line with the highest standards of the time. With the exception of the Somascan schools in Cividale, Udine was surrounded by a huge potential catchment area.[20]

In addition to these problems there were also issues of an economic and political nature. In the mid-1700s, the Friulian area experienced a profound renewal of its economy, particularly a rationalization and modernization of its agrarian structures, which required the education of individuals capable of overseeing such changes.[21] A key figure in adapting Barnabite education to these new needs was Angelo Maria Cortenovis.[22] He arrived in Udine in 1764 as head of the local community after having taught in the colleges of Macerata, Pisa, and Milan. Cortenovis's experience ranged from scientific disciplines to liberal arts, and despite a certain predilection for medieval history, he never neglected the importance of science and technology, aware of their contributions to civil progress. Following the example of the agronomist Antonio Zanon, who in 1762 had founded the Society of Practical Agriculture in Udine, Cortenovis had the study of agronomy introduced into local colleges run by Barnabites, which became one of the most important disciplines of these schools.[23]

Overall, therefore, the process of calling and integrating Barnabites into the institutional mechanism of Udine was anything but linear and was

---

20   The nearest schools were those of the Piarists in Koper (100 km distant), the Jesuits and the Somascans in Belluno (130 km distant) and the Somascan schools of Treviso (120 km distant).

21   Alessandro Della Salvia, "Della statistica agraria," in *Atti dell'Accademia di Udine per il biennio 1867–1868* (Udine: Tipografia di Giuseppe Seitz, 1870), 113–22. Among the main innovations in Friulian agricultural structures of the eighteenth century was the introduction of the mulberry and silkworm which gave impetus to silk production in the region. See Romano Molesti, *Economisti e accademici nel Settecento veneto. Una visione organica dell'economia* (Milan: FrancoAngeli, 2006), 79–88.

22   On the Barnabite father Angelo Maria Cortenovis, see Roberto Volpi, "Cortenovis Angelo Maria," *Italian Biographical Dictionary*, 29 (1983), and Giuseppe Boffito, *Scrittori barnabiti o della Congregazione dei chierici regolari di San Paolo 1533–1933*, 1 (Florence: Olschki, 1933–1937), 517–30.

23   *I Barnabiti*, 253.

re-structured over time in response to various social, political and economic circumstances and needs that the community expressed to the religious. This, in part, was due to the decentralized location of Udine and its border town nature in an already difficult political context such as that of the Republic of Venice. However, it was perhaps because of these difficulties that the Barnabite college of Udine represented an important experiment for the future development of the boarding schools of the congregation after the Napoleonic restoration. Dealing with such different problems from time to time allowed the cleric teachers of Saint Paul to develop a particular resistance that favored their rebirth in the following nineteenth century.[24]

1.2 Jesuits and Piarists in the Duchy of Modena: A Competition between Local Networks

Let us now shift our attention from the political borders of the Italian Peninsula to another center set in the heart of the great plains of northern Italy, namely Correggio. This small town (which officially obtained the title of 'city' in 1559) had for centuries hosted a princely dynasty that took its name from its place of origin, the Da Correggio family. Despite its decentralized location, the *Correggese* dynasty succeeded in creating a vast base of power in the contiguous region that allowed the family to play an important political role during the late Middle Ages. A prominent family member, Giberto III, became for a short time the lord of the city of Parma. Thus, the Correggio dynasty remained, until the first half of the sixteenth century, an important actor in international politics, serving as a diplomatic mediator between Italian and European powers at least until the Italian Wars.[25]

---

24 In general, for the last years before the French Revolution and the Napoleonic domination of Italy, see Alain Pillepich, *Napoléon et les Italiens. République Italienne et Royaume d'Italie 1802–1814*, (Paris: Nouveau monde éditions, 2002) in particular chapter 7: *La crise religieuse*, 131–50, where the problem posed by public education is analyzed. On the suppression of the Barnabites, refer to: *I barnabiti*, 259–60; Gentili, *Les Barnabites*, 174–79, and Orazio Maria Premoli, *Storia dei barnabiti dal 1700 al 1825* (Rome: Società tipografica Aldo Manuzio, 1925), 364–73.

25 On the concept of the small Italian and European Renaissance state, see Giorgio Chittolini, "Stati padani, 'Stato del Rinascimento': problemi di ricerca," in *Persistenze feudali e autonomie comunitative in stati padani fra '500 e '700*, ed. Giovanni Tocci (Bologna: Clueb, 1988), 9–29; Maurizio Bazzoli, *Il piccolo stato nell'età moderna. Studi su un concetto della politica internazionale tra XVI e XVIII secolo* (Milan: Jaca Book, 1990); Alice Blythe Raviola, L'Europa dei piccoli stati. Dalla prima età moderna al declino dell'Antico Regime (Rome: Carocci, 2008); Giovanni Tocci, "Sul piccolo stato nel Cinquecento padano," in *Ferrante Gonzaga. Il Mediterraneo, l'Impero (1507–1557)*, ed. Gianvittorio Signorotto, (Rome: Bulzoni, 2009), 37–58.

As was frequently the case with Italian princely dynasties, in addition to hiring private tutors for their children, the Da Correggio family took charge of schools and education in their own lordship.[26] The presence of a court with its organs of chancellery had created conditions for lively culture and education that lasted until the beginning of the seventeenth century. Moreover, local schools, perhaps due to the peripheral position of Correggio (compared to the larger neighboring cities, namely Mantua, Modena, Reggio Emilia and Parma), remained more closely linked to the humanistic educational model, following the example of Vittorino da Feltre. The schools in Correggio resisted the post Tridentine penetration of religious people into the educational sphere.[27] However, in 1635 the Correggio State passed from the homonymous family to the dukes of Modena. The Este dinasty had long plotted to get hold of it, and did so by accusing Siro, the last family descendant, of felony for having unduly coined money.

After several centuries, the sudden absence of the ruling dynasty and the distance of the new dominant family inaugurated a period of decline that was heavily reflected in the cultural and educational sphere. In the following decades, the municipal schools were served by lay teachers salaried by the community, and the local convent of Dominican friars proved incapable of responding to local educational needs. However, the local noble class was still alive and demanded education consistent with its social level, while the slow but steady development of the merchant class required education in line with their own work needs. In addition to this, the population of young people was growing consistently along with overall seventeenth century demographic trends.[28]

The existing educational apparatus of the new capital city, Modena, could hardly provide a solution to these needs. The distrust between the central and peripheral aristocracy persisted, making it difficult for the aristocrats of the suburbs to access the Modena College of Nobles. The mercantile bourgeoisie faced an even harder situation. In addition to the normal difficulties of accessing the schools in Modena, the children of the merchants also needed to stay close to home to follow the family business. It therefore became necessary to

---

26   Salomoni, *Scuola, maestri e scolari*, 173–81.
27   David Salomoni, "Sulle orme di Vittorino da Feltre. Profili di maestri tra Mantova e l'area gonzaghesca (XVXVI secc.)," in *Maestri e pratiche educative in età umanistica*, ed. Monica Ferrari, Matteo Morandi, Federico Piseri (Brescia: Morcelliana, 2019), 219–37.
28   Maria Grazia Lasagni, "La presenza degli scolopi a Correggio dal 1722 al 1810," in *Istruzione, educazione e collegio in Correggio dal XVII al XX secolo*, ed. Alberto Ghidini (Correggio: Convitto Nazionale R. Corso, 1999), 33–80.

open a new school in Correggio that could satisfy the educational needs of the nobility as well as the emerging merchant classes.

In 1707, the choice fell to the Barnabites of Bologna; however, the congregation was reluctant and procrastinated over the negotiations for several years, eventually breaking the agreement.[29] It is possible that the Regular Clerics of Saint Paul were not particularly attracted by a small town; we have seen how the schools of this congregation were mainly present in major centers, with a few exceptions. The second choice fell upon the Piarist order. To better understand this option, we must look for a moment at the religious-educational geography of the territory.

If we look at the Duchy of Modena, or its immediate surroundings, we find a particularly dense population of Jesuit colleges. The Society of Jesus, for obvious chronological reasons, arrived before the Piarists to establish its houses and schools in that territory. The first two foundations occurred before the Estense capital passed from Ferrara to Modena in 1598. The arrival of the Society in the towns of the duchy took place in the most classic forms as an answer to different needs. In Modena, the Jesuits were called by the City council in 1552 in order to take care of the local schools. In Novellara they were called by the local lord, Count Camillo Gonzaga, in 1571, on the advice of his wife Barbara Borromeo. Barbara, in turn, was pushed towards the Jesuits by her cousin the Archibishop of Milan, namely Carlo Borromeo. The aim was to transform Novellara, which was little more than a country village, into a center of cultural importance. In the case of Reggio Emilia, the Society arrived in 1610 as a result of its temporary expulsion from the Venetian states in 1606 and the opportunity seized by the Duke of Modena Caesar d'Este to create a Jesuit college in Reggio. In Mirandola, at that time under the diocese of Reggio, the Society was called in 1611 by the local lord Alexander Pico (a descendant of the more famous Giovanni Pico della Mirandola) because he also wanted to establish a Jesuit college in his town. In Carpi, it was by the will of the Duke of Modena that the Society arrived in 1622, while in Guastalla the Jesuits arrived in 1728 thanks to the legacy of a rich private citizen.

The foregoing list includes the main towns of the region, which is no surprise given the inveterate Jesuit attitude regarding connecting with university centers and educating the ruling classes. These statements are not intended to deny the difficulties that the Jesuits had in penetrating several contexts, or the time required for effective entry into universities, some created almost specifically for them as, for example, the University of Parma in 1601 and the

---

29   Giovanni Giovannozzi, *Il Calasanzio e l'opera sua*, (Florence: Le Monnier, 1930), 12.

University of Mantua in 1625. Even in Modena and Reggio Emilia, the only two higher education centers listed here, the Jesuits failed in creating a university; however, from the list of foundations and the map shown here, two themes clearly emerge. The first is the well-known link to the ruling classes that the Society created. Even without universities, the schools founded were all boarding schools for nobles. As has been shown, in most cases the Society was called by aristocrats to establish their schools. Another important aspect is that these boarding schools were all located on the plain, the productive agricultural heart of the State, one of the most technologically advanced areas of the world in terms of the agricultural sciences of that time. From this evident but not obvious fact, it emerges that the ruling classes of the Duchy of Modena came largely, though not exclusively, from the lowlands where the Jesuits founded their schools. Moreover, if we look at the chronological establishment of the foundations, we see that almost all of them occurred over a seventy-year period from 1552 to 1622, consistent with the pedagogical fervor of the generalates of Mercurian and Acquaviva. The only exception was the school of Guastalla, opened in 1728 at a time when the impulse of Jesuit foundations was slowing down.[30]

On the other hand, if we look at the schools run by the Piarists, we find their presence in smaller and poorer centers further away from the political and economic heart of the duchy. Some congregations, including the Piarists, knew how to exploit the needs and aspirations of peripheral areas for their own interests. These places, as we have seen, were not usually considered by the Jesuits to have potential for establishing boarding schools or colleges of any importance. The economic relevance of certain mountain locations, in particular on the Apennine chain, was not significant. Rural and mountain areas were considered by the Society to be more suitable for evangelizing missions against superstition and heresy. The religious deviances in these areas were mostly limited to pagan legacies concerning the use of medicinal herbs, for which preaching was deemed sufficient.

Nonetheless, in these communities a local aristocracy persisted. These nobles were the heirs to the warlike nature and mighty feudalism of the late Middle Ages. Despite the loss of prestige, these people aspired to the same kind of education as the richest and most powerful nobility of that time. Until a few decades earlier, these nobles had availed themselves of the services of important humanists, and they certainly would not have accepted being cut off from

---

30   Sabina Pavone, "I Gesuiti in Italia 1548–1773," in *Atlante della letteratura italiana*. Vol. 2: *Dalla Controriforma alla Restaurazione*, ed. Sergio Luzzatto, Gabriele Pedullà, Eriminia Irace (Torino: Einaudi, 2011), 359–73.

such an important element of social status. The followers of Calasanz knew that, and they were ready to exploit these claims for their own benefit. The first school foundations in these remote places were an effect of the recommencement of the order after the reduction suffered in 1646, and in a crowded educational market they had to be satisfied with this. Nonetheless, it was also an intelligent political move. By exploiting the claims of the nobility, the Piarists were able to create a new power base and demonstrate their pious activity to the duke. The Piarists had been active in the Apennine mountain center of Fanano since 1621, where they were called by the city council and by the local aristocracy. After their restoration in 1669 following the 1646 reduction, the Piarists were asked to reach another mountain center, namely Pavullo, in 1690.[31] The turning point occurred a few decades later when the Piarists were called, again by the city council, to Correggio in 1722 and to Mirandola in 1774 to replace the newly suppressed Jesuits. In this last case, we can see the fathers of the Pious Schools retaliating against Jesuit rivals by replacing them in the important lowland center of Mirandola. These dynamics moved the Piarists from the periphery to the center, rather than from the center to the periphery, as was the case for the Jesuits. We can observe that the timing and motives that determined the spread of the Piarist and Jesuit schools partially overlapped. It is true that the Jesuits eventually penetrated some peripheral locations, as in the case of Guastalla, but this happened later during the eighteenth century, at a time of decline. The fathers of the Pious Schools had already been able to exploit the social and educational regions that had been relatively abandoned by the main religious teaching congregations.[32]

Returning to the case of Correggio, we can affirm that the arrival of the Piarists was the first step of the congregation from mountain isolation towards a richer and more politically centered part of the duchy into the heart of the Jesuit school network in the Modena State, almost an anticipation of what would happen in Mirandola fifty years later in 1774. An important role in bringing the Pious Schools to Correggio was carried out by the Piarist Giuliano Sabbatini, future bishop of Modena. This connection testifies to the rapprochement of the Piarist network in the political heart of the duchy. Giuliano Sabbatini had been involved in important preaching missions in the Modenese rural territory during the early eighteenth century and his pious activity had brought him

---

31   Giuseppe Bedogni, "Il pedagogista Bruno Bruni docente nelle Scuole Pie correggesi," *Bollettino storico reggiano* III, (1970): 1–15.
32   Maurizio Sangalli, "Le congregazioni religiose insegnanti in Italia in età moderna: nuove acquisizioni e piste di ricerca," *Dimensioni e problemi della ricerca storica*, no. 1 (2005): 25–47.

close to Duke Rinaldo d'Este.[33] Sabbatini was a pupil of the Piarist schools in Fanano, and his proximity to the Duke of Modena proved to be a key element for the congregation getting to Correggio.[34]

During the early years of the Piarist presence in Correggio, their schools continued to be largely financed by the community. This can be seen as evidence of how the old municipal pride was not yet completely dormant at the threshold of contemporaneity.[35] As the Barnabites had in Udine, the Piarists had arrived in the Emilian town as teachers for public schools, although a Piarist convent had opened. The turning point came in 1783, when the Dominicans were expelled from their monastery, which was then given to the followers of Calasanz to convert into their own college. At that time the Piarist fathers had already entered into the possession of the Jesuit college of Mirandola. With the establishment of this second collegiate center they sealed their educational supremacy in the heart of the Duchy of Modena.

Supremacy, however, did not mean monopoly. Other religious orders were active in the educational sphere in the Modenese territory between the sixteenth and eighteenth centuries. The Capuchins and Servites had been active in Mirandola since 1580 and 1630, respectively. The Capuchin friars were introduced into Carpi, the small capital of the humanist prince Alberto III Pio, in 1584, but the Jesuits didn't arrive until 1622. In the village of Brescello, home of the Aristotelian philosopher Mario Nizzoli, it was the Benedictine monks who continued to take care of the education of young people. In Viadana, a big commercial village bordering the Duchy of Modena, the Conventual Franciscans and Augustinians were teaching in public schools during the sixteenth and seventeenth centuries.[36] In the town of Guastalla, before the arrival of the Jesuits in 1728, the Servites had arrived in 1568, the Observant Franciscans in 1572, the Capuchins in 1591, and the Theatines in 1616. They were all active in public schools.

---

33 Matteo Al Kalak, "Sabbatini Giuliano," *Dizionario Biografico degli Italiani*, vol. 89 (2017).
34 The future bishop of Modena had also been a student of the Jesuits, thus demonstrating not only an apparently unexpected impartiality, but also farsightedness in grasping the ascendant parable of the followers of Calasanz if compared to the descending one of the Italian Jesuits. See Francesco Ferrari, *Il collegio delle Scuole Pie di Fanano* (Modena: Società Tipografica Modenese, 1917), 132.
35 The funding amounted to 640 lire of Modena for teaching and 43 lire for teaching materials per annum. See Lasagni, *La presenza degli scolopi a Correggio*, 40.
36 We see that in Viadana the Augustinians were specialized in the teaching of letters, natural sciences and mathematics, while the Franciscans were more oriented towards philosophy and theology.

In the Duchy of Modena, the Capuchin friars were introduced into the community of Vignola at the beginning of the sixteenth century. They arrived in the city of Modena in 1539, Sassuolo, belonging to the Pio family, in 1570, Reggio Emilia in 1573, Finale in 1576, Correggio in 1601, and Novellara where, despite the presence of the Jesuits since 1571, the Capuchin order arrived in 1603. They arrived in the small village of San Martino in Rio in 1614, and in Scandiano, birthplace of the poet Matteo Maria Boiardo, in 1622.

So, what was the main difference between all these religious orders and the Jesuits and Piarists that allows us to detect real competition between these two congregations which eventually led to a switch of primacy? It was the fact that Jesuits and Piarists opened their own colleges and boarding schools, while the other congregations were just employed by public schools. The orders working in public schools were less likely to direct their own educational policies within the communities belonging to the Este dominion. The orders that had their own schools, despite struggles and difficulties, could try to exercise more effective action.

These foundations were not only useful for the congregation but also for its main supporter, the Duke of Modena Ercole III.[37] In the framework of a long process of centralization and control over public education by the Este government, which started at the beginning of the sixteenth century, the governor of the region, based in Carpi, was also the president of the Piarist College, with the right to intervene in every aspect of its life. The fathers always reacted to these interferences, but they eventually had to adapt to this type of dialectic and interaction between powers.[38] The congregation also took great advantage of this dialectic.

For the Piarists, gaining the trust of the ruling dynasty was consistent with the expansion of the schools of the congregation in central and eastern Europe, given the increasingly close ties between the Este and Habsburg families.[39] In 1725 the Piarist father Giuliano Sabbatini, who favored the arrival of the Pious Schools in Correggio, was sent by Duke Rinaldo to Vienna, where he soon became an extraordinary ambassador to the emperor Charles VI. The penetration of the Piarists into the Duchy of Modena shows us a strategic foresight of the order in approaching the high spheres of power through gradual

---

37 From this moment on the best source for the history of the Piarist College of Correggio is represented by the "*Memorie cronologiche della casa dei primi ragazzi poveri della Madre di Dio delle Scuole Pie, nella città di Correggio*," manuscript (eighteenth to the nineteenth century), preserved at the *Biblioteca Comunale* of Correggio.
38 Lasagni, *La presenza degli scolopi a Correggio*, 40.
39 Sangalli, *Le smanie per l'educazione*, 351–52.

steps that only partially recall the Jesuits' moves between the sixteenth and seventeenth centuries.

On the one hand, the Jesuits had quickly shifted their focus from the education of the poor to that of the ruling and aristocratic classes, reminiscent of the aspirations of the Renaissance humanists.[40] On the other hand, the Piarists, through the education of the lower social classes, had found an alternative way to win the trust and favor of princes and monarchs. In doing so they succeeded in creating educational institutions for the nobles. The Piarists approached the higher spheres of government instilling less suspicion than the Jesuits, thus succeeding in their competition with other congregations.

From an institutional point of view, the presence of the Piarists in Correggio was formalized in the distinction between their activity in public schools and the opening of their own colleges. External students could access public schools, while there was a selection process to enter the colleges for students ranging in age from seven to fourteen years. The college typically required five years of attendance, the time it took to complete courses in philosophy and rhetoric, but it was not uncommon for some students to leave the institution before the end of their studies. From the time of their arrival in 1723, the fathers offered classes in order of difficulty in distinct schools of grammar, humanity, and rhetoric. At the end of the year, based on the Jesuit model, a public debate was staged in which students demonstrated their speaking skills and the coronation of the "emperor of diligent pupils" took place.[41]

While philosophy courses began in 1725, by 1747 the teaching of moral theology had begun, and in 1784 French and violin lessons were both included in the curriculum.[42] The teachers, however, were not all Piarist fathers, they were also secular priests and laymen under the supervision of the congregation. From the two fathers who had initially arrived in 1723, their number increased rapidly; the following year they were six. Due to the success of the schools, it became difficult to secure an adequate number of teachers, customary for the *ancien régime* schools. The task of providing trained teachers was particularly difficult for the more specialized subjects, such as civil institutions, architecture, perspective, drawing, calligraphy, arithmetic, French, piano, violin, cello, dance and fencing, for which the college had to hire laypeople.

---

40   See chapter 1.
41   The first public debate was held on April 30th, and the coronation on May 7th, both in 1723. See *Memorie cronologiche*.
42   Municipal Library of Correggio, fund: *Archivio Memorie Patrie*, envelope 73, *Scolopi convitto chiesa di S. Giuseppe*, 1747. For the French and violin classes, see the letters of March 3rd and April 17th both written in 1784.

As in the case of Udine, the school system was impacted by the 1789 Revolution and the arrival of French troops, first in 1796/'97 and then again with the return of Napoleon in 1801. After the French arrived in 1796, many families removed their children from the college, and only after an agreement was made between General Bonaparte and the Duke Ercole III was the student population partially reinstated. In 1798, with the withdrawal of the revolutionary armies, a temporary Estense restoration was possible under the protection of the Habsburg arms; however, with the return in 1800 of French domination, the Piarists of Correggio (together with the Franciscans) suffered a heavy fine from the occupying government on charges of acclaiming Austrian troops when they entered the city.[43] This was only a preamble to the closure of the Pious Schools in Correggio and the Duchy of Modena in light of the 1810 decree of Compiègne which suppressed all religious congregations in Italy. From the 1810/'11 school year on the Kingdom of Italy took charge of education and, even after the Restoration of 1814, the Piarists no longer considered returning to the Emilian town. The assets belonging to the former Piarist College were confiscated partly by the State and partly by the municipality, and it wasn't until 1819 that the school management returned to operating under a religious order, though this time it was the Missionary Oblates of Mary Immaculate.

1.3 Guastalla: A Multi-layered Religious Education for the Community

Regarding the arrival of the religious to work in pre-existing public schools, interesting case studies are offered by some towns located in the heart of northern Italy. A significant example is the community of Guastalla, a small renaissance town purchased in 1539 by Ferrante Gonzaga, a trusted man of Emperor Charles V, who was at that time Viceroy of Sicily.[44] The Jesuits did not go to Guastalla during the sixteenth and seventeenth centuries and, except for a monastery of Augustinian nuns established in the early 1470s, there were no other religious orders.[45] The absence of congregations specifically engaged in education, especially Mendicant orders, characterized Guastalla in the late Middle Ages. Such a feature emphasizes its rurality and distance from the

---

43 Lasagni, *La presenza degli scolopi a Correggio*, 59.

44 On Ferrante Gonzaga and the purchase of Guastalla, see Gianvittorio Signorotto, ed., *Ferrante Gonzaga. Il Mediterraneo, l'Impero 1507–1557* (Rome: Bulzoni Editore, 2009).

45 The Society of Jesus did not arrive in Guastalla until the first half of the eighteenth century. See Gino Badini, ed., *I gesuiti a Guastalla*, (Reggio Emilia: La Nuova Tipolito, 2003) and Sergio Ciroldi, "Ordini e congregazioni religiose nel Guastallese," in *Storia della Diocesi di Reggio Emilia-Guastalla*, vol. III, *Dalla Riforma tridentina alla Rivoluzione francese*, ed. Giovanni Costi and Giuseppe Giovanelli (Brescia: Morcelliana, 2014), 185–203.

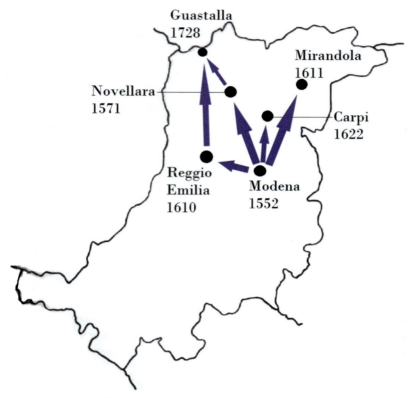

MAP 6   Map of Jesuit schools in the Duchy of Modena

urban world. The arrival within the communal territory of such orders can be considered a major historical turning point. In 1568, the Servite fathers eventually arrived in the community, followed by the Observant Franciscans. The eighteenth-century historian Ireneo Affò wrote that the decision to call them was taken by Cesare Gonzaga, the son of Ferrante, who was in search of a "religious order useful and advantageous to the people."[46]

The Minor Observants of Saint Francis entered the county in 1572. In 1591, the Capuchins also arrived, joined by the Theatines in 1616.[47] The two Franciscan branches, the Observants and the Capuchins, and the order of the Theatines, as we have seen, were all involved in the education that characterized the

---

46   Original quote: "un ordine di religiosi utile al popolo, e vantaggioso." Ireneo Affò, *Istoria della città e ducato di Guastalla*, III (Guastalla: Presso Salvatore Costa, 1787), 41.

47   Ciroldi, "Ordini e congregazioni religiose nel Guastallese," Observants: 192–93; Capuchins: 194–96; Servites: 196–97; Theatines: 199.

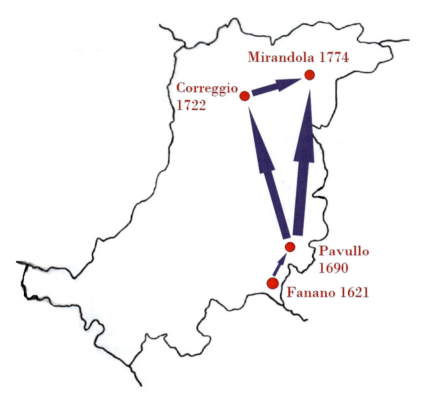

MAP 7   Map of Piarist schools in the Duchy of Modena

Catholic Reformation. The case of Guastalla shows us how interactions between these orders could sometimes translate into complex balances, even within small centers. In 1640 the priest Domenico Campi, belonging to the order of the Servants of Mary, was active in the local public schools.[48] A few years later, however, in a municipal resolution of 1646, Duke Ferrante III Gonzaga informed the city council of his "desire that three teachers of school were to be introduced in Guastalla, one for grammar and humanity, one for the rhetoric and the other for logic, and that they had to be three religious, one Theatine, the other Franciscan and the third Servite and that with 200 *scudi* all three masters could be satisfied."[49] Again in 1650, we find another Servite in

---

48   Biblioteca Maldotti di Guastalla (BMGu), *Registro delle Deliberazioni del Consiglio Comunale*, September 22nd, 1640.
49   Original extended quote: "Radunati n. 9 consiglieri il Sindaco espose che il Duca avrebbe desiderio che s'introducessero in Guastalla 3 Maestri di Scuola, e così uno per

charge of public schools, the priest Carlo Aguzzani, hired by the city council. It is interesting to note that in the contract for the hiring of Aguzzani in 1652, it was recommended that the Servite teacher use the "manner, way and order observed by the Jesuit fathers in teaching."[50] He was also obliged to keep a school of Christian doctrine in the city church every Sunday.

The overlapping of assignments and pedagogical suggestions towards Aguzzani show us that members of religious orders, in this case the Servants of Mary who had a precise *Ratio Studiorum*, could be exposed to a series of contaminations and solicitations from other pedagogical experiences when entering into a communal public school as in the case of Jesuit education and the schools of Christian doctrine.[51] A small turning point in the educational guidelines of schools in Guastalla took place in 1655, when a Theatine was chosen instead of a Servite to teach in the local schools. The new teacher was supposed to lodge at the local Theatine house but, because of a broken floor in the room assigned to him, the authorities moved him to an independent house in which he would hold school, exactly as had happened a century before with the lay masters. Even more significant was the prohibition to open an alternative school in the city.[52] This shows how there was a political will to give an official profile to local education following the pedagogical forms of the Theatines, and how within the community there were also efforts to push education in a different direction from the official one. Despite the desire to conform the local schools to the educational norms of a specific religious order, the material contingencies did not allow the project to be completed. Circumstances related to military upheavals and economic and social issues made the continuous

---

la Grammatica ed umanità; uno per la Rettorica e l'altro per la logica; e che fossero tre Religiosi, uno Teatino; l'altro Francescano ed il terzo Servita e che con 200 Scudi si soddisfacevano tutti e tre i Maestri, il qual danaro si poteva ricavare dalla Macina col pagare due soldi di più per sacco di frumento da macinare. I consiglieri ciò sentito dissero di differire la delibera ad altro Consiglio." BMGu, *Registro delle Deliberazioni del Consiglio Comunale*, August 18th, 1646.

50 Original quote: "Inoltre insegnerà la grammatica, umanità e retorica se vi saranno figliuoli per essa con la maniera modo et ordine che tengono et osservano i PP. Gesuiti nell'insegnare." BMGu, *Registro delle Deliberazioni del Consiglio Comunale*, May 29th, 1652.

51 The methods and the educational paths within the Order of the Servants of Mary experienced a long process of elaboration characterized by fairly frequent additions and reforms. For the early modern age, among the most important we recall are those made by the Constitutions of Budrio (1548), Bologna (1556), Florence (1569) and Parma (1580). Refer to Pacifico Maria Branchesi, "Gli studia delle province italiane dell'Ordine dei Servi di Maria negli anni 1597–1601 ed il loro contesto legislativo," *Studi Storici OSM*, 23 (1973): 168–70.

52 BMGu, Registers, October 6th 1655.

presence of Theatine teachers impossible. In the following decades, secular priests and lay teachers continued to alternate, with a relative increase of the latter in the last years of the seventeenth century. This somewhat chaotic alternation of the religious in the classrooms of the town stopped in 1738, when the Jesuits, who had opened a small college, were also introduced in Guastalla. Within a few years the number of students attending these schools reached 150 and in 1747 the seminarians and the young local priests were also admitted. However, this experience turned out to be short-lived. Guastalla, with the Treaty of Aix-la-Chapelle (1748), had lost its political autonomy by passing definitively under the Duchy of Parma, governed by the Bourbon dynasty. In 1768 the seventeen-year-old Duke Ferdinand of Bourbon decreed the expulsion of the Jesuits from all his dominions, including Guastalla, in line with what had been done a few years earlier in France by his uncle King Louis XV.[53]

We can find other examples of regular clerics and friars engaged in public municipal schools rather than colleges or institutes of a precise order. By the end of the sixteenth century in the commercial borough of Viadana inside the borders of the Duchy of Mantua, Augustinian monks taught mathematics and natural philosophy while Franciscan friars oversaw theology and philosophy.[54]

In addition to religious orders, the number of secular priests during the seventeenth century also increased among teachers in Guastalla. This, it is legitimate to suppose, was the result of a greater influence of noble authority in the governing of municipal public schools. We see that the council was more appreciative of employing lay masters, while the grievances became evident when hiring a master priest, as in the case of Giacomo Vezzani. His education took place mainly in Rome at the Somascan and Jesuit schools. Vezzani was taught by Bernardino Stefonio S. J. and Famiano Strada S. J., the latter among the teachers of Giulio Rospigliosi, the future pope Clement IX.[55] Vezzani studied mainly Aristotelian philosophy. Returning to Reggio in 1606, he took the sacred orders and began his public teaching until his call to Guastalla by the will of Ferrante II Gonzaga.[56]

---

53   Badini, *I gesuiti a Guastalla*, 75; and Ciroldi, "Ordini e congregazioni religiose nel Guastallese," 202–03.
54   David Salomoni, "Fragments of Renaissance schools on the banks of the Po River," *Educazione. Giornale di pedagogia critica*, VI, 1 (2017): 7–30.
55   On Bernardino Stefonio and Famiano Strada, see respectively: Mirella Saulini, *Bernardino Stefonio S.J. Un gesuita sabino nella storia del teatro* (Rome: Edizioni Espera, 2014) and Jozef Ijsewijn, "Scrittori latini a Roma dal Barocco al Neoclassicismo," *Studi romani*, 36 (1988): 229–51. See also Girolamo Tiraboschi, *Biblioteca modenese*, V (Modena: Presso la Società Tipografica, 1784), 366.
56   Affò, *Istoria*, 43.

Vezzani's teaching resembled that of the Jesuits in the nearby community of Novellara, where they had been teaching for forty years. Ferrante II, in "wishing that young people, in order to become worthy of the priesthood, in addition to piety also possessed the right doctrine," entrusted Vezzani with the task of setting up a school. This institution, as the one in Novellara, imparted basic grammatical instruction without necessarily including the way of the priesthood, while in higher grades it was aimed at the education of the religious or of those who wanted to become religious. In January 1612, Vezzani was called by the Chapter of Reggio Emilia Cathedral to be a "professor of grammar of the school of the same cathedral for five years with the annual pension of 100 *ducatoni*," but he refused; he must have found a suitable environment in Guastalla thanks to the favor of a wise and benevolent prince (*doctissimum* and *humanissimos*). Illustrious students were educated in his school:

> among them Persio Caracci, who was then bishop of Larino. Virginio Ghisolfi, a young man with a singular talent, who deserved to be strongly recommended to the teacher by *Monsignor* Baldi himself, a very learned man, although coming from a family with scarce economic means (*ob rei familiaris angustias*), as Vezzani declared, applied to the profession of music. Jacopo Soragna, who also studied the Greek letters in Piacenza, and was therefore appointed archpriest of Barbasso and Francesco Tolosa succeeded as last Archdeacon of our Cathedral (of Guastalla), who left various works in verse and prose in Italian and Latin.[57]

In these lines we observe the presence of a small but significant group of intellectuals cultivated by Vezzani in Guastalla. The young people mentioned were all from the local aristocracy. Our pedagogist, nonetheless, also taught the children and students of the community, who could study and learn at a school run by an important scholar and humanist. It is possible to find some reference in Ireneo Affò *Istoria* to former students who did not choose the consecrated life. This shows that the activity of the teacher did not only address future religious men. Among the one hundred spearmen given in 1614 as military conduct to

---

57 Original quote: "tra' quali Persio Caracci, che fu poi vescovo di Larino; Virginio Ghisolfi giovane di particolare talento, che meritò di essere raccomandato caldamente al maestro dallo stesso Monsignor Baldi, assai dotto, benché poi *ob rei familiaris angustias*, come dice il Vezzano, si applicasse alla profession della musica; Jacopo Soragna, che in Piacenza studiò poi anche le lettere greche, e fu quindi arciprete di Barbasso; e Francesco Tolosa, riuscito alfine arcidiacono della nostra Cattedrale, che varie opere in versi e in prosa nell'una e nell'atra lingua lasciò." Affò, *Istoria*, 105–06.

Francesco Gonzaga, Ferrante II's younger brother, we find Francesco Rinaldi from Guastalla, defined by Vezzani as a young man very passionate about studying.[58] It is interesting to look at the chronological proximity between the activity of our teacher and Rinaldi's militancy in Francesco Gonzaga's troops. Giacomo Vezzani was active in Guastalla between 1611 and 1613, and only a few months later, in 1614, the young spearman appeared in the service of his captain. This shows how different the human and professional vocations of the young people educated in the school of *maestro* Vezzani could be.

2 Episcopal Requests

Urban magistrates were not the only authorities promoting the arrival of religious orders in urban centers to take charge of education; there were also bishops. In the course of this section, several known such cases will be examined. In general, medieval schools attached to cathedrals had gradually reduced their activities and their student bodies with the rise of communal and public schools during the twelfth and thirteenth centuries. These transformations did not necessarily mean a decline, but rather a specialization in the education of the clergy. In particular, the universities founded during the twelfth century represented new educational institutions with universal vocations (at least in their intention), while cathedral schools rediscovered a more local and urban attitude.[59]

Although during the Middle Ages the education provided by cathedral schools addressed mainly religious people or future clergy, there were also secular listeners who, after their studies there, would return to their secular careers. Alongside the cathedral schools were some colleges that accommodated students from the countryside, and even from other cities. Within the school, lessons were imparted in grammar, philosophy, biblical studies, theology and canon law, and often entrusted to teachers with a university degree. The best students could then continue their education at a university.[60]

---

58 Affò, *Istoria*, 110.
59 The stark distinction between universities and episcopal schools and between the secular and the religious dimension is, of course, a schematization for explanatory purposes. The members of the clergy, in fact, often held up to advanced early modern times a very important role, if not an effective government, in several important universities, for example the Franciscans at the Sorbonne in Paris. See Bert Roest, *Franciscan Learning, Preaching and Mission c. 1220–1650* (Leiden-Boston: Brill, 2015).
60 On the cathedral schools and the evolution of their social, cultural and educational role between the late Middle Ages and the early modern age I refer to classical works that remain solid starting points for understanding this type of education. In particular: Pierre

Despite the survival and vitality of the cathedral schools until the end of the Middle Ages, the new challenges posed by the Protestant and Catholic reformations during the sixteenth century found these educational institutions unprepared. Although the internal transformations of medieval culture and society had had an impact on the physiognomies and aims of the cathedral schools, the institutions had nevertheless continued to operate within the same religious and anthropological framework acquired over the preceding eras. It was in reaction to this new situation that the Catholic bishops themselves, starting in the 1500s, began to promote the arrival of new religious orders in their cities and dioceses. Such support was required in the new seminaries in line with the activities of cathedral schools for the education of future priests and for the establishment of new schools and colleges for laypeople, sometimes in collaboration with communal authorities. Indeed, as Angelo Turchini explained, the Church considered the schools necessary, "contributing with its own investments in the reorganization of structures and in the qualification of men; its main purpose, the cultural growth of the ecclesiastical institution, had obvious repercussions on the local society that was willing to bear some burden in support of the initiative, in an interested participation."[61]

Concrete actions came quickly. From the fifth session of the Council of Trent in 1546, education connected to religious institutions was regulated. It was decided that in the cathedrals and collegiate churches of the most important communities, a theological prebend had to be established. This was to be a paid position for a religious person able to teach sacred scripture. A similar measure had already been taken at the Fourth Lateran Council and at the Basel Council. Both the clergy and laypeople were targets of this type of educational institution. Cardinal Carlo Borromeo was particularly diligent in the implementation of this decree within his archdiocese.[62] The intention was to make it

---

Riché and Jacques Verger, *Des nains sur des épaules de géants. Maîtres et élèves au Moyen Âge* (Paris: Éditions Tallandier, 2006), 289–91. Other important elements of analysis are present in Paul Grendler, *Schooling in Renaissance Italy* (Baltimore and London: The Johns Hopkins University Press, 1989), 3–10.

61 Angelo Turchini, *Sotto l'occhio del padre. Società confessionale e istruzione primaria nello Stato di Milano* (Bologna: Il Mulino, 1996), 133.

62 Turchini, *Sotto l'occhio del padre*, 131–37. See also: Eleuterio Chinea, "Le scuole del Ducato di Milano dal Concilio tridentino alla riforma teresiana (1562–1773)," *Rivista pedagogica*, XXIV (1931): 43144; and Guerrino Pelliccia, *La scuola primaria a Roma dal secolo XVI al XIX. L'istruzione popolare e la catechesi ai fanciulli nell'ambito della parrocchia e dello "Studium Urbis" da Leone X a Leone XII 1513–1829* (Rome: Edizione dell'Ateneo, 1985), 25. On the role played by Carlo Borromeo, refer to: Giovanni Pietro Giussano, *Vita di San Carlo Borromeo* (Naples: Tipografia arcivescovile, 1855) and Federico Rossi di Marignano, *Carlo Borromeo. Un uomo, una vita, un secolo* (Milan: Mondadori, 2010), 223–24.

widespread. In an undated written record, plausibly from the 1570s and kept in the diocesan historical Archive of Milan, the following places are listed: Monza, Pontirolo, Varese, Gallarate, Vimercate, Desio, Gorgonzola, Corbetta, Incino, Massaglia, Galiano, Appiano, Castelseprio, Castiglione, Melegnano, Canobio, Brebbia, Marliano, and Valtravaglia.[63]

Another decisive step taken by the Church for the renewal of its educational structures took place on July 15th, 1563. On that date, the XXIII overall session of the Council of Trent unanimously approved the decree *Cum adolescentium aetas*, a truly epoch-making measure that established the seminaries as centers for the education and vocational care of future priests. It was not immediately clear what structure and model was to be used for these new schools. Initially, the Council Fathers were inspired by Cardinal Reginald Pole's project for the London Synod of 1556, which took place during the brief English Catholic Restoration. Pole had in mind a school that was to be like a plant nursery, hence the name "seminary" (*seminarium*), but in practice it was the model of the Roman College of the Jesuits that was imposed. Many bishops, in fact, turned to the Society of Jesus to find teachers capable of preparing the future priests of their dioceses.[64] In many cases it was the Society of Jesus which was called to take care of the government of the new seminaries after the Council of Trent.

The most important case is represented by the Pontifical Roman Major Seminary, which became exemplary for seminaries organized in many other Italian cities.[65] Despite the Jesuits' pioneering habit of providing models on which to structure the new educational undertakings of the Tridentine Church, other religious orders of the new course were soon involved in the governance and management of diocesan seminaries. This type of experience was often a general rehearsal for teaching congregations that were to open new schools or colleges.

2.1 *The Somascans between Schools and Diocesan Seminaries*

A recurrent dynamic within the sources shows bishops of the Italian cities attempting to call religious teaching congregations to their dioceses. Regular

---

63 The source (cited in Turchini, *ibid*, 133) is kept in the Diocesan Historical Archive of Milan, section 14, number 65, booklet 56.
64 Adriano Prosperi, *Il Concilio di Trento: una introduzione storica* (Torino: Einaudi, 2001), 85.
65 On the activity of the Jesuits in the Roman seminary and in other Italian cities, see Luca Testa, *Fondazione e sviluppo del Seminario romano 1565–1608* (Rome: Pontificia Università Gregoriana, 2002) and Samuel Overloop, "Rules of the Congregation for Members of the Roman Seminary," *The Way* XLVII, 4 (2008): 93–98.

clerics were initially quite often reluctant to take charge of the schools, preferring the management of the diocesan seminaries. In their initial phase, for example, the Somascan Fathers, still suspended between the desire to establish orphanages and educate young people, often preferred to accept roles in seminaries.[66] Their path towards governing these institutions was gradual. Initially, they preferred to help bishops who were asking for support or aid by sending one or two fathers to assist with seminary governance or lecturing. For example, in 1574, during the chapter held on April 25th in Milan, the decision was made to send some fathers to help in the seminary of Naples, while during another Milanese chapter, held in 1578, a priest was sent to assist at the seminary of Pavia. Another example is the General Somascan Chapter held in Pavia at the college of Saint *Majolo* on April 29th 1607, where the decision was made to take charge of the diocesan seminaries in the city of Ravenna and in the village of Tonone, near Biella, in western Lombardy, in addition to the education of orphans (*orfanelli*).[67]

However, it is possible that the Somascans refused to help bishops seeking assistance or that they threatened to withdraw from seminaries that they already took care of. During the Chapter of Pavia in 1583, the Somascan assembly refused to allow a rector from its own congregation to enter the seminary of Vicenza as requested by the local bishop.[68] In 1580 the Somascans were active in the seminary of Alessandria, but threatened to withdraw in 1587 if certain conditions imposed by the congregation were not accepted.[69] We do not know exactly what those conditions were, but another example gives us an idea. In 1593, a similar situation occurred in Tortona, in eastern Piedmont. The Somascans, called by the local bishop, agreed to take charge of the seminary on the condition that the bishop had schools and student dormitories built onto the seminary to be governed.[70] Thus, we can see how gradually, between

---

[66] Raviolo Sebastiano C.R.S., "Il contributo dei Somaschi alla Controriforma e lo sviluppo dei loro ordinamenti scolastici dagli inizi alla prima metà del '700" (M.A. diss., Milan Catholic University of the Sacred Heart, 1942). The typewritten copy of this dissertation is kept at the Genoese Somascan General Archives. See also: Maurilio Guasco, "La formazione del clero: i seminari," in *Storia d'Italia, Annali IX, La Chiesa e il potere politico*, ed. Giorgio Chittolini and Giovanni Miccoli (Torino: Einaudi, 1986), 629–715.

[67] ACTA CONGREGATIONIS (1603–1663). Vol. 2. Fonti per la storia dei Somaschi, ed. Maurizio Brioli C.R.S. (Rome: Curia generalizia dei padri Somaschi, 2006), 22.

[68] ACTA CONGREGATIONIS (1528–1602). Vol. 1, Fonti per la storia dei Somaschi, ed. Maurizio Brioli C.R.S. (Rome: Curia generalizia dei padri Somaschi, 2006), 85.

[69] ACTA, Vol. 1, 79, 95.

[70] ACTA. Vol. 1, 123. The source specifies the amount of tax that students would have to pay, ranging between 42 and 45 *scudi* per year, at the discretion of the father general.

the end of the sixteenth and the beginning of the seventeenth century, *tout-court* schools were beginning to be part of the pastoral priorities of the Regular Clerics of Somascha together with orphanages and diocesan seminaries.

To illustrate these dynamics, the case of the Patriarchal Seminary of Venice is particularly instructive. The Somascan Fathers had an orphanage in the city of Saint Mark, which had been operating since 1557. During the chapter held in Ferrara during May 1579, they agreed to help the Patriarch of Venice, Giovanni Trevisan, to establish the first diocesan seminary in his city, although this institution didn't actually begin to operate until 1581.[71] The return to the Republic of Venice in order to take part in such an important foundation was favored by Cardinal Aldobrandini, as we can see from a letter addressed to him before 1590, and it took place after half a century of Somascan expansion, mainly in the Lombard area.[72] In 1589 the seminary was already in full swing and the number of aspiring priests who were attending it was increasing; however, the Somascan fathers were only helping with the new seminary, not fully directing it. They made a proposal to the patriarch of Venice to add another four members of the order to make their presence more influential inside the seminary, but the patriarch refused to pay them more money.[73] In 1590, in addition to the patriarchal seminary, a new ducal seminary was created under the protection of the *doge* (duke), the primicerius and the procurator of Saint Mark's.[74] In that year, Somascans were called upon to teach theology in the ducal seminary, and at the same time they received full governing of the patriarchal seminary.[75] The organization of the patriarchal seminary consisted of the following system: the fathers were housed in the convent of Saint Cyprian of Murano, previously inhabited by the Premonstratensian fathers. The furniture for the church, the wax for the candles and the oil were provided partly by the diocesan administrators of the seminary, partly by the Somascan congregation and partly by

---

[71] ACTA. Vol. 1, 69, 77. On the Patriarchal Seminary of Venice, see also: Flaminio Cornaro and Giovanni Manfré, *Notizie storiche delle chiese e monasteri di Venezia, e di Torcello: tratte dalle chiese veneziane, e torcellane* (Padova: Nella stamperia del Seminario, appresso Giovanni Manfré, 1758); Giannantonio Moschini, *La chiesa e il seminario di Santa Maria della Salute in Venezia* (Venice: Tipi di G. Antonelli, 1842).

[72] The source [quoted in: *I Somaschi*, ed. Luigi Mascilli Migliorini (Rome: Edizioni di storia e letteratura, 1992), 29], is kept in the Venice State Archives (Archivio di Stato di Venezia), Section: *Ordini religiosi*, Somaschi, Vol. 1.

[73] "May the government of the seminary of Venice continue; but being the number of convicts increased and not wanting the *clarissimo* [patriarch] our emolument to be satisfied at least that part of the greater effort should be made to introduce another 4 of our members into that seminary." ACTA Vol. 1, 102.

[74] Migliorini, ed., *I Somaschi*, 134–35.

[75] ACTA. Vol. 1, 110.

two congregations of secular priests consecrated to the Virgin Mary and Saint Jerome. In the seminary, as written in the contract, twenty-four seminarians were to be educated in accordance with the decrees of the Council of Trent, with six priest teachers and four laypeople in 1650.[76]

In 1593 the seminaries of Trent and Como and in 1596 and 1597 respectively, the seminaries of Udine and Treviso had also been taken over by Somascans; however, these new commitments didn't lessen the strong dedication they had to the seminaries already held in Venice where they actually wanted to increase their work. In Saint Mark's Republic Capital City, the Somascans wanted to annex schools to the patriarchal seminary. Eventually, in January 1670, twenty years after they had been given the Venetian seminary, the regular clerics were given the task of opening their public schools in Venice.[77] What had taken shape before 1670 had been a 'college-seminary,' similar to others in the Venetian lagoon, for example that of Torcello where Piarists were called to operate in 1734 by bishop Marco Giustinian.[78] In 1633 the Somascans decided to annex boarding schools to only some of the seminaries governed by their congregation, among them the Patriarchal Seminary of Venice. As Luigi Mascilli Migliorini wrote, the arrival of the Somascans in Venice in the 1590s sanctioned a new phase of diffusion and activity of the fathers after about fifty years of difficult attempts to enter the Venetian Republic, the first place of the apostolate of the founder of the Somascans, Girolamo Emiliani. In addition to the earlier, purely charitable intent of the congregation, the motivations that supported the opening of new schools and houses were increasingly accompanied by the task of "educating and raising young people in the fear of God." The local episcopate, therefore, was increasingly involved in these foundations, especially the bishops, and were ready to carry out their human and social task as defenders of the authentic faith. The foundations of the patriarchal seminary and of the ducal seminary, to which the erection of the College of the Most Holy Trinity for the officiating of novices of the order was added at the end of the 1500s, refer more explicitly to the forms established by the Council of Trent, accentuating the educational moment typical of the Tridentine Church, which would have characterized the Italian educational panorama

---

76   ACTA. Vol. 1, 110–11.
77   Moschini, *La chiesa e il seminario*, 53.
78   Maurizio Sangalli, *Le smanie per l'educazione. Gli scolopi a Venezia tra Sei e Settecento* (Rome: Viella, 2012), 173, 210–11. As Sangalli explains, the seminary, before the arrival of the Piarists, was always opened by Bishop Giustinian in 1720, and only afterwards were the schools annexed.

throughout the eighteenth century.[79] Still, we know that there were teachers of the humanities, including philosophy, theology, and Greek, at this college in 1725.[80]

There are other examples in the Italian Peninsula of Somascan schools opened at the request of bishops; one was opened in 1662 in Alba, another in 1689 in Tolentino at the request of the bishop of Macerata and yet another in 1696 in Caserta, where the Regular Clerics were asked to establish both a seminary and a public school.

3 Other Types of Schools Operated by Religious Orders

The call of religious orders to direct schools, colleges, and seminaries by the will of urban magistracies and religious authorities are the most common cases a historian can find amongst sources; however, these were not the only ones. An important role was retained by private citizens, often aristocrats but also rich merchants or landowners. They usually opened schools for the children of their cities and villages as an act of charity and philanthropy. Of course, this was not without social and political implications which highlighted their distinct and superior role within their community. In many cases these aristocrats were also clergy members and often diocesan priests. The religious people who belonged to the ranks of the urban aristocracy felt a strong obligation to contribute to the work of re-establishing post-Tridentine Catholic identity in the field of education and youth care. On the opposite side of this educational model we find religious teachers working as private tutors for the children of nobles. Some examples of these two educational models will be described in the course of this section in order to better understand their social, cultural and political implications.

3.1 *Barnabite Schools Established by Notables and Aristocrats*
During the previous chapters we have seen cases of princes and nobles who lived during the Renaissance and Reformation committed to establishing new

---

79 Migliorini, ed., *I Somaschi*, 29. To better understand the Venetian political context of the time, see Gino Benzoni, *Venezia nell'età della Controriforma* (Milan: Mursia, 1973) and Alvise Zorzi, *La Repubblica del Leone. Storia di Venezia* (Milan: Rusconi, 1979). For the early modern Venetian educational panorama, see Vittorio Baldo, *Alunni maestri e scuole in Venezia alla fine del XVI secolo* (Como: New Press, 1976).
80 ACTA CONGREGATIONIS (1664–1737). Vol. 3, Fonti per la storia dei Somaschi, ed. Maurizio Brioli C.R.S. (Rome: Curia generalizia dei padri Somaschi, 2006), 149.

schools in their states to prepare their subjects for public service. The most famous case was that of the *Ca' Zoiosa*, the well-known school created by Vittorino da Feltre in Mantua during the fifteenth century. Similar cases can also be found in Novellara during the sixteenth century, where Count Camillo Gonzaga called the Jesuits to create a college for the local people. In both cases, it should be emphasized that the founders of these schools were actual princes (heads of their states), and not simply nobles or aristocrats. Nonetheless, these two social categories, princes and aristocrats, were both active in the educational sphere and they were not lacking in initiative to establish educational institutions through generous endowments.

Among the most famous cases is that of the Barnabite Arcimboldi schools in Milan which were established in 1608 through a legacy left by Monsieur Giambattista Arcimboldi.[81] He came from a patrician family of Milan and carried out important tasks at the Roman Curia. The testament in which he set the sum of money to be allocated to the foundation of this school was written in 1603. As Angelo Bianchi explains, it is a document of great interest because it establishes in detail all the rules for the functioning of the school. As seen above, Arcimboldi wanted young laypeople to be educated in the school, marking a real turning point in the history of the Barnabites' pastoral activity.

The money allocated for the school was deposited in Milan, Cremona, and Rome. The deed stated that the Congregation of the Clerics Regular of Saint Paul, represented by its superior general, had to undertake the opening and governing of two schools in perpetuity, one of humanity and one of rhetoric, both at the College of Saint Alexander, to educate young laypeople admitted free of charge after being interviewed by the fathers.[82] The executors of the wills were the Archbishop of Milan, the Vicar of Provisione (*Vicario di Provvisione*) and the Superior General of the Barnabites.

The Barnabites were entrusted with every aspect of the management of the new college, from the administrative and financial government to the pedagogical, supplying and recruiting teaching staff.[83] In fact, in the deed of foundation of 1608, all the rules for the direction of the institution (*Regule*) were

---

81   On the Arcimboldi schools, see Angelo Bianchi, "Le suole Arcimboldi a Milano nel XVII secolo: professori, studenti, cultura scolastica," *Barnabiti Studi* 19, (2002): 55–78. The act of its founding is kept in the historical archives of the Barnabites in Milan (*Archivio Storico dei Barnabiti di Milano*, ASBMi), section B, folder II, booklet IV, *Instromento dell'erettione del Collegio Arcimboldo rog. dal Sig. Hieronimo Bolino*, and *Ex donatione Rev.mi Arcimboldi; Ivi, Ex instrumento fundationis*.
82   Bianchi, *Le scuole Arcimboldi*, 58.
83   For example, the professor of rhetoric was always a member of the congregation while the professor of humanity was hired by the ranks of public teachers of Milan.

drawn up in a real Barnabite *Ratio Studiorum*.[84] In the first part of the *Regule*, the method for appointing the positions of the college was determined. Among these positions were the *praefectus studiorum* (the actual head of the school, to whom all students and teachers had to refer), the three members of the committee for the acceptance of students, the school (with the task of keeping the register of admissions and resignations from the college up to date) and the *pater spiritualis*, charged with the spiritual direction of the students and leader of the congregation of the Blessed Virgin to which all the boarders had to belong.[85] In the second part of the *Regule*, all aspects relating to the calendar of lessons and holidays were established, as well as disciplinary rules.[86]

In the case of the Arcimboldi schools, therefore, we find not only an important example of an ecclesiastical Milanese patrician engaged in a project that summarized various aspects of his social, civic, and religious role, we also find a proud aristocrat who contributed to the prestige of his household by providing his city with a service of public utility. Giambattista Arcimboldi was an original pedagogical genius, able to use his ideas to influence one of the most important educational experiences in the history of the Regular Clerics of Saint Paul. This school, in fact, was the first one to be opened by the Barnabites for laypeople, as Arcimboldi had clearly expressed in his will. This school indelibly marked the entire Barnabite educational experience.[87]

Nonetheless, Arcimboldi was not the only munificent creator of schools run by religious congregations in post Tridentine Italy. In southern Latium, for example, in the town of Arpino, a Barnabite College was opened in 1627 by the local nobleman Desiderio Merolla. In the Arpino college the fathers taught philosophy and theology until the end of the eighteenth century.[88] Desiderio Merolla, unlike Arcimboldi, was a layman, but there are other cases in which we find clergy members calling religious orders to establish schools in their communities. In the Lombard city of Lodi, for instance, Archdeacon Paolo Dunieri provided in his testament an endowment for the opening of a Barnabite school of logic, metaphysics, and theology attached to the college of San Giovanni delle Vigne. Thanks to this provision, the school was able to serve

---

84 See Chapter 2.
85 Bianchi, *Le scuole Arcimboldi*, 60–61.
86 Bianchi, *Le scuole Arcimboldi*, 62–63.
87 *I Barnabiti nel IV centenario dalla fondazione 1533–1933* (Genova: Tipografia Artigianelli, 1933), 247.
88 *I Barnabiti*, 257 and Luigi Barelli, *Memorie dell'origine, fondazione, avanzamenti, successi ed uomini illustri in lettere e santità della congregazione de' Chierici Regolari di S. Paolo*, Vol. II (Bologna: Per Costantino Pisarri, 1707), 631–32.

as an aid to the diocesan seminary, educating young priests-to-be until 1726.[89] Outside Italy, in the bordering region of Savoy and even in the heart of France, private patrimonies contributed to the opening or consolidation of Barnabite schools and colleges. Such was the case of Étampes at the gates of Paris, where in 1629 the Fouldier family, of which two members had entered the Barnabites, contributed to the expansion of schools that had been operating in the community since 1626. In Bonneville in Savoy, a school of the Regular Clerics of Saint Paul was opened in 1659 thanks to the legacy of the Cocastel family.[90] The list of examples could continue with Barnabite schools being created in other cities and small towns, as in the case of Genoa in 1674 at the behest of Bartolomeo Gavanto in Finalmarina in 1711 as requested by the priest Carlo Agostino Ghislieri, and even in Florence where in 1735 the College of Saint Charles was open to students from all backgrounds by the will of Francesco Boddi.[91]

3.2 *The Religious as Private Teachers*

On the opposite side of creating new educational institutions, we find the imperishable practice of wealthy classes, both aristocratic and bourgeois, of hiring private tutors for their children. By hiring private teachers, their goal to provide their children with the best possible education was combined with their desire to emphasize their distinct and privileged social status.[92] In most

---

89   *I Barnabiti*, 249. See also Paolo Pissavino and Gianvittorio Signorotto, eds., *Lombardia borromaica Lombardia spagnola: 1554–1659* (Rome: Bulzoni, 1995), 797; Simona Negruzzo, *Collegij a forma di Seminario. Il sistema di formazione teologica nello Stato di Milano in età spagnola* (Brescia: Editrice La Scuola, 2001), 165ss; Emanuele Colombo, "Benefici e costruzioni di élites a Lodi (XVIII–XIX secolo)," in *Ambizioni e reputazioni. Élite nel Lodigiano tra età moderna e contemporanea*, ed. Pietro Cafaro (Milan: FrancoAngeli, 2013), 47–76.

90   On the cases of Étampes and Bonneville, see Basile Fleureau, *Les antiquitez de la ville et du duché d'Estampes* (Paris: chez Jean Baptiste Coignard, 1683), 420–24 (Chapter 14: *Du College d'Estampes*) and Goffredo Casalis, *Dizionario geografico, storico, statistico, commerciale degli Stati di S. M. il re di Sardegna* (Torino: Presso Maspero libraio e Marzorati tipografo, 1849), 599.

91   On the cases of Geona and Finalmarina, see *I barnabiti*, 252; and Davide Bertolotti, *Viaggio nella Liguria marittima* (Torino: Tipografi Eredi Botta, 1834), 350. For the College of St. Charles in Florence, see Licia Bertani, Giuseppe Cagni, Eugenio Castellani, Giampaolo Trotta, *San Carlo dei Barnabiti a Firenze: una chiesa ed un collegio all'ombra dei Granduchi e dell'Impero* (Florence: Comune di Firenze, 1995), 33.

92   As Angelo Turchini writes, "the model of the private tutor as a sign of distinction is destined to become the rule," see Turchini, *Sotto l'occhio del padre*, 235. This practice would have lasted until the 19th and 20th centuries; see Rita Benigni, *Educazione religiosa e modernità. Linee evolutive e prospettive di riforma* (Torino: Giappicchelli editore, 2017), 135.

cases, however, hired teachers were religious, most frequently diocesan priests and sometimes members of congregations. The reason for this lies in the fact that secular priests, because of their high number, could often remain without specific tasks within a parish and therefore without remuneration. A private teaching position, therefore, could represent a good source of income to which was added the comfort provided by board and lodging, that often (though not always) went with the assignment. Diocesan priests, unlike members of religious orders, were subject to the authority of the local bishop; hence, they did not take the vow of poverty and could accept salaries to teach. To underline the fluidity of educational models, a private clergyman teacher could also hold school publicly in addition to the assignment in a private house, proof of the permeability of existing situations. An example of this is the teacher Alessio Grambini, who in 1574 was working in the house of Paolo Sormani in the Lombard commune of Missaglia; Grambrini gave public as well as private lessons.[93]

The option of receiving private tutoring fell also to daughters. The 1624 testament of Giovanni Casotti, a parish priest residing in Guastalla, lists some credits claimed by the prelate, including "four and a half years of salary for teaching" the three daughters of Count Ferrante II Gonzaga and his wife Vittoria Doria "to write, to sing and the grammar."[94] Young women often had the option to choose between a private education at home or at a convent, which was often the basis for taking a religious habit.

3.3 Women, Nuns, Teachers: The 'Educandato' of Saint Charles

In addition to the examples in the second chapter regarding female instruction, another institution representative of educational attention paid to women was the *Educandato*. The *Educandato* was usually represented by a female convent or monastery where girls were hosted and educated by the nuns who resided there. The nature of this institution was not too different from the regular clerics' boarding schools seen so far; the main difference was that these structures were not born as schools but were fully religious institutions that took charge of education for certain groups of people, such as girls

---

93 Turchini, *Sotto l'occhio del padre*, 236.
94 Municipal Archives of Guastalla (kept in the Maldotti Library), *Curia del Podestà*, Civil Lawsuits, 1626. Original text: "Prima, dall'Illustrissimo et Eccellentissimo Sig. Duca Sig. Ferrante Gonzaga io avanzo la mercede di quattr'anni e mezzo per haver insegnato a tre sue figliole di scrivere, cantare et grammatica [...]." The source is reported in Elisa Bertazzoni, *Il monastero di San Carlo in Guastalla e le giovani Gonzaga* (Guastalla: Umberto Soncini editore, 2008), 196–97.

for whom a private education was not possible or desirable. The young women were formally distinct from the nuns, and their destiny was not necessarily to take vows, unless they wanted to, once they reached the appropriate age. Their other option was marriage. The nuns were responsible for the education of the young women entrusted to them, who could be of various social backgrounds, such as orphans, abandoned girls or young noblewomen waiting to get married. A well-documented example can be found in the town of Guastalla, namely in the monastery of San Carlo, which housed an important *educandato* between the sixteenth and seventeenth centuries. In the Episcopal Abbey Archive of Guastalla (*Archivio Episcopale Abbaziale di Guastalla*), an entire documentary fund relating to the entrance of girls to this educational institution is preserved.[95]

These documents explain the aims of the institution, stating that "the said monastery can and is used to keep spinsters," that is, unmarried girls (*zittelle*).[96] The source specifies that the monastery was a "special place for girls to be educated (*educande*), which was comfortable, distinct and separate from the professed nuns and from the young novices."[97] The source specifies that there was "a fixed number of *educande* in accordance with the capacity of the place, and that numbers could not be higher than half of the nuns, without counting the novices and converse."[98] With regard to the requirements for the girls to enter, we read that the aspiring *educanda* had to show "all the necessary requisites" and had to be "accepted by the nuns' chapter and by secret ballot."[99] The main condition was that the girl should be "older than seven years of age and less than twenty-five, and [...] at twenty-five, she must leave immediately."[100] The existential and pedagogical dimension found by a girl when she entered the *educandato* is emphasized by the obligation that she "enter alone, modestly clothed, and observe the law of the cloister, the parlor, like the nuns

---

95   *Archivio Episcopale Abbaziale di Guastalla*, Envelope 32, April 23rd, 1652. This document is also published in Elisa Bertazzoni, *Il monastero di San Carlo in Guastalla e le giovani Gonzaga* (Guastalla: Biblioteca Maldotti, 2008), 194.

96   Original quote: "il detto monastero possa et sia solito tener zittelle." All the quotes come from the above-mentioned source: Envelope 32, April 23rd, 1652.

97   Original quote: "luogo particolare per l'educande, commodo, distinto e separato da quello dove le monache professe et anco le novitie sogliono habitare."

98   Original quote: "un numero fisso d'educande conforme alla capacità del luogo, et che detto numero non possi passar la metà delle monache, non computatevi le novizie et le converse."

99   Original quotes: "tutti i requisiti necessarii"; "accettata dalle monache capitolarmente e per voti segreti."

100   Original quote: "maggiore di sette anni et minore di venticinque, et [...] alli venticinque, debba uscire subito."

themselves" and that "going out once, she cannot, without a new license, be received in that or any other monastery, except in order to become a nun."[101]

The entry into the *educandato*, as mentioned, could not take place before a girl attained seven years of age; however, there were exceptions where girls were admitted as young as three years of age. In most cases, time spent at this type of institution ended with the entry of the girl into the religious order; however, there were also families who couldn't afford proper wedding dowries for their daughters and hoped to assure them a better chance to get married by giving up their parental rights and letting them enter the *educandato*. Most of the girls who entered the boarding school were orphans, clearly shown in the registers of the monastery. Another document from the first half of the seventeenth century mentions the education that was given to the *educande* of the monastery of San Carlo. Some elements reveal an education centered on domestic works; however, there are also traces of richer types of education.

> The *educande* are trained every day in reading and writing [...] and in arithmetic. They also receive lessons of Italian and French grammar, geography, cosmography and Christian doctrine. Sacred history is read and explained on public holidays. In addition to domestic works, manual works are done such as embroidery in white and silk, making lace and bags, and many other works that costume and circumstances present. All this, however, is taught to them according to their age.[102]

We can see that next to embroidery, foreign languages and geography were taught, as well as arithmetic and writing, a type of education that, alongside traditional elements, was intended for the education of housewives yet placed next to avant-garde disciplines, such as cosmography, important in male boarding schools.

Another important issue related to the lives of these girls was that this type of education implied a segregated existence, far from the world. The cloistered life was characterized by a strong limitation of interaction with the outside

---

[101] Original quotes: "entri sola, modestamente vestita, et osservi la legge della clausura, parlatorio, come le monache stesse» and "uscendo una volta, non possi, senza nuova licenza, esser più ricevuta in quello o altro monisterio, eccetto per farvisi monaca."

[102] Original quote: "Sono esercitate le educande giornalmente nel leggere e scrivere [...] e nell'aritmetica. Ricevono inoltre lezione e spiegazione di grammatica italiana e francese, di geografia, di sfera e di dottrina cristiana. La storia sacra viene letta e spiegata ne' giorni festivi. Le opere manuali sono, oltre i lavori proprj del sesso, il ricamo in bianco ed in seta, il far merletti e borse a telajo, e molti altri lavori che il costume e le circostanze presentono. Tutto questo però viene loro insegnato a norma dell'età."

world, reduced to a few letters and visits by family members. The monastery and its *educandato* was a small and closed world, where the relational sphere was limited to its components.

The girls were welcomed into the monastery with a symbolic gesture, usually a kiss. "At the entrance of the *educanda*, the mother prioress and the mother teacher may remain at the door; [...] once the young girl entered and gave the kiss, then all the people must leave from the door."[103] If a girl died by misfortune after entering the monastery, she would be buried there. In the Catalogue of the Dead Religious of the Monastery of San Carlo, there is a list of schoolgirls who died there.[104] We read, for example, of Maria Teresa Bianchi who, after four years and one month of education, died "at fifteen years, ten months and eight days. And she was buried in this interior of our tomb." Another girl "passed to the eternal rest [...], here at the *educanda*, at the age of eleven years." Another interesting example concerns a schoolgirl who died when she was fourteen years old and whose death record informs us that she had entered the boarding school when she was three years old: "Miss Luigia Curti of Casalmaggiore, a schoolgirl, passed to the eternal rest, having come to the monastery at three years old, and of education eleven years old, and of her age when she went to enjoy the Lord fourteen years, three months, five days."[105]

In conclusion, in addition to the detachment of these girls from the world and their families, there is another painful detachment that we should consider, namely the one suffered by the nuns. It is legitimate to believe that the nuns, especially those closest to the girls, such as the mother teacher, suffered greatly from the loss of the girls. These nuns were for the most part young women themselves who perhaps had been denied marriage and children because of a claustration dictated by the tyranny of family or poverty. How can we not think that they must have had a deep affection for the girls under their care, some of whom were very young?[106]

---

103 Original quote: "Nell'entrare delle signore educande, potranno restare sulla porta la Madre Priora e la Madre Maestra; [...] entrata la giovine e dato il bacio, dovranno tutti partire dalla porta."

104 *Biblioteca Maldotti of Gustalla* (Guastalla Maldotti Libarry), Fondo Cani, Envelope 59, *Catalogo delle Religiose defunte* (Catalogue of Dead Religious).

105 Original quote: "passò alli eterni riposi la Sig.a Luigia Curti di Casalmaggiore, educanda, essendo venuta in monastero d'anni tre e di educazione anni undici, e di sua età quando è andata a godere il Signore anni 14, mesi tre, giorni 5."

106 Bertazzoni, *Il monastero di San Carlo in Guastalla e le giovani Gonzaga*, 204.

CHAPTER 5

The End of an Educational Season
The Schools of Religious Orders between Scientific and Political Revolutions (17th–18th cc.)

The early modern age for the schools of the religious congregations ended as it had begun, namely with a great upheaval of European scope. Since the collapse of continental religious cohesion in the first half of the sixteenth century, Napoleonic armies were exporting the values of the French Revolution by the end of the eighteenth century, inflicting a severe blow to religious orders across the continent.[1] The Italian pre-unitarian states followed or adapted to these new policies, sometimes spontaneously, dazzled by the possibility of controlling the important economic resources of the congregations. However, it is necessary to take a step back to understand the overall educational situation in Italy on the eve of the French Revolution.

The great educational effort made by religious teaching orders during the previous period had yielded important results. In the transition from the seventeenth to the eighteenth century the situation between Catholics and Protestants had reached a balance. In a less conflictual atmosphere, the Church of Rome felt strong. Despite the rigor of its official positions regarding seventeenth century scientific debates on Copernicanism and heliocentrism, Catholicism had in part mitigated the degree of its control over scientific research. In this new climate, scientific studies had flourished within teaching congregations. The result was that actual scientific research traditions were created within the religious orders. This evolution, as we have seen, had not been without traumas. During the first half of the seventeenth century, the adherence of some orders to Copernican and heliocentric theories had led to strong conflicts with the Inquisition. The attendance of some Piarist clerics at the school of Galileo Galilei had contributed to bringing the order founded

---

[1] In general, for the last years before the French Revolution and the Napoleonic domination of Italy, see Alain Pillepich, *Napoléon et les Italiens. République Italienne et Royaume d'Italie 1802–1814*, (Paris: Nouveau monde éditions, 2002) in particular chapter 7: *La crise religieuse*, 131–50, where the problem posed by public education is analyzed. On the suppression of the Barnabites, refer to: *I Barnabiti nel IV Centenario della Fondazione*, 259–260; Gentili, *Les Barnabites*, 174–79, and Orazio Maria Premoli, *Storia dei barnabiti dal 1700 al 1825*, (Rome: Società tipografica Aldo Manuzio, 1925), 364–73.

by Calasanz to the brink of suppression. However, these adversities also contributed to the development of the new identity of the congregation of the Pious Schools in the second half of the seventeenth century. In the new cultural climate of the Enlightenment, teaching congregations, especially Piarists, could re-evaluate the Galilean heritage, using it as an element of conjunction with the Newtonianism that was rapidly spreading across Europe. On the eve of the French Revolution, the research and teaching of the religious orders had reached their highest point. In the following section I will outline in general terms the premises and developments of this path.

1 The Scientific Culture: Religious Orders on the Eve of Modernity

Among the most controversial features of the research and teaching of early modern religious congregations is their relationship with the new scientific paradigms. The involvement of the teaching orders in the scientific world was a distinctive element in the pedagogical change of the late early modern period. Among all the scientific fields in which important changes of perspective took place, we find a particular interest in physics, more precisely astronomy and the passage from the Aristotelian Ptolemaic paradigm to Copernican heliocentricity. As is well known, Copernicus himself was a member of a religious order, the Canons Regular of Saint Augustine, proof of the constant commitment of religious orders to astronomical research.[2]

Although it is now well established that after the Council of Trent there was not always a conflict between the Catholic Church and scientific research, most historians of early modern science still feel the need to clarify this at the beginning of their books. It is evident that in the collective perception, the dark legend of an uncompromising opposition of the Catholic world to any kind of technical-scientific innovation during the apogee of the Counter-Reformation persists very strongly. The dramatic experiences of key figures such as Tommaso Campanella, Giordano Bruno and Galileo Galilei still have such an important role in determining this general perception that it is possible to forget how

---

2 See Francesco Agnoli, Andrea Bartelloni, *Da Copernico padre dell'Eliocentrismo a Lemaître padre del Big Bang* (Torino: La Fontana di Siloe, 2018), 23–29. The bibliography on Copernicus is now very vast; here I refer to André Goddu, *Copernicus and the Aristotelian Tradition* (Leiden: Brill, 2010); Kenneth Howell, *God's two books: Copernican cosmology and biblical interpretation in early modern science* (Notre Dame: University of Notre Dame Press, 2002); Thomas Kuhn, *The Copernican Revolution. Planetary Astronomy in the Development of Western Thought* (Cambridge: Harvard University Press, 1957).

much Protestant and anti-Catholic propaganda contributed to the legend.[3] In addition, academic literature often forgets that the first and hardest attacks on Copernicus came from the Protestant world, at least from a theological point of view. Luther, for example, called Copernicus a "fool" who was eager to upset the whole of astronomy. Even the more moderate Protestant theologian Philip Melanchthon saw in the Copernican system a set of intellectual bizarreness and sacrilegious doubt cast on the "inerrancy" of the Holy Scriptures. These facts were rightly opposed to the widespread belief that the Catholic Church had a special hostility towards science; on the contrary, for more than seventy years it had had no difficulty accepting the Copernican system, even if only as a mathematical hypothesis. The commission of experts established by Pope Gregory XIII to reform the calendar believed that Copernicus' calculations established the exact length of the calendar year, but Protestant countries rejected the Gregorian calendar, which was decreed by the papal bull of February 24, 1582 and effected on October 15 with the elimination of ten days from October 5 to 14. Only in 1700 did Protestant Germany admit to the correctness of the manner in which the Catholic calendar passed directly from February 18 to March 1; England followed even later, in 1752.

Nonetheless, Galileo Galilei seems to evoke a particularly strong fascination in historians. His case became almost paradigmatic of a conflict between new forms of knowledge and obscurantist forces. The changed attitude of the Catholic Church was clearly revealed in 1615, when the Roman court of the Inquisition had to consider for the first time a complaint against Copernicus and his followers, among whom Galilei was expressly mentioned. The decree of March 1616 judged the thesis that placed the motionless sun at the center of the universe as philosophically "foolish and absurd" and "formally heretical."[4] An equally foolish and erroneous theory (at least from the theological point of view) was the thesis that attributed movements to the earth around the sun. Copernicus' work was momentarily forbidden until it was corrected. An openly Copernican book was condemned as contrary to Sacred Scripture. The

---

3 See Ronald Numbers, *Galileo goes to jail and other myths about science and religion* (Cambridge: Harvard University Press, 2009); Richard Orson, *Science and Religion, 1450–1900: from Copernicus to Darwin* (Westport: Greenwood Press, 2004); David Lindberg; Ronald Numbers, *When science and Christianity meet* (Chicago: University of Chicago Press, 2003); John Hedley Brooke, *Science and religion. Some historical perspectives* (Cambridge: Cambridge University Press, 1991).

4 The quotation is reported in Michael Sharrat, *Galileo: Decisive Innovator* (Cambridge: Cambridge University Press, 1994), 127–31; and Maurice A. Finocchiaro, *Defending Copernicus and Galileo: Critical Reasoning in the two Affairs* (New York: Springer, 2010), 74.

sentence did not mention Galileo and his works; however, he was expressly urged not to defend or profess Copernicus' theses.

However, a trial against Galileo did occur. In 1623, Cardinal Maffeo Barberini was elected pope with the name Urban VIII. In the past, the new pope had been a friend of Galilei, and received him in Rome in 1624. The Tuscan astronomer was given the impression that the sentence of 1616 could be changed. Galilei therefore set out to write the *Dialogo sopra i due massimi sistemi del mondo* ('Dialogue on the two greatest systems in the world'), going beyond a merely hypothetical and geometric repetition of the heliocentric system. Nevertheless, the book was able to have the approval of ecclesiastical censorship and appear in February 1632. Eight months later Galilei was summoned before the Inquisition, and from April to June of 1633 he had to face a formal trial. The Tuscan scientist was confronted with long interrogations and the threat of torture, and eventually retracted his heliocentric theses.

Galilei accepted the sentence, resulting in perpetual confinement in his villa in Arcetri. The condemnation of heliocentrism, however, in no way led to a systematic persecution of scientists in the countries subject to the Inquisition. Despite the outcome of the Galileo trial, scientists and astronomers did not openly deal with questions of cosmology and generally became more cautious in making their convictions public. The accumulated evidence against the Ptolemaic system was about to appear overwhelmingly in Protestant countries. The condemnations of 1616 and 1633 seemed, on the part of the Catholic Church, a confirmation of the official scientific character attributed to Aristotelianism.[5] Lutheran and Calvinist traditions had proved rather reluctant to engage with Aristotle's philosophy and had admitted that the Bible had to be sometimes read allegorically. In order to portray a more complex picture of the relationship between Galileo and the Catholic world, we should consider that Galileo often worked closely with members of religious orders. During his retreat in Arcetri, his assistants were fathers of the Pious Schools, mathematicians engaged in technological and scientific research.

1.1 *Famiano Michelini and the Galilean Piarists*

The Piarist's relation with science is certainly an interesting case study to better understand some of the dynamics that caused scientific research to be included amongst the religious orders' main activities. In chapter four, rivalries between religious orders concerning the educational market were discussed.

---

5 Charles Bernard Schmitt, *The Aristotelian Tradition and Renaissance Universities* (London: Aldershot-Brookfield, 1998).

We have seen the competitive dynamic between Jesuits and Piarists in a limited geopolitical context, the small Italian Duchy of Modena and Reggio Emilia, but the implications can be extended. One historiographic trend of thought believes this competition to have been the cause, or at least the premise, of the reduction of the order of the Pious Schools to a simple congregation without vows, which took place in February 1646 under the pontificate of Innocent x. As mentioned earlier, the process involved the removal of all internal hierarchies and the submission of the fathers to the bishops of each diocese, as well as the option, for those who requested it, to enter other orders and the impossibility of new members to be admitted to the novitiate without papal approval; in short, extinction.[6]

The reason why this action against the Piarists was misattributed to the Society of Jesus lies in the fact that this sentence resulted from an investigation on the internal state of the order entrusted to a Jesuit, namely Silvestro Pietrasanta. The investigation had begun a few years earlier in 1641, when the Piarist Mario Sozzi arrived in the Florentine Pious Schools. Sozzi, after fighting with some of his fellow clerics, decided to retaliate, denouncing some of them to the Holy Office for their proximity to Galileo Galilei. These colleagues were Famiano Michelini, Ambrogio Ambrosi, Clemente Settimi, Angelo Morelli and Carlo Conti, mathematicians who were close to Galileo Galilei. Sozzi denounced them for teaching heresies, including heliocentrism, atomism and the denial of God's omnipotence. Although the accusation of heresy linked to scientific research soon gave way to a simple but no less delicate investigation into the internal policies of the order (an investigation that lasted, with ups and downs, for five years), the starting point for the crisis remains interesting. In Pietrasanta's reports, in fact, we do not find the will to eradicate the Pious Schools. Of course, during the investigation, critical points and problems requiring correction were highlighted, but nothing that couldn't be dealt with. It is important to note, though, that Sozzi's accusation occurred only eight years after Galileo's conviction in 1633, when the controversy over his sentence was still alive and burning.

Among the protagonists in this story was the mathematician Famiano Michelini. He is an example of the entanglement of the tensions caused by the intersection of science, education, and heresy. Michelini's biography also shows how dense the network of scientists belonging to the religious orders of

---

6 Mario Spinelli, *Giuseppe Calasanzio: il pioniere della scuola popolare* (Rome: Città Nuova, 2001), 201–03; Antonio Lezáun, *Storia delle Scuole Pie*, (Madrid: Instituto Calasanz de Ciencias de la Educación, 2011), 26–27.

the early modern age was.[7] Famiano was born in Rome in 1604 to parents of humble conditions. His first teacher was Ventura Sarafellini, a collaborator of Calasanz, who encouraged him to study mathematics. In 1627, he was sent to Genoa, where he attended the lessons of Antonio Santini, a Somascan mathematician, and met the Jesuit mathematician Giovanni Battista Baliani, who would later present him to Galileo Galilei. In 1629, he was sent to teach mathematics in the Pious Schools opened in Florence at the behest of the Grand Duke of Tuscany, Ferdinando II de' Medici. In 1635, he became a mathematics teacher at the Medici court. These were the very years of Michelini's Galilean attendance; however, his scientific network was not limited to the home of the famous scientist. In 1634, he was sent twice to Rome on behalf of the Order. It was an opportunity for Michelini to expand his scientific connections. There he met the prominent mathematician and Benedictine monk Benedetto Castelli, another friend of Galilei, and his guests, namely the young Giovanni Alfonso Borelli, perhaps Evangelista Torricelli, and certainly Raffaello Magiotti.[8] These are just a few examples of members of Michelini's scientific network. The type of research verging on heresy of such characters is additional proof of Michelini's own orientation. During the Florentine years, he was probably teaching new scientific theories in his school of mathematics. Evidence of this is given by Sozzi's own complaint to the Holy Office in 1641. He wrote about Michelini and his companions that

> all of them believe that there is no science truer and more certain than the one Galileo teaches following the mathematical way, calling it the new philosophy and the real way to do natural philosophy. The above mentioned, and Fathers Francesco Clemente and Ambrogio in particular, have often said that this was the true way to know God. And time and again Father Clemente tried to convince me to take up the study of their theories. They said that this philosophy had been proved and that it was the true way to convert the heretics and to know God.[9]

---

7   On Famiano Michelini's life and scientific network, see Federica Favino, *Famiano Michelini*, Dizionario Biografico degli Italiani, vol. 74 (2010); Id., "Scienza ed erudizione nei collegi degli ordini religiosi a Roma tra Sei e Settecento," *Cheiron*, 43–44 (2006), 331–70.
8   Favino, *Famiano Michelini*.
9   Original quote: "Tutti li sopradetti tengono che non ci sia né più vera, né più certa scienza di questa del Galileo che insegna per via di mattematica, chiamandola nova filosofia, e vero modo di filosofare; e più volte hanno detto i sopradetti e particolarmente il Padre Francesco Clemente et Ambrogio che questo è il vero modo di conoscere Dio, e più volte mi ha essortato il Padre Clemente a darmi a questo studio hanno detto che questa filosofia è provata, che questo è il vero modo di convertire gli heretici e conoscere Dio." In Leodegario Picanyol,

Through this lens, it is easier to understand how the teaching of certain theories within schools could influence religious teaching orders, particularly with respect to the Roman Inquisition. Famiano Michelini was not tried for spreading Protestant doctrines in his school; nonetheless, some traits of his teaching can be compared to those of the humanist teachers who had been persecuted by the Inquisition for adhering to Protestantism during the sixteenth century. Michelini, indeed, was active in urban and densely populated environments. He attended and had access to intellectual groups from high social levels. He taught dangerous theories in his school and shaped his students' minds with such theories. Eventually, he was also investigated by the Holy Office. The only difference between him and sixteenth-century schoolteachers was the content of the forbidden teaching. Michelini shifted from religious to scientific content with huge doctrinal implications, doubtless a man of his time. His Treaty on the Direction of Rivers (*Trattatto sulla direzione de' fiumi*), an important work on the canalization of running waters, shows us his engagement in the resolution of practical problems concerning the development of the economy through the changing of rural structures. Economics, politics, philosophy, science, and religion thus merged in the profile of a teacher who perfectly embodied the tensions and characteristics of an era and its educational culture. With Famiano Michelini, we can say that we passed from the age of doctrinal heresies to the age of scientific heresies.

To dwell briefly on Michelini's experience is useful to understand an important aspect of the Piarists' gradual opening towards the major sciences, which occurred between the end of the seventeenth and the beginning of the eighteenth century. Michelini's case, in fact, was more of an exception than the rule since mathematical teaching in the early days of the Pious Schools was more directed towards simple abacus use and practical questions. Thanks to the Galilean premise of the Tuscan pious school, a critical reception and the subsequent triumph over Descartes made it possible to welcome Newtonian thought in connection to Galileo.[10] The schools of the religious orders were

---

Le Scuole Pie e Galileo Galilei (Rome: Ed. PP. Scolopi di S. Pantaleo, 1942), 141–43. The English translation reported here was made by V. R. Remmert and can be found in Volker R. Remmert, "Galileo, God and Mathematics," in *Mathematics and the Divine: A Historical Study*, ed. Teun Koetsier and Luc Bergmans, 347–60, (Amsterdam: Elsevier, 2005), 357.

10   Sangalli, *Le smanie per l'educazione*, 67. Refer also to Alessandra Ferraresi, "La fisica sperimentale fra università e ginnasi nella Lombardia austriaca," in *Dalla filosofia naturale alla fisica. Discipline e didattica in Italia all'epoca di Volta*, ed. Alessandra Ferraresi and Franco Giudice, *Studi Settecenteschi*, 18 (1998): 279–315; Gabriele Baroncini, "L'insegnamento della filosofia naturale nei collegi italiani dei gesuiti (1610–1670): un esempio di nuovo aristotelismo," in *La Ratio Studiorum. Modelli culturali e pratiche educative dei Gesuiti in Italia tra Cinque e Seicento*, ed. Gian Paolo Brizzi (Roma: Bulzoni, 1981), 163–215. See also: Baldini,

fundamental to the development of mathematical, scientific, and astronomical research in the seventeenth and eighteenth centuries, despite the fact that they could not openly teach heliocentrism as a physical reality. In this sense, the story of the Piarists is particularly important. From the beginning of the eighteenth century, their colleges influenced individuals well versed in the sciences, such as Paolino Chelucci (1681–1754) and Odoardo Corsini (1651–1750), and it is no coincidence that they later became generals of the order.

As Maurizio Sangalli has shown, an interesting example of the depth reached by Newtonian theories within the Piarist order is provided by a short but significant correspondence between Father Gaetano Davini of the Pious School of Murano and his pupil, Marquis Girolamo Gravisi, between 1740 and 1741.[11] Within this brief but important correspondence we find the cultural interests and deep Piarist involvement that were at the forefront of the eighteenth century's scientific research. Those years, in fact, represent an important turning point in Italian scientific culture. In November 1740, Giovanni Poleni inaugurated his *Teatro di filosofia sperimentale* (Theater of Experimental Philosophy) in Padua, following the example of other "theaters" founded in Paris by Jean Antoine Nollet and in Leiden by Willem Gravesande and Pieter Van Musschenbroek.[12] Father Davini wrote to Gravisi that he was extremely interested in Poleni's experimental activity, remarkably interesting since Poleni was at that time the most representative heir of Galileo's experimental activity in Padua. Poleni's scientific research, indeed, was aimed at the

---

Saggi sulla cultura della Compagnia di Gesù, secoli XVI-XVIII (Padova: Cleup, 2000), in particular the chapters: "L'evoluzione della 'fisica dei gesuiti in Italia, 1550–1700: un approccio strutturale," 239–79; "Teoria boscoviana, newtonismo, eliocentrismo: dibattiti nel Collegio Romano e nella Congregazione dell'Indice a metà Settecento," 281–347. In addition: Id., *Legem impone subactis. Studi su filosofia e scienza dei gesuiti in Italia 1540–1632* (Rome: Bulzoni, 1992); and Id. "La scuola galileiana," in *Scienza e tecnica nella cultura e nella società dal Rinascimento a oggi*, ed. Gianni Micheli, in *Storia d'Italia, Annali*, 3, (Torino: Einaudi, 1980), 381–463.

11 As reported in Maurizio Sangalli, *Le smanie*, 69, these letters are kept at the *Pokrajinski Arhiv Koper* (Koper Provincial Archives) and at *Družinski Arhiv Gravisi* (Gravisi Family Archives), envelope 40.

12 Sangalli, *Le smanie per l'educazione*, 70. On Poleni's activity, see Ivano Dal Prete, *Scienze e società nel Settecento veneto. Il caso veronese 1680–1796* (Milan: FrancoAngeli, 2008), 277–301; and Maria Pancino, "La didattica di Giovanni Poleni," in *Il teatro di filosofia sperimentale di Giovanni Poleni*, ed. Maria Pancino and Gian Antonio Salandin (Trieste: Lint, 1986), XV-XXII.

implementation of a systematic use of the Galilean-Newtonian experimental method, in an open break from Aristotelianism.[13]

This example shows two elements that need to be highlighted. The first is that peripheral areas were not necessarily backward in relation to the most recent technical and theoretical scientific acquisitions of the European Enlightenment, when compared to the great Roman colleges of religious orders. The second is the evidence of how the Galilean legacy became a true element of identity for the Piarist order, not only in Florence but throughout the Italian Peninsula. Galileo was not only a methodological example for the Piarists of the Pious Schools, but also for other congregations, within which the teaching of heliocentric theories was paid for at a high price.

1.2 Baranzano Redento

The Piarist order was not the only congregation committed to scientific research and to its teaching in schools; Barnabite fathers were also active in this field. One of the most representative Barnabites engaged in research and scientific teaching was Redento Baranzano (1590–1622). He was born in 1590 in Serravalle Sesia in the Italian northwest pre-alpine Piedmont region, not far from Savoy and Switzerland.[14] Not long before Baranzano's birth, this region had received particular attention from religious authorities because of its exposure to the Protestant world. We recall the 1560s' missions of Antonio Possevino with special regard to schoolteachers. For centuries, the Piedmont area has been filled with tension, but it was also a place of ferment and rapid transformation, a frontier subject to cultural contamination at the crossroads of French, Italian and Occitan traditions. Baranzano Redento completed his studies in this environment in the cities of Vercelli, Novara, and Milan, eventually joining the Barnabites in 1609. He later studied philosophy and theology and in 1615 he was sent by the Barnabite general Antonio Mazenta to teach philosophy in the college of Annecy in Savoy, entrusted in 1614 by Charles Emmanuel I to the Regular Clerics of Saint Paul. During this period, Baranzano was also engaged in a vast activity of preaching against Calvinism, using all the weapons of his dialectical ability and his philosophical expertise in Thonon, Geneva and in Béarn, where his congregation had opened a mission at the behest of the French king Henry IV.[15]

---

13 Vincenzo Ferrone, *Scienza natura e religione: mondo newtoniano e cultura italiana nel primo Settecento* (Naples: Jovene, 1982), in particular chapter 4, "Newton e le tradizioni scientifiche venete," 235–313.
14 On Baranzano Redento's life, see Mario Tronti, "Baranzano Redento," *Dizionario Biografico degli Italiani*, vol. 5, (1963).
15 Tronti, *Baranzano Redento*.

It was during these years that he held a series of scientific lectures on the system of planets in the school of Annecy. These lessons led to the publication of the *Uranoscopia seu de Caelo*, which appeared in Geneva in 1617 without the author's consent. The work is composed of a preface in ten parts and two main sections, in which Baranzano explains the heliocentric structure of the universe. This work aroused bitter controversy as it apparently supported the Copernican system, and was withdrawn in 1618 when the heliocentric paradigm was condemned by Pope Paul V. He was then forced to retract it, which he did by writing *Nova de motu terrae copernicaeo iuxta Summi Pontificis mentem disputatio*. The case of Baranzano is exemplary of the relationship between scientific progress and education. An important aspect of the *Uranoscopia*, as Michela Malpangotto points out, is that it was written precisely to give his students a modern and complete vision of the progress of research in science, astronomy in particular.[16] This choice was far from trivial. After all, why teach students such theories? Were they just a mathematical model or did they represent the true reality of the cosmos? As in the case of Michelini, and perhaps even more clearly his students, Baranzano's teachings had an impact. Two students, in fact, Giovanni Battista Muratori and Ludovic des Hayes, went on to edit and publish the *Uranoscopia* in Geneva, without his consent. In their preface of the publication, they stated their commitment to saving the abundance of information in their teacher's work.[17] We have no decisive evidence that Baranzano was a firm supporter of heliocentrism, but he was an objective descriptor for his students of the most recent state of scientific research.[18]

Only in 1757, under the pontificate of Benedict XIV, would the Barnabites obtain justice. In that year, Father Pietro Lazzari presented a report to the Congregation of the Index to abolish the decree of Paul V, obtaining satisfaction, and in 1820 the Holy Office approved the heliocentric theory. This example is useful because it highlights how Barnabite scientific research and teaching

---

16   Michela Malpangotto, "Discussions coperniciennes au début du XVIII siècle: Le système du monde du P. Redento Baranzano enseignant en Savoie," *Archives internationales d'Histoire des sciences*, 60/2 (2010): 369–422.
17   Malpangotto, *Discussions*, 374–75.
18   In this regard, however, as Michela Malpangotto argues, there are doubts. From some statements made by Muratori and des Hayes in the preface to the *Uranoscopia*, in fact, it is possible that Baranzano simply didn't want to let his opinions be revealed in order to provide an unconditioned and objective view of the state of research or perhaps he just wanted to protect himself from the risk of suspicion of heresy. At the time of the condemnation to abjure, in fact, he would have declared himself mortified to have spread heliocentric theories, but the doubt about his personal beliefs exists. See Malpangotto, *Discussions*, 394.

was at the forefront of its time. Baranzano's heritage was instrumental in shaping a tradition of research inside of the order. During the eighteenth century, another Barnabite made prominent headway in the astronomical field, Paolo Frisi (1728–1784).[19] He entered the Barnabites in 1743 and, at the age of twenty-one, wrote a "dissertation on the figure of the earth" that earned him great popularity in the Enlightenment scientific circles. Even in the case of Frisi, the legacy of the memory of Galileo and Baranzano was instrumental in receiving and spreading Newton's theories in Italy.

From these few but significant examples we can draw two important conclusions. The first is the importance of some dramatic experiences in certain fields of knowledge in determining (to a certain extent) the scientific openness of religious orders in the transition from the world of the militant Counter-reformation to the world of the Enlightenment. The second conclusion concerns the entry of the teaching religious orders into the new cultural climate of the eighteenth century. Religious congregations entered as protagonists, with a spirit of intellectual curiosity towards the new technical and scientific achievements. Nevertheless, during the eighteenth century, religious teaching orders were subject to strong attacks and radical reforms by the modern Enlightened European states. What was the reason for this?

2   School Reforms in the Age of Enlightenment

The absolute monarchies of the second half of the eighteenth century had triggered a season of economic and administrative reforms that had not forgotten the world of education. This interest in the educational sphere emerged for several reasons. First, there was the will to snatch the monopoly of education from the church and put it under the control of the state, which was becoming more and more centralized. Emperors, kings, and princes made the school a political instrument, as they had between the sixteenth and seventeenth centuries to fight against the Protestant danger, at least on the Catholic side. Another aim in taking over the reins of education was the desire to form a small bourgeoisie within the school to faithfully serve the enlightened authority of the state and the monarchy.[20]

---

19   Gennaro Barbarisi, ed., *Ideologia e scienza nell'opera di Paolo Frisi, 172–81784* (Milan: FrancoAngeli, 1987), 129–47.
20   In general, see Maurizio Piseri, *La scuola primaria nel Regno Italico, 1796–1814* (Milan: FrancoAngeli, 2017), 21–60; and Ernesto Lama, *Il pensiero pedagogico dell'Illuminismo* (Florence: Giuntine-Sansoni, 1958). For some local examples, see Maurizio Piseri,

2.1 The European Situation

The first European state to begin these reforms was the Prussia of Frederick William I in 1716. The monarch, under the influence of a rapidly growing religious movement, Pietism, had reorganized the school system. He made the opening of elementary schools mandatory and established normal schools for the preparation of teachers. The son of Frederick William, Frederick II the Great, issued the General School Regulations in 1763 and "The General School Regulations for Roman Catholics in Silesia and in the county of Glatz" in 1765. The abbot of Sagan, Ignatius Felbiger, who wrote the Prussian scholastic Ordinance of 1765, was then called by Empress Maria Theresa of Habsburg in Austria, where he composed a "General scholastic Ordinance for normal, main and elementary German schools in all imperial and royal provinces" in 1774. This regulation was not fully applied except in the Sovereign Edict of 1783 and the Regulations of 1805. The aim of this legislation was to achieve the highest degree of uniformity in the school system in all the provinces of the Empire, including the Italian ones.

The education system was thus divided into four parts, namely rural schools, main primary schools, normal schools, and royal schools. Rural schools (*Trivialschulen*) or 'minor elementary,' were to be opened in every village and wherever parish registers existed. Three subjects were taught: the first was religion, the second was reading and writing, and the third was arithmetic. The duration could vary from one to two years. Main primary schools (*Hauptschulen*) were to be opened in each district, even within the cloisters of the Orders of Regular Clerics, at their expense. Their programs lasted four years during which Latin, drawing, domestic science, agriculture, geography, and history were taught. At least one normal school (*Normalschule*) was to be opened in each province for the training of teachers of the aforementioned schools. Finally, royal schools (*Realschulen*) corresponded to technical schools, and were used to train state employees in commerce and economics.[21]

We dwelt on Austrian school reforms because, as we shall see, they were the ones that most influenced the history of the religious teacher congregations in Italy. While in England primary and secondary education was still largely

---

L'alfabeto delle riforme. Scuola e alfabetismo nel basso cremonese da Maria Teresa all'Unità (Milan: Vita & Pensiero, 2002).

[21] On the Prussian and Austrian early modern school system, refer to Van Horn Melton, James. *Absolutism and the eighteenth-century origins of compulsory schooling in Prussia and Austria* (New York: Cambridge University Press, 1988). See also Karl Heinz Gruber, "Higher Education and the State in Austria: An Historical and Institutional Approach," *European Journal of Education*, 17/3, (1982): 259–70.

in the hands of confessional churches, in Russia Tsarina Catherine II was the first sovereign to take an initiative in the field of education. She looked primarily to Austria, which at that time was the beacon of school reform in Europe. Emperor Joseph II of Habsburg sent qualified personnel to Russia to help the imperial administration promulgate a "Statute of Popular Schools" in 1786. This reform provided for the opening of a state primary school and a high school in each capital of the sixteen provinces. These schools were free of charge for young people of all social backgrounds and teachers were paid by the state. Textbooks were also provided free of charge. In ten years, the schools grew slowly. By 1796, the number of active teachers had risen from 136 to 744 and the number of schools from 40 to 316.[22]

In France, prior to the Revolution, not much had been achieved in terms of school reforms. Despite this, there was no lack of projects, which only after 1789 found fertile ground.[23] Two intellectuals embodied this trend, namely the Breton magistrate Louis René de Caradeuc de La Chalotais (1701–1785) and Barthélemy-Gabriel Rolland d'Erceville (1734–1794), authors of the *Essai d'éducation nationale* in 1763, and the *Plan d'éducation* in 1784, respectively. These profiles are of particular interest to us because they defined the orientations of school policies in revolutionary France and consequently in the countries where its principles were exported. La Chalotais and d'Erceville were strongly anticlerical and particularly opposed to the Jesuits. They claimed the principle of the centrality of the state in popular education, and wanted to replace the confessional school system forged in the sixteenth century with a secular and national one. La Chatolais had contributed decisively in 1764 to the expulsion of the Jesuits from France. In that year, he published the *Comptes Rendus des Constitutions des Jésuites*, in which he not only denounced the evils deriving from the presence of these "ultramontane hypocrites" in the kingdom of France, but also criticized the work of all religious orders to which education had been entrusted throughout history, from the mendicant orders, passing

---

22   On England's educational history, see Deborah Reed-Danahay, *Education and Identity in Rural France. The Politics of Schooling* (Cambridge: Cambridge University Press, 1996); John Lawson and Harold Silver, *A Social History of Education in England* (New York: Routledge, 1973, 2007). On Russian educational history, see Ben Eklof, ed., School and Society in Tsarist and Soviet Russia. Selected Papers from the Fourth World Congress for Soviet and East European Studies (New York: St. Martin's Press, 1993); Id., *Russian Peasant Schools. Officialdom, Village Culture, and Popular Pedagogy 1861–1914* (Berkeley, Los Angeles, London: University of California Press, 1990), 19–49.

23   For France's educational history, see *Deborah Reed-Danahay, Education and Identity in Rural France. The Politics of Schooling* (Cambridge: Cambridge University Press, 1996).

through Barnabites, Somascans and Piarists, up to the Lasallian Brothers and the French Fathers of the Oratory.[24]

From a didactic point of view, La Chalotais claimed an educational culture more suited to the new national needs aimed at action, civil and social industriousness. He wanted a school system at the service of a centralized state, not based on moral and religious edification. He supported the teaching of the national language, French, at the expense of Latin, which was reduced to a formal study. Other important subjects in the new school system were technical drawing, history, geography, physics, mathematics, and physical education. In this context, the militaristic principles were characteristic not only of Napoleonic France but of the whole of nineteenth century Europe, which was ready to start its colonial and imperialist conquest for world domination.

La Chalotais' thought was not limited to France, but soon spread south of the Alps. In Italy, as we shall see, other intellectuals followed the example of this French magistrate. With respect to Europe, where were the Italian pre-unitarian states in their process of reforming educational institutions and, above all, how did they deal with the religious orders that for almost three centuries had been the main promoters and guardians of schooling and education in Italy?

2.2 *The Situation in Italy: The Italian States and the Religious Orders*

During the eighteenth century, as we have seen, the schools of the religious orders enjoyed good health. Despite the suppression of the Society in 1773, the Jesuits, during the Age of Enlightenment, produced some of their greatest intellectuals. The founding process of new colleges slowed, but did not stop.[25] State administrations were not necessarily opposed to the educational activity of the teaching congregations. The schools of the religious orders, in fact, did an important job of subsidiarity that relieved the state coffers of this expenditure. As we have seen, moreover, the education provided in the schools and colleges of the religious orders was not necessarily reduced to clerical instruction but was able to integrate the most recent acquisitions of European scientific culture, in particular Newtonianism, with the rules of study elaborated by each congregation during two centuries of history.

---

24   Louis René Caradeuc de La Chalotais, *Essai d'éducation nationale ou plan d'études pour la jeunesse* (Geneva: chez Philibert, 1763) ; Id., *Comptes Rendus des Constitutions des Jésuites* (Paris: Ponthieu Librairie, 1826), 11.
25   Sabina Pavone, "I Gesuiti in Italia 1548–1773," in *Atlante Storico della Letteratura Italiana*, ed. Sergio Luzzatto, Gabriele Pedullà, Erminia Irace (Torino: Einaudi, 2011), 359–73.

Even in Italy, voices of intellectuals and politicians spoke out in favor of a national and secular centralization of public education. In the middle of the eighteenth century, an anonymous Venetian reformer compared "the reform of public studies to the reform of the army," while in Florence, another school reformer whose name has not been handed down, drew up "a plan for the education of this noble youth," which had to be "convenient to a republican citizen."[26] In Italy, perhaps more so than in the rest Europe, the problem of education concerned the need to give new impulse to a sluggish political class. In this respect, religious orders, from the educational point of view, were not without responsibility. It was necessary to get the nobles on the move again to make them officials for public service. In 1780 Gaetano Filangieri (1753–1788) complained about the ignorance of the "populace," hoping for school reform led by the state.[27] In the Kingdom of Naples by 1767, the year of the Neapolitan expulsion of the Jesuits, the minister Bernardo Tanucci (1698–1783) entrusted Antonio Genovesi (1713–1769) with a reorganization of the school system. Genovesi produced a "School Plan" (*Piano delle Scuole*), but it was not implemented because of Minister Tanucci's fall into disgrace.

In the Kingdom of Naples, however, schools for women, "*Conservatori,*" experienced a better fate. These institutions were established in 1768 by King Ferdinand IV and were meant for the professional education of orphan girls. In 1779, the "*Educandato Carolino*" was founded in Palermo. This *educandato*, with the same name as the one seen in the previous chapter, was partially different; it was a public boarding school to educate impoverished noble girls in religion but also in Latin, French, history, geography, music and the arts of embroidery, sewing and knitting. The *Educandato Carolino* maintained a type of education which resembled the one seen earlier in the nuns' monastery, but this time was completely secular. Similar institutions began to be quite common in eighteenth century Italy and Europe. These were the first completely lay examples of schools for women inspired by the Ursulines, the Venerini and Filippini Pious Schools, and the colleges were based on the model of the one founded in Milan by Ludovica Torelli.

---

26 Venice State Archives, *Consultori in jure 165. Nuovo piano di studi per l'università di Padova*. Both sources are reported in Franco Venturi, *Settecento Riformatore*, Vol. II, *La chiesa e la repubblica dentro i loro limiti, 1758–1774* (Torino: Einaudi, 1976), 153.

27 For an overview of the Italian Enlightenment, see Franco Venturi, *Settecento Riformatore*, Vol. I, *Da Muratori a Beccaria* and Vol. III, *La prima crisi dell'Antico Regime* (Torino: Einaudi, 1969–1979).

At the same time, in Peter Leopold's Tuscany, similar schools were created exclusively for women.[28] A good number of monasteries were converted into schools for girls, and in 1785 a *motu proprio* of the grand duke formally established the "Conservatories for the education of spinsters from their earliest age." In Tuscany, a first general reorganization of the scholastic system took place thanks to the bishop of Prato and Pistoia Scipione de' Ricci (1741–1810), but it was with the suppression of the Jesuits in 1773 that Peter Leopold was able to centralize all the school policies in his own hands. The anti-Jesuit controversy had found fertile ground in Florence. The aforementioned anonymous Florentine reformer, for example, had stated in his plan (very similar to La Chalotais') that the endless rules with which Latin was taught constituted "very serious damage" in "all the schools of Italy." Attention had to be shifted to contemporary languages such as French and English, in addition to Italian. It was in this cultural and political climate that Peter Leopold abolished some of the existing religious private institutes, entrusting all the remaining schools only to Piarists, Barnabites, and Vallombrosians. In addition, the Grand Duke standardized the study programs, establishing a system of competition for the recruitment of teaching staff.

Even in the small Duchy of Parma, Piacenza and Guastalla, radical reforms were made in the field of education. The small size of this state made it easier to implement such policies. The duchy was ruled by the Bourbons, and because of its governability it was a good experimental laboratory and a showcase for policies to be applied in bigger Bourbon monarchies, namely France and Spain. In Parma, under the governments of the ministers Guillaume Du Tillot (1711–1774) and Paolo Maria Paciaudi (1710–1785), the latter belonging to the Theatine order, a "Magistrate of the Reformer to Studies" (*Magistrato dei riformatori degli studi*) was established after the expulsion of the Jesuits in 1768 and a "Constitution for royal studies" (*Costituzione per i regi studi*) was drafted. The expulsion of the Jesuits in Parma was particularly traumatic. As Ugo Baldini wrote, the Jesuit presence in Parma had reached "a degree of penetration into the nervous folds of society that had few analogues in other areas not only

---

28   Peter Leopold was the Grand Duke of Tuscany from 1765 to 1790. He later became the Emperor of the Holy Roman Empire and King of Hungary and Bohemia from 1790 to 1792. He was the son of Emperor Francis I and his wife Maria Theresa of Austria, and the brother of Marie Antoinette, queen of France, and Marie Caroline, queen of Naples. Leopold, who succeeded his brother Joseph II, was a moderate proponent of enlightened absolutism and advocate of the Leopoldine Code, a law that led the Grand Duchy of Tuscany to be the first state in history to formally abolish the death penalty. On Peter Leopold's educational thought, refer to Luciana Bellatalla, *Pietro Leopoldo di Toscana granduca-educatore: teoria e pratica di un despota illuminato* (Lucca: Editore Pacini Fazzi, 1984).

of Italy, but of Europe."[29] The Jesuits dominated education in the Duchy of Parma, Piacenza, and Guastalla until they were expelled in 1768.[30] After 1768, private teaching was prohibited, seminarists were required to attend public institutions, the use of texts unapproved by the civil authorities was forbidden and the teaching of doctrines that violated the authority of the prince was prevented. There were also initiatives by the local aristocracy for the creation of original pedagogical experiences. One of these was the "House of Education and Industry" (*Casa di educazione e di industria*), opened in 1801 by Count Stefano Sanvitale in Fontanellato, an ancient fief of his family, for the professional training of young orphans.[31]

Similar to the Duchy of Parma and Piacenza, although less traumatic, was the situation in the nearby Duchy of Modena and Reggio Emilia. During the government of Ercole III (1727–1803), the Este monarchy, like the other Italian ruling houses, had undertaken a policy of state reform. Measures had also been taken with respect to the religious congregations to rationalize their activities and assets in the interests of the state, although sometimes with contradictory results.[32] Measures were taken concerning the *mortmain* and real estate of religious orders. As far as school policies were concerned, there was no fervor, although initiatives were not lacking. On the eve of the Jesuit suppression, the members of the Society, together with the Piarists, were the main teaching congregation within the dukedom. With the brief *Dominus ac Redentor* of 21 July 1773, however, which suppressed the Jesuits, the lieutenant of the Duke of Modena took possession of their properties within the small State. The colleges of Modena and Reggio were dissolved in 1774. The novices returned to their families and some fathers remained to teach in public schools or as private tutors. All the assets of the ex-Jesuit colleges of Modena, Carpi, Reggio and Novellara were destined to finance the new university of Modena. The college of Mirandola was taken over by the Piarists. For the management of these

---

29 Ugo Baldini, "I gesuiti nella cultura del ducato," in *Un Borbone tra Parma e l'Europa. Don Ferdinando e il suo tempo, 1751–1802*, ed. Alba Mora (Reggio Emilia: Diabasis, 2005), 98–135.

30 On the Jesuit arrival in the Duchy of Parma, see Casalini, "Building a Duchy to the Greater Glory of God. The Jesuits and the Farnesian Educational Policy in Parma (1539–1604)," *Educazione. Giornale di pedagogia critica* IV, 1 (2015): 29–48.

31 For Parma, see Alba Mora, ed., *Un Borbone tra Parma e l'Europa. Don Ferdinando e il suo tempo, 1751–1802* (Reggio Emilia: Diabasis, 2005) and Moreau de Saint-Méry, *Historique. Etats de Parme 1749–1808*, ed. Carla Corradi Martini (Reggio Emilia: Diabasis, 2003).

32 Giuseppe Orlandi, "I religiosi dello Stato di Modena nel Settecento tra riforme e rivoluzione," in *Lo stato di Modena. Una capitale, una dinastia, una civiltà nella storio d'Europa*, ed. Angelo Spaggiari and Giuseppe Trenti (Rome: Ministero per i beni e le attività culturali Direzione generale per gli Archivi, 2001), 743–81.

assets, ErcoleIII instituted the foundation *Patrimonio degli Studi*, a depository of the archives of the suppressed Jesuit houses.[33] The suppression of the Society of Jesus represents the main form the scholastic turning point for the teaching congregations took in the Duchy of Modena. However, their schools were not closed, but passed under the dependence of municipal authorities and the diocese. Within ex-Jesuit schools, teaching continued with the *Ratio Studiorum*. The lower schools of the duchy were entrusted to diocesan priests, and the schools of the Piarists also continued to operate. The turning point came in 1796, with the first descent of Bonaparte into Italy. The colleges and their buildings were requisitioned by the troops and used as barracks and quarters. This put an end to educational activity, both municipal and religious.[34]

The model that inspired Count Sanvitale in Parma was the *Rosine* Congregation of Turin, founded in the middle of the eighteenth century by the Dominican Tertiary Rosa Govone (1716–1776). This is another fine example of female educational initiative, directly in line with all those seen so far. With the help of Charles Emmanuel III of Savoy (1701–1773), Govone had opened a school in Turin for the professional training of young orphaned or poor girls. The example of Govone, a pious woman, although not a nun, shows how even in the Catholic world a sensitivity for the nascent working class was being developed. In the case of the Piedmontese Govone, we glimpse an embryo of Giovanni Bosco's sensitivity. It is no coincidence that both were located in the same region, one of Italy's future industrial hubs. King Charles Emmanuel started an important period of educational reforms in the Kingdom of Sardinia. The Constitutions of the University of Turin of 1772 placed all the secondary schools under the direction of the "Magistrate for the Reform of Studies." With this reform, a peripheral direction of public education was also introduced. Local reformers were given the task of implementing reform decrees even in small towns. It was also established that in each provincial capital a royal

---

33 Modena State Archives, Suppressed Jesuits Fund (*Fondo Gesuiti Soppressi*): strands 1–83; and Jesuit School Assets Fund (*Fondo Gesuiti Patrimonio degli Studi*). See also: *Inventario generale dei rogiti, scritture e libri economici ritrovati nell'archivio dei soppressi Gesuiti di Modena, Reggio, Mirandola, Carpi e Novellara*, kept in the Eca Fund located in the Modena State Archives.

34 Ilaria Giovanelli, *Educazione e istruzione durante il periodo della restaurazione con particolare riferimento all'Appennino reggiano* (Reggio Emilia: Deputazione di storia patria per le antiche province modenesi, 2005), 49–72.

college for the teaching of Latin, philosophy, theology and surgery had to be established.[35]

Venice also presented an overly complex situation, perhaps the most emblematic on the Italian scene. The Venetian Republic had remained the only Italian sovereign state spared from foreign interference, at least formally; however, by the end of the eighteenth century, the *Serenissima* was terminally ill. In Venice, more than elsewhere, school reform meant political reform. In a Republic, rather than a monarchy, the political life of the state depended on the activity of its officials, who in Venice had for centuries been its patricians. This aspect is of interest. The first chapter emphasized how the affirmation of the Venetian territorial state gave impetus to the spread of the educational principles of humanism in Italy. Renaissance humanists of the Padua school, including Vittorino Rambaldoni, Guarino of Verona and Gasparino Barzizza, were driven out of the city after Venice's conquest in the early fifteenth century, and were forced to take refuge in the other capitals of Italy. Their aim was to educate the social elites of Venetian cities according to humanistic educational principles, but Venice preferred to rely on the traditional education of its patricians but in the eighteenth century these values could no longer compete with modernity.

The need for a modernized educational system triggered a series of projects, surveys, and discussions. The debate which started at the beginning of the 1770s concerned the methods of reforming or creating new schools based on new ideas. Many authoritative intellectual voices engaged in the debate. Some echoed the opinion of la Chalotais and the controversy with the Jesuits. Gasparo Gozzi insisted on the establishment of "colleges for the education of the noble youth" where languages would be taught. "I would begin with Italian," wrote Gozzi, "because it is the closest to the mother tongue and yet easier to learn and especially of greater use throughout life. I would add French, almost the sister of Italian, and made necessary by now for people of literary and civil profession, for whom two languages will be keys to Latin, which I would like to reserve for the other class, for lack of tedium and toil of the children."[36]

---

35 On Rosa Govone and the educational season of reforms in the Kingdom of Sardinia, see Italo Lana, *Storia della Facoltà di lettere e filosofia dell'Università di Torino* (Florence: Olschki, 2000); and Casimiro Turletti, *Vita di Rosa Govone* (Torino: Artigianelli, 1876).

36 Venturi, *Settecento Riformatore* II, 153. Gasparo Gozzi introduced modern journalism in Italy. He was among the main characters on the Venetian eighteenth-century cultural scene. See Alvise Zorzi, *La Repubblica del Leone. Storia di Venezia* (Milan: Rusconi, 1979), 461. These fragments are taken from: Gasparo Gozzi, "Intorno all'educazione. Frammenti," in *Scritti di Gasparo Gozzi*, ed. Niccolò Tommaseo (Florence: Le Monnier, 1849), 371–95.

Other voices that joined Gozzi were those of Andrea Tron, Natal Delle Laste, and Sebastiano Foscarini. They wanted to implement the teachings of Venetian history and strengthen scientific subjects according to Newton's principles. The school reorganization culminated with the opening of the College of San Marco in Padua, which allowed access to a large number of impoverished nobles from the Venetian province; however, a serious clash occurred between the religious orders and the Church. In Venice, the replacement of the Jesuits did not have the character of a decisive turning point as it had had in Naples, Parma and Milan between 1767 and 1773. As Franco Venturi wrote, a series of clashes broke out in the *Serenissima* between the seminary and San Marco College concerning a possible chair to be established in favor of or against a college that depended on the patriarch of Venice. However, as we have seen, the attitude of the Venetian Republic towards religious orders had been anything but tender over the centuries. A series of clashes and expulsions had marked the centuries. Barnabites and Angelic Sisters were expelled in 1551, Jesuits in 1606, and Somascans in 1769. Although these expulsions were mostly temporary, they show how difficult the relationship between Venice and the early modern religious teaching orders had been.

Another central aspect that deserves to be considered is the incredible attraction and driving force that Venice and its territory exerted on these pedagogical experiences. Venice was almost always a decisive junction for the development of the educational identities of all the teaching congregations. In 1527, the Theatines opened their first house outside of Rome in Venice. Between 1536 and 1537, the first Jesuits, unable to leave for Jerusalem, carried out their first apostolic activities in the streets of Venice. There they took their vows of chastity and poverty, and Ignatius was ordained a priest.[37] Girolamo Emiliani, founder of the Somascans, was born in Venice and developed his religious vocation in the Venetian army, similarly to Ignatius of Loyola. Barnabites and Ursulines also experienced an early spread in the State of Venice. Angela Merici was born in Desenzano within the borders of Saint Mark's Republic.

Even for the Piarists, Venice represented a promised land. As for the Jesuits before them, it represented a new Jerusalem, a new Byzantium, a new Rome.[38] When the Sicilian Piarist Giovanni Alacchi arrived in Venice in 1630, Calasanz struggled to curb the enthusiasm of his envoy, something that did not fail to arouse suspicion on the part of the Venetian authorities. A series of economic,

---

37 Hans Peter Kolvenbach, "Ignazio a Venezia. Simbolismo di un passaggio," *in I Gesuiti e Venezia. Momenti e problemi di una storia veneziana della Compagnia di Gesù*, ed., Mario Zanardi (Padova: Gregoriana, 1994), 37–56.

38 Sangalli, *Le smanie per l'educazione*, 79.

political, cultural, and symbolic reasons intertwine in the bond between Venice and the religious teaching congregations. Its traditional proximity to the East, Constantinople, and Jerusalem made it the heir to a centuries-old tradition of western projection towards the lands of the origins of Christianity. Its fertile territory, straddling the Alps, the Po River and western Padania, was the basis of a rapid development of economic structures that increased the demand for literate and qualified personnel. The proximity to the central European area made the Venetian state attractive for religious orders that aimed to expand their missionary activity in those parts of Europe.

Perhaps it was because of this profound historical entanglement that, despite attempts at reform, the Venetian patriciate was unable to create a type of school that met its political and social needs. A new university did not emerge and Padua, as Venturi writes, could never compare to Pavia.[39] The pro-clerical turning point of the last years of the Republic contributed to this. The last act of the Lion of Saint Mark took place in 1797. The year before, in 1796, the French troops of General Bonaparte had freely entered the borders of the Republic in pursuit of the retreating Austrian army. At the end of the conflict, in a wise political move devised in order not to exacerbate the humiliation of the enemy with the treaty signed in Campoformio, Bonaparte put an end to Venetian sovereignty and ceded its territory to Austria. We shall see how, a few years later, Napoleon played a decisive role in marking the destiny of all the teaching congregations in Italy.

Before the arrival of Bonaparte, the Barnabite colleges in the Kingdom of Sardinia were closed in 1799 and the fathers, in exchange, were offered public professorships in some universities. In Tuscany, between 1783 and 1785, Grand Duke Leopold closed all the schools of the order. From 1781 onward, in Lombardy, the Barnabite fathers were removed from the control of the congregation and placed under the control of the bishops. Only a few Barnabites were retained in some parishes in Milan, where the former fathers officiated as simple diocesan priests, ready to rebuild their institutes as soon as the opportunity was offered.[40]

A similar fate awaited the Somascan fathers. In the mid-eighteenth century, the congregation was divided into three provinces, namely Lombardy, Veneto, and Rome. A first step towards the decline of the Clerics of Somascha was made in Venice, where in 1769 the decision was made to suppress the small convents within the Republic. At that time, several houses of the congregation

---

39   Venturi, *Settecento riformatore*, 156.
40   *I barnabiti nel IV centenario dalla fondazione*, 259–60.

were closed, and secular parish priests were introduced. In 1783, the Austrian government imposed the division of the Somascan Lombard province into the provinces of Lombardy and Genoa. In the latter, two new houses were created in 1784 in Novi and Genoa (Maddalena and Santo Spirito). With the arrival of Napoleon, the order was almost destroyed. In 1802, the province of Piedmont was suppressed while in Naples the Capece, Caracciolo and Macedonio colleges were closed. In Rome, when Pope Pius VI was kidnapped by the French, the Clementine college was also suppressed.[41]

The Piarists, on the other hand, had to cope with the forces of division from within their order, especially from their more peripheral provinces, such as Poland and Hungary. In 1744, the pope decreed that the General Congregation in Italy, when electing the provincial superior of a province or the rector of a house, could not choose a candidate outside of three presented by the province itself. This 1759 obligation was extended to all the other European provinces; however, the disintegrating tendencies gained more and more strength with the reformist policies of many contemporary states. The Austrian Empire was the first. The laws issued by Emperor Joseph II in 1781 disconnected the provinces of Austria, Hungary, and Bohemia from Rome. For this reason, these provinces could not participate in the General Chapter of 1784. The Bourbons of the Kingdom of Naples acted similarly. In 1788, they separated the provinces of Naples, Sicily, and Apulia from Rome. The Spanish crown did the same. Because of this, the General Chapter of 1796 was only able to count on the presence of the Italian Piarists. The Order remained divided into three parts, namely the Austrian Empire, Spain, and Italy. Even in Poland and Lithuania, the Piarists led an autonomous life while still trying to maintain connections with Rome.[42]

After 1797, the Italian states fell one by one under French control. In northern Italy, the Cisalpine Republic was created by the Treaty of Campoformio. This state became the Italian Republic from 1802 until 1805, and from 1805 to 1814 it was transformed into the Kingdom of Italy, ruled by Eugène de Beauharnais, Napoleon's adopted son. At the time of its maximum expansion, the Kingdom of Italy included the regions of Lombardy, Veneto, most of Emilia and the northwestern part of the Church State. The Grand Duchy of Tuscany became the Kingdom of Etruria from 1801 to 1807 and was later annexed to the French Empire. A similar fate was suffered by the Papal State which was annexed in 1808. The kingdom of Sardinia was divided. Sardinia remained under the

---

41   L'ordine dei Chierici Regolari Somaschi nel IV centenario della sua fondazione, 240.
42   Lezáun, Storia delle scuole pie, 86–87.

sovereignty of the Savoy dynasty while Piedmont was annexed to the French Empire in 1802. The Kingdom of Naples, on the other hand, remained a formally independent state governed by dynasties of Napoleonids. From 1806 to 1808, Naples was under the rule of Napoleon's elder brother, Joseph Bonaparte, and from 1808 to 1815 under Napoleon's brother-in-law, Joachim Murat. Sicily, however, remained under Bourbon's sovereignty, protected, along with Sardinia, by the English navy.

The decree of the National Constituent Assembly on February 23rd, 1790, had suppressed religious orders in France and abolished the monastic vows, harshly affecting the schools. The Civil Constitution of the Clergy of July 12th, finding a strong opposition among the fathers, dispersed them permanently, relegating them to the same category as outlaws. In Italy, the Napoleonic decree of April 25th, 1810 suppressed all religious orders.

3   Conclusion

"The monks would be by far the best teaching staff, if it were possible to control them and submit them to a foreign leader," Napoleon said about the Italian educational situation.[43] This statement by the French Emperor sums up well the state of religious orders at the time of their suppression with particular reference to their educational role.

We have seen how, over the centuries, the evolution of the role of the religious orders in Italian society was not a systematically guided process towards education; rather, they were born in response to the eschatological and spiritual anxieties of the late fifteenth century as movements of reform within the Catholic Church. Nonetheless, religious orders were driven into the world of education by a series of social, political, economic, and religious circumstances. During the sixteenth century, the transition from a municipal to a religious school system was gradually completed. The half century of war that hit Italy during the sixteenth century was a determining factor. The wars emptied the coffers of the cities and they could no longer afford to finance schools. The new colleges opened by religious congregations very often accepted students free of charge, extremely useful in the eyes of princes and municipalities. However, the wars of Italy took place earlier than the affirmation on a large scale of the teaching congregations. With the peace of *Cateau-Cambresis* in

---

43   Hélie de Noailles, *Le comte Molé (1781–1855). Sa vie. Ses mémoires*, vol. 1 (Paris: Champion, 1922), 55.

1559, the debate on where to direct the charism of the congregation was still ongoing in many religious orders.

The decisive factor, for many orders, was internal religious ferment. As seen with the Capuchins, Barnabites and Servites, in fact, it was the risk of being judged heretical by the Holy Office that determined an educational turning point. The need of the orders to theologically train their novices meant that the congregations began to provide themselves not only with intellectual tools but also with material means. Classrooms, books, and desks put the congregations in a position to extend their teaching to the populations in which they lived, both urban and rural. In addition to this were the ongoing transformations taking place in the rural and economic structures of Italian territory, particularly in the north. The extension of the reclamations, the enlargement of the cultivated areas, and the new cultivations required a whole series of professional figures, namely engineers, surveyors, notaries and rural police. These people needed different degrees of training from the religious orders.

These educational needs were among the factors that led the religious orders to fully open themselves to the study of science and technology. The technology of water and rivers, so important for the development of agriculture, found a formidable scholar in the Piarist mathematician Famiano Michelini. The interests of this scientist active in the Florentine Pious Schools during the first half of the seventeenth century, illustrate the crossroads of concrete economic needs and scientific studies at the forefront of physics and astronomy. Michelini was the author of the fundamental "*Trattato della direzione de' fiumi*" (Treaty on the Direction of Rivers), an important work on the canalization of running waters.[44] He had also been one of the main assistants of Galileo after the years of his condemnation to abjure, and he supported Galilei's heliocentric and Copernican theses in his own school until he was denounced at the Holy Office in 1641. Economics, politics, philosophy, science, and religion thus merged in the profile of a schoolteacher who perfectly embodied the tensions and characteristics of an era and its educational culture. With Famiano Michelini, we can say that we passed from the age of doctrinal heresies to the age of scientific heresies.

With the passage from the seventeenth to the eighteenth century, however, the tensions between science and the Church eased. With the rise of the Enlightenment, Galilean heritage and its experimentalist approach was used by religious orders to explore the new ways presented by Newtonianism and the new scientific paradigms. To acknowledge this is helpful to better understand

---

44   Famiano Michelini, *Trattato della direzione de' fiumi* (Florence: Stamperia Stella, 1664).

Napoleon's statement at the beginning of the paragraph. The religious orders during the eighteenth century were not lacking valid content for their teachings, which had been at the forefront in early modern Italy and Europe. In the eighteenth century, the problem with the educational system built by religious congregations during the Reformation was the lack of uniformity between their systems and the irregularities in their government structures. The religious educational network suffered from the same lack of rationality that enlightened intellectuals rejected in the political, economic, and judicial systems of the *ancien régime*. It was widely believed that all these sectors of public life should be reformed for the good of the state and the citizens; however, the reforms that the states were unable to operate were made by the French army at the beginning of the Napoleonic wars. The *Grande Armée*, in addition to the Napoleonic Civil Code, brought new educational ideas.

As had happened two and a half centuries earlier during the Italian Wars, the arrival of an army in a semi-permanent state of war represented for the small communities an irreparable upheaval of the hierarchy. The communities to which enlightened reformism had gradually handed back the educational responsibility (at least as far as elementary education was concerned), could not bear the costs of supplying the invading troops and the costs of running the schools. Educational budgets had always been a critical point for the public coffers and had been one of the decisive factors in the affirmation of the various types of schools of religious orders between the sixteenth and seventeenth centuries. Despite the reforms, eighteenth century Italian states were still not strong enough to provide schools in times of emergency; European powers were perhaps better prepared. The fact remains that with the restoration that took place between 1814 and 1815, a first stable embryo of public schools was made possible by a reorganization of school systems and a rationalization of public education assets. Teaching congregations not only recovered but were called to work by the rulers. Religious schools completed the modern public education system.

In the nineteenth century, new challenges awaited the religious teaching orders. Industrialization and the gradual massification of societies, the uncontrolled growth of cities and the formation of the proletariat encouraged the Catholic world to engage in a new effort in the same way that the sixteenth century's upheavals had led to the rethinking of educational paradigms. It was in this context that twenty-three new religious congregations were born, of which the most famous is perhaps the Salesian Society of Saint John Bosco.

Bibliography

Consulted Archives

- Archivio Storico Diocesano di Milano (Historical Diocesan Archives of Milan)
- Archivio di Stato di Enna (Enna State Archives)
- Archivio di Stato di Modena (Modena State Archives)
- Archivio di Stato di Reggio Emilia (Reggio Emilia State Archives)
- Archivio di Stato di Mantova (Mantua State Archives)
- Archivio di Stato di Venezia (Venice State Archives)
- Archivio Storico dei Barnabiti in Milano (Historical Archives of the Barnabites in Milan)
- Archivio Storico del Collegio Guastalla (Guastalla College Historical Archives)
- Archivio Comunale di Guastalla (Municipal Archives of Guastalla)
- Archivio Comunale di Carpi (Municipal Archives of Carpi)
- Archivio Generalizio dei Somaschi (Somascan General Archives)
- Archivio Generalizio dei Teatini (Theatines General Archives)
- Biblioteca Ambrosiana (Ambrosian Library)

Published Sources

Acta Congregationis (1528–1737). 3 vols. *Fonti per la storia dei Somaschi*. Edited by Maurizio Brioli C.R.S. Rome: Curia generalizia dei padri Somaschi, 2006.

Atti dei capitoli generali (1542–1591). 2 vols. *Fonti per la storia dei Somaschi*. Edited by Carlo Pellegrini C.R.S. Rome: Curia generalizia dei padri Somaschi, 1997.

Ordini e decreti capitolari dal 1570 al 1591. *Fonti per la storia dei Somaschi*. Edited by Carlo Pellegrini C.R.S. Rome: Curia generalizia dei padri Somaschi, 1997.

Costituzioni dei Chierici Regolari di San Paolo Decollato. Prima edizione italiana delle Costituzioni del 1579. Edited by Giovanni Scalese. *Barnabiti Studi* 31, (2014).

Monumenta paedagogica Societatis Iesu, nova editio ex integro refecta. Edited by László Lukács. 7 vols. Rome: Apud "Monumenta Historica Soc. Iesu," 1965–1992.

Statuto organico del Regio Collegio della Guastalla in Milano. Milan: F. Manini, 1883.

The Ratio Studiorum: The Official Plan for Jesuit Education. Edited and translated by Claude Pavur. Boston: Institute for Advanced Jesuit Studies, 2005.

Early Printed Books (before 1830)

Affò, Ireneo. *Istoria della città e ducato di Guastalla*. 4 vols. Guastalla: Presso Salvatore Costa, 1785–1788.

Arcangelo, Giani. *Regola che diede papa Martino V e conferma Innocenzo VIII a Fratelli e Sorelle della compagnia de' Servi di Maria con sommario di tutte le indulgenze*. Florence: Marescotti, 1591.

Barelli, Francesco Luigi. *Memorie dell'origine, fondazione, avanzamenti, successi ed uomini illustri in lettere e santità della congregazione de' Chierici Regolari di S. Paolo*. Vol. II. Bologna: Per Costantino Pisarri, 1707.

Barelli, Francesco Luigi. *Vita del Venerabil Servo di Dio Alessandro Sauli*. Bologna: Per Costantino Pisarri, 1705.

Castiglione, Giambattista. *Istoria delle scuole della Dottrina Cristiana fondate in Milano e da Milano e nell'Italia altrove propagate*. Milan: Stamperia Malatesta, 1800.

Caradeuc de La Chalotais, Louis René. *Comptes Rendus des Constitutions des Jésuites*. Paris: Ponthieu Librairie, 1826.

Caradeuc de La Chalotais, Louis René. *Essai d'éducation nationale ou plan d'études pour la jeunesse*. Geneva: chez Philibert, 1763.

Carboni, Ludovico. *Dello ammaestramento de' figliuoli nella dottrina Christiana*. Venice: Appresso Giovanni Guerigli, 1596.

Chronologia Historico-Legalis Seraphici Ordinis Minorum Sancti Patris Francisci, Vol II. Naples: ex Typographia Camilli Cavalli, 1650.

Collectio bullarum, constitutionum, brevium, ac decretorum omnium ad Seraphicum Sancti Bonaventurae collegium. Rome: ex typographia Pauli Junchii, 1780.

Constitutiones urbanae fratrum ord. Min. conv. S. Francisci. Rome: apud impressore camerale, 1628.

Cornaro, Flaminio and Manfré, Giovanni. *Notizie storiche delle chiese e monasteri di Venezia, e di Torcello tratte dalle chiese veneziane, e torcellane*. Padova: Nella stamperia del Seminario, appresso Giovanni Manfré, 1758.

De Tisana, Agostino. *Chorographica descriptio Provinciarum et Conventuum Fratrum Minorum Sancti Francisci Capocinorum*. Mediolanum: Giuseppe Pandolfo Malatesta, 1712.

Del Tufo, Giambattista. *Historia della Religione de' Padri Chierici Regolari*. Rome: Presso Girolamo Facciotto e Stefano Paolini, 1609.

Di Simone, Francesco. *Della vita della serva di Dio Lucia Filippini superiora delle scuole pie*. Rome: per l'Ansillioni al corallo vicino alla Chiesa Nova, 1732.

Dizionario storico portatile degli ordini religiosi e militari e delle congregazioni regolari e secolari che contiene la loro origine, i loro progressi, la loro decadenza e le relative loro riforme. Torino: Presso Francesco Prato, 1792.

Educazione cristiana ossia catechismo universale. Venice: Eredi Curti, 1824.

Fleureau, Basile. *Les antiquitez de la ville et du duché d'Estampes*. Paris: chez Jean Baptiste Coignard, 1683.

Grazioli, Pietro. *Della vita, virtù e miracoli del Beato Alessandro Sauli*. Bologna: Per Giovanni Antonio Ghidini, 1741.

Masini, Eliseo. *Sacro arsenale ouero prattica dell'Officio della Santa Inquisitione*. Genoa: Giuseppe Pavoni, 1621.

Michelini, Famiano. *Trattato della direzione de' fiumi*. Florence: Stamperia Stella, 1664.

Moncalieri, Giovanni. *Chorographica descriptio provinciarum et conventuum fratrum minorum S. Francisci capucinorum Praedicatorum, Sacerdotum, Clericorum, et Lacos universorum eiusdem ordinis collectio*. Augustae Taurinorum: 1654.

Notizie per l'ingresso nel Collegio di Fossano de P.P. Somaschi. Torino: Presso Giammichele Briolo, 1787.

Paltrinieri, Ottavio Maria. *Elogio del nobile e pontificio Collegio Clementino di Roma*. Presso Antonio Fulgoni, 1795.

Patrignani, Giuseppe Antonio. *Menologio di pie memorie d'alcuni religiosi della compagnia de Gesù*. Vol. 2. Venice: presso Niccolò Pezzana, 1730.

Racine, Bonaventure. *Storia ecclesiastica divisa per secoli con riflessioni*. Vol. 15. Florence: Francesco Pisoni, 1781.

Regola della Compagnia delli Serui dei Puttini in Carita. Ferrara: appresso Francesco de' Rossi da Valenza, 1555.

Richia Giuseppe S.J., *Notizie Istoriche delle Chiese Fiorentine Divise ne' suoi Quartieri*, Tomo X, Parte II. Florence: Nella Stamperia di Pietri Gaetano Viviani, 1762.

Silos, Giuseppe. *Historiarum clericorum regularium a congregatione condita*, 3 vols. Rome: Typis Vitalis Mascardi, 1650–1666.

Tagliati, Giovanni Maria. *Compendium rei grammaticae*. Mutinae: apud Antoniium Gadaldinum, 1549.

Tiraboschi, Girolamo. *Biblioteca Modenese o Notizie della vita e delle opere degli scrittori nati negli stati del serenissimo signor duca di Modena*. 7 vols. Modena: Presso la Società Tipografica, 1781–1786.

Vezzosi, Antonio Francesco. *I Scrittori de' Chierici Regolari detti Teatini*. 2 vols. Rome: Nella stamperia della Sacra Congregazione di Propaganda Fide, 1780.

Modern Bibliography (after 1830)

Achilli, Giuseppina. "Castellino da Castello e le scuole della dottrina cristiana." *La scuola cattolica* LXIV, (1936): 35–40.

Adrover, Julian. "I Teatini in Monaco di Baviera." *Regnum Dei* 9, (1953): 3–18.

Agnoli, Francesco; Bartelloni Andrea. *Da Copernico padre dell'Eliocentrismo a Lemaître padre del Big Bang*. Torino: La Fontana di Siloe, 2018.

Al Kalak, Matteo. *Gli eretici di Modena. Fede e potere alla metà del Cinquecento.* Milan: Mursia, 2008.

Al Kalak, Matteo. *L'Eresia dei fratelli. Una comunità eterodossa nella Modena del Cinquecento.* Rome: Edizioni di storia e letteratura, 2011.

Al Kalak, Matteo. *Il riformatore dimenticato. Egidio Foscarari tra Inquisizione, Concilio e governo pastorale, 1512–1564.* Bologna: Il Mulino, 2016.

Al Kalak, Matteo. "Sabbatini Giuliano." *Dizionario Biografico degli Italiani*, vol. 89 (2017).

Alberzoni, Maria Pia; Annamaria Ambrosioni; Alfredo Lucioni, eds. *Sulle tracce degli Umiliati.* Milan: Vita e Pensiero, 1997.

Alcaini, Giovanni. "Origini e progressi degli istituti diretti dai Padri Somaschi." *Somascha. Bollettino di Storia dei Padri Somaschi* 4, (1979): 70–175.

Andreu, Francesco. "I chierici regolari." *Regnum Dei*, 30, (1974): 55–78.

Andreu, Francesco. "I teatini dal 1524 al 1574. Sintesi storica." *Regnum Dei*, 30 (1974): 8–54.

Andreu, Francesco. "I teatini e l'Oratorio del Divino Amore a Venezia." *Regnum Dei*, 99, (1973): 53–76.

Andreu, Francesco. "La regola dei Chierici Regolari nella lettera di Bonifacio de' Colli a Gian Matteo Giberti." *Regnum Dei*, 2, (1946): 38–53.

Arcangeli, Letizia; Susanna Peyronel, eds. *Donne di potere nel Rinascimento.* Rome: Viella, 2008.

Badini, Gino, ed. *I gesuiti a Guastalla.* Reggio Emilia: La Nuova Tipolito, 2003.

Baernstein, Renée. *A Convent Tale: A century of Sisterhood in Spanish Milan.* New York: Routledge, 2002.

Baldini, Ugo. "I gesuiti nella cultura del ducato." In *Un Borbone tra Parma e l'Europa. Don Ferdinando e il suo tempo, 1751–1802.* Edited by Alba Mora: 98–135. Reggio Emilia: Diabasis, 2005.

Baldini, Ugo. "La scuola galileiana." In *Scienza e tecnica nella cultura e nella società dal Rinascimento a oggi.* Edited by Gianni Micheli, *Storia d'Italia, Annali*, 3: 381–463. Torino: Einaudi, 1980.

Baldini, Ugo. *Legem impone subactis. Studi su filosofia e scienza dei gesuiti in Italia 1540–1632.* Rome: Bulzoni, 1992.

Baldini, Ugo. *Saggi sulla cultura della Compagnia di Gesù, secoli XVI-XVIII.* Padova: Cleup, 2000.

Baldo, Vittorio. *Alunni maestri e scuole in Venezia alla fine del XVI secolo.* Como: New Press, 1976.

Balsamo, Luigi. "Libri e biblioteche nella tradizione culturale dei frati cappuccini." In *Tra biblioteca e pulpito. Itinerari culturali dei frati minori cappuccini*, 67–78. Messina: Sicania, 1997.

Barbarisi, Gennaro, ed. *Ideologia e scienza nell'opera di Paolo Frisi (1728–1784).* Milan: FrancoAngeli, 1987.

Baroncini, Gabriele. "L'insegnamento della filosofia naturale nei collegi italiani dei gesuiti (1610–1670): un esempio di nuovo aristotelismo." In *La Ratio Studiorum. Modelli culturali e pratiche educative dei Gesuiti in Italia tra Cinque e Seicento*. Edited by Gian Paolo Brizzi: 163–215. Rome: Bulzoni, 1981.

Barzazi, Antonella. *Gli affanni dell'erudizione. Studi e organizzazione culturale degli ordini religiosi a Venezia tra Sei e Settecento*. Venice: Istituto veneto di scienze, lettere ed arti, 2004.

Bazzoli, Maurizio. *Il piccolo stato nell'età moderna. Studi su un concetto della politica internazionale tra XVI e XVIII secolo*. Milan: Jaca Book, 1990.

Bedoni, Giuseppe. "Il pedagogista Bruno Bruni docente nelle Scuole Pie correggesi." *Bollettino storico reggiano* III, (1970): 1–15.

Bellabarba, Marco. "The feudal principalities: the East (Trent, Bressanone/Brixen, Aquileia, Tyrol and Gorizia)." In *The Italian Renaissance State*. Edited by Andrea Gamberini and Isabella Lazzarini, 197–219. Cambridge: University Press, 2012.

Bellatalla, Luciana. *Pietro Leopoldo di Toscana granduca-educatore: teoria e pratica di un despota illuminato*. Lucca: Editore Pacini Fazzi, 1984.

Bellatalla, Luciana and Sira Sirenella Macchietti. *Questioni e esperienze di educazione femminile in Toscana: dalla Controriforma all'ultimo Ottocento*. Rome: Bulzoni, 1998.

Benigni, Rita. *Educazione religiosa e modernità. Linee evolutive e prospettive di riforma*. Torino: Giappicchelli editore, 2017.

Benzoni, Gino. *Venezia nell'età della Controriforma*. Milan: Mursia, 1973.

Bertani, Licia, Giuseppe Cagni, Eugenio Castellani and Giampaolo Trotta. *San Carlo dei Barnabiti a Firenze: una chiesa ed un collegio all'ombra dei Granduchi e dell'Impero*. Florence: Comune di Firenze, 1995.

Bertazzoni, Elisa. *Il monastero di San Carlo in Guastalla e le giovani Gonzaga*. Guastalla: Umberto Soncini editore, 2008.

Bertolotti, Davide. *Viaggio nella Liguria marittima*. Torino: Tipografi Eredi Botta, 1834.

Bertolotto, Claudio. *Il Real Collegio e i Barnabiti a Moncalieri: educazione e custodia delle memorie*. Torino: Celid, 1997.

Bianchi, Angelo and Giancarlo Rocca, eds. "L'educazione femminile tra Cinque e Settecento." *Annali di storia dell'educazione e delle istituzioni scolastiche*, 14, (2007).

Bianchi, Angelo. *L'istruzione in Italia tra Sette o Ottocento. Lombardia, Veneto, Umbria*. Brescia: La Scuola, 2007.

Bianchi, Angelo. *L'istruzione secondaria tra barocco ed età dei lumi. Il collegio di San Giovanni alle Vigne di Lodi e l'esperienza pedagogica dei Barnabiti*. Milan: Vita e pensiero, 1993.

Bianchi, Angelo. "Le scuole Arcimboldi a Milano nel XVII secolo: professori, studenti, cultura scolastica." *Barnabiti Studi* 19, (2002): 55–78.

Bianchi, Angelo. "Le scuole di dottrina cristiana: linguaggio e strumenti per una azione educativa 'di massa'." In *Carlo Borromeo e l'opera della "Grande Riforma." Cultura, religione e arti nella Milano del pieno Cinquecento*. Edited by Franco Buzzi and Danilo Zardin, 145–58. Milan: Credito Artigiano, 1997.

Bireley, Robert. *Religion and Politics in the Age of the Counterreformation: Emperor Ferdinand II, William Lamormaini, S.J., and the Formation of Imperial Policy*. Chapel Hill NC: University of North Carolina Press, 1981.

Bireley, Robert. *The Jesuits and the Thirty Years Wars. Kings, Courts and Confessors*. New York: Cambridge University Press, 2003.

Black, Christopher. *The Italian Inquisition*. New Haven & London: Yale University Press, 2009.

Black, Robert. *Education and Society in Florentine Tuscany. Teachers, Pupils and Schools, c. 1250–1500*. Leiden-Boston: Brill, 2007.

Boero, Giuseppe. *Sentimenti e fatti del p. Silvestro Pietrasanta della Compagnia di Gesù in difesa di San Giuseppe Calasanzio e delle Scuole Pie*. Rome: Dalla Tipografia di Marini e Morini, 1847.

Boffito, Giuseppe. *Scrittori barnabiti o della Congregazione dei chierici regolari di San Paolo 1533–1933*, I. Florence: Olschki, 1933–1937.

Bond, Bradley G., ed. *French Colonial Louisiana and the Atlantic World*. New Orleans: Louisiana State University Press, 2005.

Bonora, Elena. *I conflitti della Controriforma. Santità e obbedienza nell'esperienza dei primi barnabiti*. Florence: Le Lettere, 1998.

Bonora, Elena. *La Controriforma*. Rome-Bari: Laterza, 2005.

Borraccini Verducci, Maria Rosa. "La scuola pubblica a Recanati nel sec. XV." *Università di Macerata. Annali della facoltà di lettere e filosofia* 8, (1975): 121–62.

Bouwsma, William. *Venice and the Defense of Republican Liberty. Renaissance Values in the Age of the Counter Reformation*. Berkeley: University of California Press, 1968.

Brancati, Mario. *L'organizzazione scolastica nella Contea principesca di Gorizia e Gradisca dal 1615 al 1874*. Udine: Grillo, 1978.

Branchesi, Pacifico Maria. "Gli studia delle province italiane dell'Ordine dei Servi di Maria negli anni 1597–1601 ed il loro contesto legislativo." *Studi Storici OSM*, 23 (1973): 168–70.

Brereton, John and Cinthia Gannet, eds. *Traditions of Eloquence: The Jesuits and Modern Rhetorical Studies*. New York: Fordham University Press, 2016.

Bressan, Edoardo, Marco Bona Castellotti and Paola Vismara, eds. *Politica, vita religiosa, carità. Milano nel primo Settecento*. Milan: Jaca Book, 1997.

Brizzi, Gian Paolo. "Scuole e collegi nell'antica Provincia Veneta della Compagnia di Gesù (1542–1773)." In *I Gesuiti e Venezia. Momenti e problemi di storia veneziana della Compagnia di Gesù*. Edited by Mario Zanardi, 467–511. Padova: Gregoriana Libreria Editrice, 1994.

Burke, Peter. *The European Renaissance. Centres and Peripheries*. Oxford: Basil Blackwell, 1998.

Caccamo, Domenico. "La diplomazia della Controriforma e la crociata: dai piani del Possevino alla 'lunga guerra' di Clemente VIII." *Archivio Storico Italiano*, 2/128, (1979): 255–81.

Caimmi, Riccardo. *La guerra del Friuli 1615–1617 altrimenti nota come Guerra di Gradisca o degli Uscocchi*. Gorizia: Confine Orientale, 2007.

Cajani, Luigi. "Castellino da Castello." *Dizionario Biografico degli Italiani*, vol. 21, (1978).

Campanelli, Marcella, ed. *I Teatini*. Rome: Edizioni di storia e letteratura, 1987.

Carlsmith, Christopher. *A Renaissance Education. Schooling in Bergamo and the Venetian Republic 1500–1650*. Toronto, Buffalo, London: University of Toronto Press, 2010.

Casalini, Cristiano. *Aristotle in Coimbra: The Cursus Conimbricensis and the education at the College of Arts*, translated by Luana Salvarani. New York: Routledge, 2017.

Casalini, Cristiano. *Benet Perera and Early Jesuit Pedagogy. Human Knowledge Freedom Superstition*. Rome: Anicia, 2016.

Casalini, Cristiano. "Building a Duchy to the Greater Glory of God. The Jesuits and the Farnesian Educational Policy in Parma (1539–1604)." *Educazione. Giornale di pedagogia critica* IV, 1 (2015): 29–48.

Casalini, Cristiano, ed. *Jesuit Logic and Late Ming China: Lectures on the Cursus Conimbricensis*. Boston: Institute of Advanced Jesuit Studies, 2029.

Casalini, Cristiano and Claude Pavur, eds. *Jesuit Pedagogy, 1540–1616: A Reader*. Boston: Institute for Advanced Jesuit Studies, 2016.

Casalini, Cristiano and Luana Salvarani, eds., *Coltura Degl'Ingegni* written by Antonio Possevino. Rome: Anicia, 2008.

Casalis, Goffredo. *Dizionario geografico, storico, statistico, commerciale degli Stati di S. M. il re di Sardegna*. Torino: Presso Maspero libraio e Marzorati tipografo, 1849.

Casati, Stefano. "I preti riformati di Santa Maria Piccola e i Somaschi." *Somascha* XI, (1986): 55–72.

Catto, Michela. *Un panopticon catechistico. L'arciconfraternita della dottrina cristiana a Roma in età moderna*. Rome: Edizioni di storia e letteratura, 2003.

Cavazza, Silvano. "Un'eresia di frontiera. Propaganda luterana e dissenso religioso sul confine austro-veneto nel Cinquecento." *Annali di storia isontina*, 4, (1991): 7–33.

Cecotti, Franco and Giulio Mellinato, eds. *Archivi e fonti per la storia delle istituzioni educative giuliane*, Vol. 1/XXIX, *Qualestoria: Bollettino dell'Istituto regionale per la storia del movimento di liberazione nel Friuli Venezia-Giulia*. Trieste: Istituto regionale per la storia del movimento di liberazione nel Friuli Venezia-Giulia, 2001.

Chiappa, Franco. *Una pubblica scuola di grammatica a Palazzolo nella seconda metà del '400*. Brescia: Tipografia Fiorucci, 1964.

Chiappa Mauri, Luisa. *Paesaggi rurali di Lombardia*. Rome-Bari: Laterza, 1990.

Chiesa, Innocenzo. *Vita di Carlo Bascapè: barnabita e vescovo di Novara, 1550–1615*. Florence: Olschki, 1993.

Chiminelli, Piero. *S. Gaetano da Thiene cuore della riforma cattolica*. Vicenza: Cattolici vicentini editrice, 1948.

Chinea, Eleuterio. *L'istruzione pubblica e privata nello Stato di Milano dal Concilio Tridentino alla Riforma Teresiana (1563–1773)*. Florence: La nuova Italia, 1953.

Chinea, Eleuterio. "Le scuole del Ducato di Milano dal Concilio tridentino alla riforma teresiana (1562–1773)." *Rivista pedagogica*, XXIV (1931): 431–44. XXV, (1932): 65–99.

Chinea, Eleuterio. "Le scuole del Ducato di Milano dal Concilio tridentino alla riforma teresiana (1562–1773)." *Rivista pedagogica*, XXV, (1932): 65–99.

Chinea, Eleuterio. *Le scuole di dottrina cristiana nella diocesi di Milano (1536–1796)*. Gallarate: Stabilimento Tipo-Litografico Carlo Lazzati, 1930.

Chittolini, Giorgio. *La formazione dello stato regionale e le istituzioni del contado. Secoli XIV e XV*. Torino: Einaudi, 1979.

Chittolini, Giorgio. "Stati padani, 'Stato del Rinascimento': problemi di ricerca." In *Persistenze feudali e autonomie comunitative in stati padani fra '500 e '700*. Edited by Giovanni Tocci, 9–29. Bologna: Clueb, 1988.

Churchill Semple, Henry. S.J. *The Ursulines in New Orleans and Our Lady of Prompt Succor: A Record of Two Centuries 1727–1925*. New York: P.J. Kennedy & Sons, 1925.

Cibrario, Luigi. *Origini e progresso delle istituzioni della Monarchia di Savoia*, parte seconda. Torino: Dalla Stamperia Reale, 1855.

Cipolla, Carlo Maria. *Istruzione e sviluppo: il declino dell'analfabetismo nel mondo occidentale*. Bologna: Il Mulino, 2002.

Ciroldi, Sergio. "Ordini e congregazioni religiose nel Guastallese." in *Storia della Diocesi di Reggio Emilia-Guastalla*, vol. III, *Dalla Riforma tridentina alla Rivoluzione francese*. Edited by Giovanni Costi and Giuseppe Giovanelli, 185–203. Brescia: Morcelliana, 2014.

Colini Baldeschi, Luigi. "L'insegnamento pubblico in Macerata nel '300 e nel '400." *Rivista delle biblioteche e degli archivi* 9, (1900): 19–26.

Colombo, Emanuele. "Benefici e costruzioni di élites a Lodi (XVIII–XIX secolo)." In *Ambizioni e reputazioni. Élite nel Lodigiano tra età moderna e contemporanea*. Edited by Pietro Cafaro 47–76. Milan: FrancoAngeli, 2013.

Colombo, Giuseppe. *Profili biografici di illustri barnabiti effigiati sotto i portici del Collegio S. Francesco in Lodi*. Crema: Tipografia Campanini, 1870.

Corsetti, Luigi and Giuseppe Filippi. *Alcuni cenni statistico economici della città di Velletri*. Rome: Tipografia Menicanti, 1851.

Cruz, Anne J. and Rosilie Hernández, ed. *Woman's Literacy in Early Modern Spain and the New World*. New York: Routledge, 2011.

Cueva, Edmund, Shannon Byrne, Frederick Joseph Benda. *Jesuit Education and the Classics*. Newcastle upon Tyne: Cambridge Scholars, 2009.

Culpepper, Danielle. "'Our Particular Cloister': Ursulines and Female Education in Seventeenth Century Parma and Piacenza." *Sixteenth Century Journal*, 4 (2005): 1017–37.

D'Amico, Nicola. *Un libro per Eva. Il difficile cammino dell'istruzione della donna in Italia: la storia, le protagoniste*. Milan: FrancoAngeli, 2016.

Dabalà, Giuseppe. "Le scuole pubbliche di Udine dal 1297 al 1851." *Annuario del R. Liceo Ginnasio 'Iacopo Stellini,'* (1925–1926): 13–70.

Dal Pino, Franco Andrea. *Spazi e figure lungo la storia dei Servi di Santa Maria (secoli XIII–XX)*. Rome: Herder, 1997.

Dal Prete, Ivano. *Scienze e società nel Settecento veneto. Il caso veronese 1680–1796*. Milan: FrancoAngeli, 2008.

Damioli, Giovanni Battista. *Date e fatti degli Istituti di vita consacrata a Livorno*. Livorno: Centro Diocesano Stampa, 1984.

Damioli, Giovanni Battista. "Ordine dei Padri Barnabiti." In *I religiosi a Livorno. Fratelli e Padri*. Edited by Giovanni Battista Damioli, 55–67. Livorno: Centro Diocesano Stampa, 1984.

Davari, Stefano. *Notizie storiche intorno allo studio pubblico ed ai maestri del secolo XV e XVI che tennero scuola in Mantova tratte dall'Archivio Storico di Mantova*. Mantova: Tipografia Eredi Segna, 1876.

De Capua, Donato. "I Teatini a Bitonto." *Regnum Dei* 25, (1969): 3–143.

De Leturia, Pietro. "Il papa Paolo IV e la fondazione del Collegio Romano." *Regnum Dei* 10 (1954): 3–16.

De Lorenzo, Antonio. *Memorie da servire alla storia sacra e civile di Reggio e delle Calabrie*. Reggio Calabria: Stamperia Siclari, 1873.

De Maio, Romeo. *Riforme e miti nella Chiesa del Cinquecento*. Naples: Guida Editori, 1973.

De Rosa, Diana. *Libro di scorno, libro d'onore: la scuola elementare triestina durante l'amministrazione austriaca (1761–1918)*. Udine: Del Bianco, 1991.

De Seta, Cesare. *Storia della città di Napoli dalle origini al Settecento*. Rome-Bari: Laterza, 1973.

Del Panta, Lorenzo. "I processi demografici." In *Storia degli antichi stati italiani*. Edited by Gaetano Greco and Mario Rosa, 215–48. Rome-Bari: Laterza, 2009.

Del Tredici, Federico. "Maestri per il contado. Istruzione primaria e società locale nelle campagne milanesi (secolo XV)." In *Medioevo dei poteri. Studi di storia per Giorgio Chittolini*. Edited by Maria Nadia Covini, Massimo Della Misericordia, Andrea Gamberini and Francesco Somaini, 275–99. Rome: Viella, 2012.

Del Tredici, Federico. *Un'altra nobiltà. Storie di (in)distinzione a Milano. Secoli XIV–XV*. Milan: FrancoAngeli, 2017.

Della Bona, Giuseppe Domenico. *Osservazioni ed aggiunte sopra alcuni passi dell'Istoria della contea di Gorizia di Carlo Morelli di Schönfeld*. Gorizia: Tipografia Paternolli, 1856.

Della Guardia, Anita. *Gaspare Tribraco de' Trimbocchi. Maestro Modenese della II metà del secolo XV.* Modena: Antica tipografia Soliani, 1910.

Della Salvia, Alessandro. "Della statistica agraria," in *Atti dell'Accademia di Udine per il biennio 1867–1868*, 113–22. Udine: Tipografia di Giuseppe Seitz, 1870.

DeMolen, Richard, ed. *Religious Orders of the Catholic Reformation.* New York: Fordham University Press, 1994.

Denley, Peter. "Governments and schools in Late Medieval Italy." In *City and Countryside in Late Medieval and Renaissance Italy. Essays presented to Philip Jones.* Edited by Trevor Dean and Chris Wickham, 93–108. London: The Hambledon Press, 1990.

Di Bella, Saverio. *Caino Barocco. Messina e la Spagna 16721–678.* Cosenza: Luigi Pellegrini editore, 2005.

Di Filippo, Claudia. "The Reformation and the Catholic Revival in the Borromeo's Age." In *A Companion to Late Medieval and Early Modern Milan. The Distinctive Features of an Italian State.* Edited by Andrea Gamberini, 93–117. Leiden-Boston: Brill, 2014.

Di Fonzo, Lorenzo, Giovanni Odoardi and Alfonso Pompei, eds., *I frati minori conventuali. Storia e vita 1209–1976.* Rome: Curia generalizia O.F.M. Conv., 1978.

Diaz, Ernesto. *Jesuit Education and Mathematics: Review of Literature on the History of Jesuit Education and Mathematics.* Saarbrücken: VDM Dr. Müller, 2009.

Diemoz, Maria Caterina. "L'istruzione a Udine tra Repubblica Veneta e Regno Italico. L'impatto di un modello accentrato." PhD diss., University of Udine, 2012.

Diemoz, Maria Caterina. "L'istruzione di base maschile a Udine tra la Repubblica di Venezia e il Regno dItalia (1798–1813)," *Annali di storia dell'educazione e delle istituzioni scolastiche* 21, (2014): 161–92.

Dortel-Cloudot, Michel. "Chierici Regolari del Buon Gesù." In *Dizionario degli Istituti di Perfezione*, vol II, 909. Roma: Edizioni Paoline, 1974.

Eklof, Ben. *Russian Peasant Schools. Officialdom, Village Culture, and Popular Pedagogy 1861–1914.* Berkeley, Los Angeles, London: University of California Press, 1990.

Eklof, Ben, ed. *School and Society in Tsarist and Soviet Russia. Selected Papers from the Fourth World Congress for Soviet and East European Studies.* New York: St. Martin's Press, 1993.

Esposizione pratica della Regola di Sant'Angela Merici: per uso delle vergini della Compagnia. Brescia: Tipografia Queriniana, 1895.

Evangelisti, Silvia. "A Female Idea of Religious Perfection: Angela Merici and the Company of St. Ursula (1535–1540)." *Renaissance Studies*, 18 (2004): 391–411.

Evangelisti, Silvia. *Nuns: A History of Convent Life.* Oxford: Oxford University Press, 2007.

Farrell, Allan P. *The Jesuit Code of Liberal Education: Development and Scope of the Ratio Studiorum.* Milwaukee: Bruce Publishing Company, 1938.

Favino, Federica. "Famiano Michelini." *Dizionario Biografico degli Italiani*, vol. 74 (2010).

Favino, Federica. "Matematiche e matematici alla 'Sapienza' romana (XVII–XVIII secolo)." In *Mélanges de l'école française de Rome. Italie et Méditerranée*, 116, 11 (2004): 423–69.

Favino, Federica. "Scienza ed erudizione nei collegi degli ordini religiosi a Roma tra Sei e Settecento." *Cheiron*, 43–44 (2006): 331–70.

Ferente, Serena. "Le donne e lo Stato." In *Lo Stato del Rinascimento in Italia*. Edited by Andrea Gamberini and Isabella Lazzarini, 313–32. Rome: Viella, 2014.

Ferlan, Claudio. *Dentro e fuori le aule. La Compagnia di Gesù a Gorizia e nell'Austria interna (secoli XVI–XVII)*. Bologna: Il Mulino, 2012.

Ferlan, Claudio. "La fondazione del collegio dei Gesuiti di Gorizia. Progetti e realizzazione." *Quaderni giuliani di storia*, 2/XXVII (2006): 435–64.

Ferraresi, Alessandra. "La fisica sperimentale fra università e ginnasi nella Lombardia austriaca." In *Dalla filosofia naturale alla fisica. Discipline e didattica in Italia all'epoca di Volta*. Edited by Alessandra Ferraresi and Franco Giudice, *Studi Settecenteschi*, 18 (1998): 279–315.

Ferrari, Francesco. *Il collegio delle Scuole Pie di Fanano*. Modena: Società Tipografica Modenese, 1917.

Ferrari, S., E. Frecassetti, O. Galli and R. Gilardi. "La chiesa e la casa teatina di Sant'Agata in Bergamo alta." *Regnum Dei* 46, (1990): 81–106.

Ferrone, Vincenzo. *Scienza natura e religione: mondo newtoniano e cultura italiana nel primo Settecento*. Naples: Jovene, 1982.

Finocchiaro, Maurice A. *Defending Copernicus and Galileo: Critical Reasoning in the Two Affairs*. New York: Springer, 2010.

Firpo, Massimo. *Juan de Valdés and the Italian Reformation*. New York: Routledge, 2016.

Florensa, Joan. "La reforma de la sociedad depende de la diligente educación de los niños: el proyecto de Pere Gervàs de les Eres (1580)," *Archivum Scholarum Piarum* 83, XLII (2018) : 139–202.

Floris, Francesco. *Storia della Sardegna*. Rome: Newton Compton, 2008.

Fois, Mario. "La questione degli studi nell'Osservanza e la soluzione di S. Bernardino da Siena." *In Atti del Simposio Cateriniano-Bernardiniano*. Edited by Domenico Maffei, Paolo Nardi, 477–97. Siena: Accademia degli Intronati, 1982.

Fragnito, Gigliola. "Gli ordini religiosi tra Riforma e Controriforma." In *Clero e società nell'Italia moderna*. Edited by Mario Rosa, 115–205. Roma-Bari: Laterza, 1997.

Frova, Carla. *Istruzione e educazione nel medioevo*. Torino: Loescher, 1973.

Frova, Carla. "La scuola nella città tardomedievale: un impegno pedagogico e organizzativo." In *Le città in Italia e in Germania nel Medioevo: cultura, istituzioni, vita religiosa*. Edited by Reinhard Elze and Gina Fasoli, 119–43. Bologna: Il Mulino, 1981.

Furet, François and Jacques Ozouf. *Lire et écrire. L'alphabétisation des français de Calvin à Jules Ferry*. Paris: Editions de Minuit, 1977.

Gabotto, Ferdinando. *Lo Stato sabaudo da Amedeo VIII ad Emanuele Filiberto I (1451–1467)*. Torino-Rome: Luigi Roux Editore, 1892.

Gabotto, Ferdinando. "Supplemento al dizionario dei maestri che insegnarono in Piemonte fino al 1500," *Bollettino storico-bibliografico subalpino* 11, (1906): 102–41.

Gabrielli, Attilio. "I padri somaschi a Velletri." *Somascha. Bolletino di storia dei padri somaschi*, III, 2 (1917): 3–27.

Gabrielli, Attilio. *L'istruzione pubblica in Velletri attraverso i tempi*. Velletri: Tipografia Stracca, 1916.

Gamba, Giovanna. "Catechesi e scuole di alfabetizzazione," in *A servizio del Vangelo. Il cammino storico dell'evangelizzazione a Brescia. Vol. II L'età moderna*. Edited by Xenio Toscani, 143–73. Brescia: La Scuola, 2007.

Gamba, Giovanna. "Guidati alla virtù. Le scuole di dottrina cristiana a Brescia." In *Dalla virtù al precetto. L'educazione del gentiluomo dal '500 al '700*. Edited by Maurizio Tagliaferri, 71–100. Brescia: Fondazione Civiltà Bresciana, 2015.

Gamba, Giovanna. *La scoperta delle lettere. Scuole di dottrina e di alfabeto a Brescia in età moderna*. Milan: FrancoAngeli, 2008.

Gamberini, Andrea, and Isabella Lazzarini, eds. *The Italian Renaissance State*. Cambridge: Cambridge University Press, 2012.

Garibotto, Celestino. *I maestri di grammatica a Verona dal '200 a tutto il '500*. Verona: La tipografia veronese, 1921.

Garin, Eugenio, ed. *Il pensiero pedagogico dello umanesimo*. Florence: Giuntine-Sansoni, 1958.

Garstein, Oskar. *Rome and the Counter-Reformation in Scandinavia. Jesuit Educational Strategy 1553–1622*. Leiden-New York-Copenhagen-Cologne: Brill, 1992.

Gaudio, Angelo. "I Barnabiti a Livorno: note da una ricerca in corso." *Rassegna Volterrana*, LXXXVII (2010): 591–97.

Gavanti, Bartolomeo. *Vita del venerabile Cosimo Dossena vescovo di Tortona*. Milan: Ditta Boniardi Pogliani di Ermen. Besozzi, 1860.

Gazzini, Marina. "Scuola, libri e cultura nelle confraternite milanesi fra tardo medioevo e prima età moderna." *La Bibliofilìa* 103, 3 (2001): 215–61.

Gazzini, Marina. "Cultura e Welfare: l'istruzione gratuita per i giovani nella Milano sforzesca." In *Maestri e pratiche educative in età umanistica (Italia settentrionale, XV secolo)*. Edited by Monica Ferrari, Federico Piseri and Matteo Morandi, 141–57. Brescia: Morcelliana, 2019.

Gentili, Antonio Maria. *Les Barnabites. Manuel d'histoire et de spiritualité de l'Ordre des Clercs Réguliers de Saint Paul Decapité*. Rome: 2012.

Gianesini, Raffaele. "Istituti di istruzione a Udine nell'età moderna," in *La lavagna nera. Le fonti per la storia dell'istruzione nel Friuli-Venezia-Giulia*. Edited by Grazia Tatò, 1–40. Trieste: Associazione nazionale archivistica italiana. Sez. Friuli-Venezia-Giulia, 1995.

Ginatempo, Maria; Sandri Lucia. *L'Italia delle città: il popolamento urbano tra Medioevo e Rinascimento (secoli XIII–XVI)*. Florence: Le Lettere, 1990.

Giovanelli, Ilaria. *Educazione e istruzione durante il periodo della restaurazione con particolare riferimento all'Appennino reggiano*. Reggio Emilia: Deputazione di storia patria per le antiche province modenesi, 2005.

Giovannozzi, Giovanni. *Il Calasanzio e l'opera sua*. Florence: Le Monnier, 1930.

Giussano, Giovanni Pietro. *Vita di San Carlo Borromeo*. Naples: Tipografia arcivescovile, 1855.

Goddu, André. *Copernicus and the Aristotelian Tradition*. Leiden: Brill, 2010.

Gozzi, Gasparo. "Intorno all'educazione. Frammenti." In *Scritti di Gasparo Gozzi*. Edited by Niccolò Tommaseo: 371–95. Florence: Le Monnier, 1849.

Greco, Gaetano; Rosa, Mario, eds. *Storia degli antichi stati italiani*. Rome-Bari: Laterza, 2020³.

Greengrass, Mark. *Christendom Destroyed. Europe: 1517–1648*. London: Penguin Books, 2014.

Grendler, Paul. *Jesuit Schools and Universities in Europe 1548–1773*. Leiden-Boston: Brill, 2019.

Grendler, Paul. "Man is Almost a God: Fra Battista Carioni Between Renaissance and Catholic Reformation." In *Humanity and Divinity in Renaissance and Reformation: Essays in Honor of Charles Trinkaus*. Edited by John W. O'Malley, Thomas M. Izbicki and Gerald Christianson, 227–49. Leiden-New York-Cologne: Brill, 1993.

Grendler, Paul. *Renaissance Education Between Religion and Politics*. Aldershot-Burlington: Ashgate Variorum, 2006.

Grendler, Paul. *Schooling in Renaissance Italy. Literacy and Learning 1300–1600*. Baltimore & London: The Johns Hopkins University Press, 1989.

Grendler, Paul. *The Jesuits and Italian Universities 1548–1773*. Washington: The Catholic University of America Press, 2017.

Grendler, Paul. "The Piarist of the Pious Schools." In *Religious Orders of the Catholic Reformation: In honor of John C. Olin on his Seventy-Fifth Birthday*. Edited by Richard DeMolen, 252–78. New York: Fordham University Press, 1994.

Grendler, Paul. *The University of Mantua, the Gonzaga and the Jesuits, 1584–1630*. Baltimore: The Johns Hopkins University Press, 2009.

Gruber, Karl Heinz. "Higher Education and the State in Austria: An Historical and Institutional Approach." *European Journal of Education*, 17-3, (1982): 259–70.

Guasco, Maurilio. "La formazione del clero: i seminari." In *Storia d'Italia, Annali* IX, *La Chiesa e il potere politico*. Edited by Giorgio Chittolini and Giovanni Miccoli, 629–715. Torino: Einaudi, 1986.

Guerra, Enrica. "Guarino Veronese e la sua scuola ferrarese: cenni storiografici e di ricerca." In *Maestri e pratiche educative in età umanistica (Italia settentrionale, XV secolo*). Edited by Monica Ferrari, Federico Piseri and Matteo Morandi, 239–51. Brescia: Morcelliana, 2019.

Guerrini, Paolo. "Scuole e maestri bresciani del Cinquecento." *Commentari dell'Ateneo di Brescia* 121, (1922): 167–244.

Hébrard, Jean. "La scolarisation des savoirs élémentaires à l'époque moderne." *Histoire de l'éducation* 38, (1978): 7–58.

Howell, Kenneth. *God's two books: Copernican cosmology and biblical interpretation in early modern science*. Notre Dame: University of Notre Dame Press, 2002.

I barnabiti nel IV centenario dalla fondazione 1533–1933. Genoa: Tipografia Artigianelli, 1933.

Il regio Collegio della Guastalla. San Fruttuoso di Monza: Regio Collegio della Guastalla, 1938.

Ijsewijn, Jozef. "Scrittori latini a Roma dal Barocco al Neoclassicismo." *Studi romani*, 36 (1988): 229–51.

Kolvenbach, Hans Peter. "Ignazio a Venezia. Simbolismo di un passaggio." In *I Gesuiti e Venezia. Momenti e problemi di una storia veneziana della Compagnia di Gesù*. Edited by Mario Zanardi, 37–56. Padova: Gregoriana, 1994.

Kuhn, Thomas. *The Copernican Revolution. Planetary Astronomy in the Development of Western Thought*. Cambridge: Harvard University Press, 1957.

L'ordine dei Chierici Regolari Somaschi nel IV centenario della sua fondazione (1528–1928). Rome: Presso la Curia Generalizia, 1928.

Lama, Ernesto. *Il pensiero pedagogico dell'Illuminismo*. Florence: Giuntine-Sansoni, 1958.

Lambertini, Roberto. "Il sistema formativo degli *Studia* degli ordini mendicanti: osservazioni a partire dai risultati di recenti indagini." In *Die Ordnung der Kommunikation und die Kommunikation der Ordnungen. Bd. 1 Netzwerke: Kloster und Orden im Europa des 12. und 13. Jahrhunderts*. Edited by Cristina Andenna, Klaus Herbers, Gert Melville, 135–46. Stuttgart: Fraz Steiner Verlag, 2012.

Lasagni, Maria Grazia. "La presenza degli scolopi a Correggio dal 1722 al 1810." In *Istruzione, educazione e collegio in Correggio dal XVII al XX secolo*. Edited by Alberto Ghidini, 33–80. Correggio: Convitto Nazionale R. Corso, 1999.

Lawson, John; Silver, Harold. *A Social History of Education in England*. New York: Routledge, 2007.

Ledochowska, Thérèse. *Angèle Merici et la Compagnie de Ste. Ursule*. Rome-Milan, Ancora, 1967.

Lezàun, Antonio. *Storia delle Scuole Pie*. Madrid: Instituto Calasanz de Ciencias de la Educación, 2011.

Liberali, Giuseppe. *Le origini del seminario diocesano*. Treviso: Editrice Trevigiana, 1971.

Linari, Cleto. "Contributo dell'Ordine Teatino al Concilio di Trento." *Regnum Dei* 4, (1948): 203–29.

Lindberg, David; Numbers, Ronald. *When science and Christianity meet*. Chicago, University of Chicago Press, 2003.

Linebaugh, Peter and Markus Rediker. *The Many-Headed Hydra: Sailors, Slaves, Commoners, and The Hidden History of the Revolutionary Atlantic*. Boston: Beacon Press, 2000.

Longo-Timossi, Costanza. "I teatini e la riforma cattolica nella Repubblica di Genova nella prima metà` del seicento." *Regnum Dei* 43, (1987): 3–104.

Lovato, Italo. "I gesuiti a Gorizia 1615–1773" *Studi Goriziani* I-II (1959): 85–141, 83–130.

Lovison, Filippo. "Le scuole dei barnabiti a Udine (1679–1810)." *Barnabiti Studi* 15 (1998): 91–211.

Lovison, Filippo. "Le scuole dei barnabiti. Pietà e scienza nell'età dei lumi." *Barnabiti Studi* 26 (2009): 111–57.

Lux-Sterrit, Laurence. *Redefining Female Religious Life. French Ursulines and English Ladies in Seventeenth-Century Catholicism*. New York: Routledge, 2019.

Mac Carty, Ita. *Women and the Making of Poetry in Ariosto's Orlando Furioso*. Leicester: Troubador Publishing, 2007.

Macchietti, Sira Sirenella. *Rosa Venerini all'origine della scuola popolare femminile: l'azione educativa del suo istituto dal 1685 ad oggi*. Brescia: La Scuola, 1986.

Maierù, Alfonso. "Formazione culturale e tecniche d'insegnamento nelle scuole degli Ordini Mendicanti." In *Studio e* Studia: *le scuole degli ordini mendicanti tra XIII e XIV secolo*. Atti del XXIX Convegno internazionale di Assisi, 11–13 ottobre 2001, 3–32. Spoleto: Centro Italiano di Studi sull'Alto Medioevo, 2002.

Malpangotto, Michela. "Discussions coperniciennes au début du XVIII siècle: Le système du monde du P. Redento Baranzano enseignant en Savoie." *Archives internationales d'Histoire des sciences*, 60/2 (2010): 369–422.

Manacorda, Giuseppe. *Storia della scuola in Italia. Il Medioevo*. Palermo: Remo Sandron, 1914.

Manconi, Francesco. *La Sardegna al tempo degli Asburgo. Secoli XVI–XVIII*. Nuoro: Il Maestrale, 2010.

Marcocchi, Massimo. ed. *Il Concilio di Trento: istanze di riforma e aspetti dottrinali*. Milan: Vita e Pensiero, 1997.

Marcocchi, Massimo. "Le origini del Collegio della Beata Vergine di Cremona, istituzione della Riforma Cattolica (1610)." *Annali della Biblioteca statale e libreria civica di Cremona*, XXIV, (1974).

Mascilli Migliorini, Luigi, ed. *I somaschi*. Rome: Edizioni di storia e letteratura, 1992.

Mascilongo, Maria. *Ho creduto nell'amore. Itinerario spirituale di Rosa Venerini*. Rome: Città Nuova, 2006.

Masetti-Zannini, Gian Ludovico. "I teatini in Rimini." *Regnum Dei* 21, (1965): 87–147.

Masetti-Zannini, Gian Ludovico. "I teatini in Rimini." *Regnum Dei* 22, (1966): 58–102.

Masetti-Zannini, Gian Ludovico. *Idee sulla istruzione a Cesena ed a Rimini nel secolo XVIII*. Cesena: Badia di Santa Maria del Monte, 1972.

Materni, Marta. "Il precettore pubblico in una città italiana di provincia del Cinquecento." *Annali di Storia dell'Educazione e delle Istituzioni Scolastiche* 17, (2010): 247–264.

Maulucci, Vincenzo. "I teatini a Barletta." *Regnum Dei* 49, (1993): 3–58.

Maulucci, Vincenzo. "I teatini a Foggia." *Regnum Dei* 51, (1995): 57–172.

Mazzonis, Querciolo. "Angela Merici." In Oxford Bibliographies Online: Renaissance and Reformation. Edited by Margaret King. New York: Oxford University Press, 2012.

Mazzonis, Querciolo. "Donne devote nell'Italia post-tridentina: il caso delle compagnie di Sant'Orsola." *Rivista di Storia della Chiesa in Italia*, 2, (2014): 349–85.

Mazzonis, Querciolo. "Reforming Christianity in early sixteenth-century Italy: the Barnabites, the Somaschans, the Ursulines and the hospitals for the Incurables." *Archivium Hibernicum*, LXXI, (2018): 244–72.

Mazzonis, Querciolo. *Spirituality, Gender and the Self in Renaissance Italy: Angela Merici and the Company of St. Ursula (1474–1540)*. Washington DC: Catholic University of America Press, 2007.

Mazzonis, Querciolo. "The Company of St. Ursula in Counter-Reformation Italy." In *Devout Laywomen in the Early Modern World*. Edited by Alison Weber, 50–68. London-New York: Routledge, 2016.

Mazzonis, Querciolo. "The Impact of Renaissance Gender-Related Notions on the Female Experience of the Sacred: The Case of Angela Merici's Ursulines." In *Gender, Catholicism and Spirituality: Women and the Roman Catholic Church in Britain and Europe, 1200–1900*. Edited by Laurence Lux-Sterrit and Carmen Mangion, 51–67. London: MacMillan, 2010.

Mazzonis, Querciolo. "Ursulines." In Oxford Bibliographies Online: Renaissance and Reformation. Edited by Margaret King. New York: Oxford University Press, 2013.

Mazzotti Massimo. *The World of Maria Gaetana Agnesi, Mathematician of God*. Baltimore: The Johns Hopkins University Press, 2007.

McCoog, M. Thomas. *A Guide to Jesuit Archives*. Saint Louis-Rome: The Institute of Jesuit Sources-Institutum Historicum Societatis Jesu, 1998.

McCoog, M. Thomas, ed. *The Mercurian Project: Forming Jesuit Culture, 1573–1580*. Rome: Institutum Historicum Societatis Iesu, 2004.

McMichael, Steven, ed. *The Medieval Franciscans*. Leiden-Boston: Brill, 2019.

Michelutti, Manlio. "Scuola e istruzione in Friuli." In *Enciclopedia monografica del Friuli-Venezia Giulia*, vol. 4, 119–60. Udine: Istituto per l'enciclopedia del Friuli Venezia-Giulia, 1983.

Miglio, Luisa. *Governare l'alfabeto. Donne, scrittura e libri nel medioevo*. Rome: Viella, 2008.

Molesti, Romano. *Economisti e accademici nel Settecento veneto. Una visione organica dell'economia*. Milan: FrancoAngeli, 2006.

Molinari, Franco. "I teatini a Piacenza." *Regnum Dei* 35, (1979): 171–204.

Moncallero, Giuseppe Lorenzo. *La fondazione delle Scuole degli Scolopi nell'Europa centrale al tempo della Controriforma*. Bologna: Edizioni Domenicane, 1972.

Montanari, Daniele. *Gregorio Barbarigo a Bergamo (1657–1664). Prassi di governo e missione pastorale*. Milan: Glossa, 1997.

Mora, Alba, ed. *Un Borbone tra Parma e l'Europa. Don Ferdinando e il suo tempo (1751–1802)*. Reggio Emilia: Diabasis, 2005.

Moschini, Giannantonio. *La chiesa e il seminario di Santa Maria della Salute in Venezia*. Venice: Tipi di G. Antonelli, 1842.

Muir, Edward. "The Virgin on the Streetcorner." In *Religion and Culture in the Renaissance and Reformation*. Edited by Steven Ozment 25–6. Kirksville: Sixteenth Century Journal Publishers, 1989.

Mursia Antonio. "'Per insegnare naturali le scienze'. A proposito delle Scuole Pie dei padri Scolopi ad Adrano." *Archivum Scholarum Piarum* 79, (2016): 109–17.

Nada Patrone, Anna Maria. *Vivere nella scuola. Insegnare ed apprendere nel Piemonte del tardo medioevo*. Torino: Gribaudo, 1996.

Naphy, William. *The Protestant Revolution: From Martin Luther to Martin Luther King Jr.* London: BBC Books, 2007.

Negruzzo, Simona. "Alessandro Sauli: il professore santo." In *Almum Studium Papiense. Storia dell'Università di Pavia*, I: *Dalle origini all'età spagnola*, II, 975–76. Milan: Cisalpino, 2013.

Negruzzo, Simona. *Collegij a forma di Seminario. Il sistema di formazione teologica nello Stato di Milano in età spagnola*. Brescia. Editrice La Scuola, 2001.

Noailles, Hélie, de. *Le comte Molé (1781–1855). Sa vie. Ses mémoires*. Paris: Champion, 1922.

Novi Chavarria, Elisa. "I Teatini e 'il governo delle anime' (secoli XVI-XVII)." In *Sant'Andrea Avellino e i Teatini nella Napoli del Viceregno spagnolo. Arte religione società*. Edited by D.A. D'Alessandro 273–86. Naples: D'Auria Editore, 2011.

Numbers, Ronald. *Galileo goes to jail and other myths about science and religion*. Cambridge: Harvard University Press, 2009.

"Numero delle provincie, luoghi e padri, dei Poveri della Madre di Dio delle Scuole Pie, raccolto con l'occasione del capitolo generale celebrato in Roma a 15 d'ottobre 1637," *Archivum Scholarum Piarum*, XIII, (1954): 31–79.

O'Malley, John. *I primi gesuiti*, translated by Alberto Schena. Milan: Vita e Pensiero, 1999.

O'Malley, John. *The First Jesuits*. Cambridge: Harvard University Press, 1993.

Oleari, Paola. "L'interesse per la geografia tra i secoli XVI e XVII alla biblioteca dei teatini di Sant'Agata in Bergamo alta." *Regnum Dei* 50, (1994): 297–324.

Orlandi, Giuseppe. "I religiosi dello Stato di Modena nel Settecento tra riforme e rivoluzione." In *Lo stato di Modena. Una capitale, una dinastia, una civiltà nella storio d'Europa*, edited by Angelo Spaggiari and Giuseppe Trenti: 743–81. Rome: Ministero per i beni e le attività culturali Direzione generale per gli Archivi, 2001.

Orson, Richard. *Science and Religion, 1450–1900: from Copernicus to Darwin.* Westport: Greenwood Press, 2004.

Overloop, Samuel. "Rules of the Congregation for Members of the Roman Seminary." *The Way* XLVII, 4 (2008): 93–98.

Pacetti, Dioniso. "La necessità dello studio. Predica inedita di S. Bernardino da Siena." *Bullettino di Studi Bernardiniani* 2, (1936): 310–21.

Pagano, Sergio. "Le biblioteche dei barnabiti italiani nel 1599. In margine ai loro più antichi cataloghi." *Barnabiti studi* 3, (1986): 26–39.

Pal, Claudio Vil. "Escolapios y teations en vida de S. Josi de Calasanz." *Regnum Dei* 39, (1983) : 129–52.

Pancino, Maria. "La didattica di Giovanni Poleni." In *Il teatro di filosofia sperimentale di Giovanni Poleni*, edited by Maria Pancino and Gian Antonio Salandin: XV–XXII. Trieste: Lint, 1986.

Paone, Michele. "I teatini in Lecce." *Regnum Dei* 21, (1965): 148–72.

Paschini, Pio. *Eresia e Riforma cattolica al confine orientale d'Italia.* Rome: Lateranum, 1956.

Pasero, Dario. "Per la storia delle Scuole Pie in Dalmazia. Documenti (1776–1854)." *Archivum Scholarum Piarum* XVIII, 36 (1994): 1–127.

Pasini, Adamo. *Cronache scolastiche forlivesi.* Forlì: Valbonesi, 1925.

Patrizi, Elisabetta. *Pastoralità ed educazione. L'episcopato di Agostino Valier nella Verona post-tridentina (1565–1606).* Milan: FrancoAngeli, 2015.

Pavone, Sabina. *I gesuiti dalle origini alla soppressione.* Rome-Bari: Laterza, 2004.

Pavone, Sabina. "I Gesuiti in Italia 1548–1773." In *Atlante della letteratura italiana.* Vol. 2: *Dalla Controriforma alla Restaurazione.* Edited by Sergio Luzzatto, Gabriele Pedullà, Eriminia Irace, 359–73. Torino: Einaudi, 2011.

Pelliccia, Guerrino. *La scuola primaria a Roma dal secolo XVI al XIX. L'istruzione popolare e la catechesi ai fanciulli nell'ambito della parrocchia e dello "Studium Urbis" da Leone X a Leone XII (1513–1829).* Rome: Edizioni dell'Ateneo, 1985.

Petrino, Elizabeth and Jocelyn Boryczka, eds. *Jesuit and Feminist Education: Intersections in Teaching and Learning for the Twenty-First Century.* New York: Fordham University Press, 2012.

Picanyol, Leodegario. *Le Scuole Pie e Galileo Galilei.* Rome: Ed. PP. Scolopi di S. Pantaleo, 1942.

Piccioni, Luigi. "Città e reti insediative nel Mezzogiorno di età moderna." In *Scelte pubbliche, strategie private e sviluppo economico in Calabria.* Edited by Giovanni Anania, 217–35. Soveria Mannelli: Rubbettino, 2001.

Pillepich, Alain. *Napoléon et les italiens. République italienne et Royaume d'Italie (1802–1814).* Paris: Nouveau monde éditions, 2003.

Piseri, Federico. "L'educazione civile come problema pedagogico: il caso di Vittorino da Feltre tra continuità e innovazione." In *Maestri e pratiche educative in età umanistica*

(*Italia settentrionale XV secolo*). Edited by Federico Piseri, Monica Ferrari and Matteo Morandi, 53–72. Brescia: Morcelliana, 2019.

Piseri, Maurizio. *L'alfabeto delle riforme. Scuola e alfabetismo nel basso cremonese da Maria Teresa all'Unità*. Milan: Vita & Pensiero, 2002.

Piseri, Maurizio. *L'alfabeto in montagna. Scuola e alfabetismo nell'area alpina tra età moderna e XIX secolo*. Milan: FrancoAngeli, 2012.

Piseri, Maurizio. *La scuola primaria nel Regno Italico, 1796–1814*. Milan: FrancoAngeli, 2017.

Pissavino, Paolo and Signorotto, Gianvittorio, ed. *Lombardia borromaica Lombardia spagnola: 1554–1659*. Rome: Bulzoni, 1995.

Pititto, Rocco. "Teorie pedagogiche e pratica educativa. La *Ratio Studiorum* dei Barnabiti." *Barnabiti Studi* 26, (2009): 85–109.

Pomponio, Rita. *Il tredicesimo apostolo. Santa Lucia Filippini*. Rome: San Paolo Edizioni, 2004.

Pon, Lisa. *A Printed Icon in Early Modern Italy. Forlì's Madonna of the Fire*. Cambridge: Cambridge University Press, 2015.

Porta, Vincenzo. "I teatini a Vicenza." *Regnum Dei* 16, (1960): 85–143.

Pörtner, Regina. *The Counter-Reformation in Central Europe: Styria 1580–1630*. Oxford, Oxford University Press, 2008.

Premoli, Orazio Maria. *Storia dei barnabiti dal 1700 al 1825*. Rome: Società tipografica Aldo Manuzio, 1925.

Premoli, Orazio Maria. *Storia dei barnabiti nel Cinquecento*. Rome: Desclee editore, 1913.

Premoli, Orazio Maria. *Storia dei barnabiti nel Seicento*. Rome: Industria tipografica romana, 1922.

Prohens, Jaime. "Los teatinos en Mallorca." *Regnum Dei* 4, (1948): 121–71.

Prosperi, Adriano. "Educare gli educatori. Il prete come professione intellettuale nell'Italia tridentina." In *Problèmes d'histoire de l'éducation*, 123–40. Rome: École Française de Rome, 1988.

Prosperi, Adriano. *Il Concilio di Trento: una introduzione storica*. Torino: Einaudi, 2001.

Prosperi, Adriano. *Tribunali della coscienza. Inquisitori, confessori, missionari*. Torino: Einaudi, 2009.

Raccolta di notizie e documenti sulla fondazione, sul patrimonio e sviluppo del r. Collegio della Guastalla in Milano. Milan: F. Manini, 1881.

Rapley, Elizabeth. *The Devotes: Women and Church in Seventeenth-Century France*. Montreal and Kingston: McGill-Queen's University Press, 1990.

Ravaglioli, Fabrizio. "L'educazione umanistica nel passaggio dalla città stato tardomedievale alla città-capitale." In *Vittorino da Feltre e la sua scuola: umanesimo, pedagogia, arti*. Edited by Nella Giannetto, 95–108. Florence: Olschki, 1981.

Raviola, Blythe Alice. *L'Europa dei piccoli stati. Dalla prima età moderna al declino dell'Antico Regime*. Rome: Carocci, 2008.

Raviolo Sebastiano C.R.S. "Il contributo dei Somaschi alla Controriforma e lo sviluppo dei loro ordinamenti scolastici dagli inizi alla prima metà del '700." M.A. diss., Milan Catholic University of the Sacred Heart, 1942.

Reed-Danahay, Deborah. *Education and Identity in Rural France. The Politics of Schooling*. Cambridge: Cambridge University Press, 1996.

Regolamento interno del R. Collegio della Guastalla in Milano. Milan: Artigianelli, 1932.

Regole per maestre pie dell'istituto della serva di Dio Rosa Venerini ricavate dalla vita, dalla relazione e dai manoscritti della medesima. Rome, coi tipi vaticani, 1837.

Remmert, R., Volker. "Galileo, God and Mathematics." In *Mathematics and the Divine: A Historical Study*, edited by Teun Koetsier and Luc Bergmans: 347–60. Amsterdam: Elsevier, 2005.

Riché, Pierre and Verger, Jacques. *Des nains sur des épaules de géants. Maîtres et élèves au Moyen Âge*. Paris: Éditions Tallandier, 2006.

Rocca, Giancarlo. "Gesuiti, Gesuitesse e l'educazione femminile." In *L'educazione femminile tra Cinque e Settecento, Annali di storia dell'educazione e delle istituzioni scolastiche*, 14, (2007): 65–75.

Roest, Bert. *A History of Franciscan Education (1210–1517)*. Leiden-Boston: Brill, 2000.

Roest, Bert. *Franciscan Learning, Preaching and Mission c. 1220–1650*. Leiden-Boston: Brill, 2015.

Roggero, Marina. *Insegnar lettere: ricerche di storia dell'istruzione in età moderna*. Alessandria: Edizioni dell'Orso, 1992.

Roggero, Marina. *L'alfabeto conquistato. Apprendere e insegnare nell'Italia tra Sette e Ottocento*. Bologna: Il Mulino, 1999.

Rombaldi, Odoardo. "Maestri e scuole in Reggio Emilia nel secolo XV." In *Bartolomeo Spani 1468–1539. Atti e memorie del Convegno di studio nel V centenario della nascita*, 91–125. Modena: Aedes Muratoriana, 1970.

Rossi di Marignano, Federico. *Carlo Borromeo. Un uomo, una vita, un secolo*. Milan: Mondadori, 2010.

Rosso, Paolo. *La scuola nel Medioevo: secoli VI–XV*. Rome: Carocci, 2018.

Rozzo, Ugo. "Le biblioteche dei cappuccini nell'inchiesta della Congregazione dell'Indice (1597–1603)." In *Girolamo Mautini da Narni e l'ordine dei frati minori Cappuccini fra '500 e '600*. Edited by Vittorio Criscuolo, 50–101. Rome: Istituto storico dei cappuccini, 1998.

Rusconi, Roberto. "Gli ordini religiosi maschili dalla Controriforma alle soppressioni settecentesche. Cultura, predicazioni, missioni." In *Clero e società nell'Italia moderna*. Edited by Mario Rosa, 207–74. Rome-Bari: Laterza, 1997.

Saint-Méry, Moreau de. *Historique. Etats de Parme 1749–1808*. Edited by Carla Corradi Martini. Reggio Emilia: Diabasis, 2003.

Salomoni, David. "Fragments of Renaissance schools on the banks of the Po River." *Educazione. Giornale di pedagogia critica* 6, 1 (2017): 7–30.

Salomoni, David. "Le scuole di una comunità emiliana nel Rinascimento tra religione e politica. Il caso di Novellara." *Educazione. Giornale di pedagogia critica* 5, 2 (2016): 17–42.

Salomoni, David. "Maestri e studenti alla fine del Medioevo: il caso emiliano." In *Città, campagne e castelli. Cultura, potere e società nel Medioevo padano* Edited by Carlo Baja Guarienti, 101–18. Reggio Emilia: Antiche Porte, 2016.

Salomoni, David. "Pedagogia eretica. Note di ricerca su alcuni processi a maestri di scuola nella Modena del '500." *Educazione. Giornale di pedagogia critica* 7, 2 (2018): 7–32.

Salomoni, David. *Scuole, maestri e scolari nelle comunità degli Stati gonzagheschi e estensi.* Rome: Anicia, 2017.

Salvarani, Luana. *Nova Schola. Temi e problemi di pedagogia protestante nei primi testi della Riforma.* Rome: Anicia, 2018.

Sanders, Eve Rachele. *Gender and Literacy on Stage in Early Modern England.* Cambridge: Cambridge University Press, 1998.

Sangalli, Maurizio. *Cultura, politica e religione nella Repubblica di Venezia tra Cinque e Seicento. Gesuiti e Somaschi a Venezia.* Venice: Istituto veneto di scienze morali, lettere ed arti, 1999.

Sangalli, Maurizio. "Da Bergamo a Capodistria. Scuole, collegi, clero tra Sette e Ottocento." In *L'istruzione in Italia tra Sette e Ottocento. Lombardia-Veneto-Umbria.* I: Studi, atti del convegno nazionale di studi, Milano-Pavia 28–30 ottobre 2004. Edited by Angelo Bianchi, 235–68. Brescia: La Scuola, 2007.

Sangalli, Maurizio. "Gli scolopi e la Serenissima. Verso il riconoscimento 1630–1730." *Studi veneziani* 50, II (2005): 173–96.

Sangalli, Maurizio. "Le congregazioni religiose insegnanti in Italia in età moderna: nuove acquisizioni e piste di ricerca." *Dimensioni e problemi della ricerca storica*, no. 1 (2005): 25–47.

Sangalli, Maurizio. *Le smanie per l'educazione. Gli scolopi a Venezia tra Sei e Settecento.* Rome: Viella, 2012.

Sangalli, Maurizio, ed. *Per il Cinquecento religioso italiano. Clero, cultura, società.* Rome: Edizioni dell'Ateneo, 2003.

Sangalli, Maurizio. "Un generale alle prese con la riorganizzazione delle Scuole pie: Carlo Giovanni Pirroni e le sue prime quattro circolari 1677–1681." *Archivum Scholarum Piarum* 20, (1996): 15–44.

Sangalli, Maurizio. "The Piarist in a Frontier Region between the Republic of Venice and the Empire of the Habsburg: Economic and Educational Strategies of a Teaching Religious Congregation in the Eighteenth Century." In *Growing in the Shadow of an Empire: How Spanish Colonialism Affected Economic Development in Europe and in the World (XVI–XVIII cc.).* Edited by Giuseppe De Luca and Gaetano Sabatini, 377–92. Milan: FrancoAngeli, 2012.

Sangalli, Maurizio. *Università, accademie, gesuiti. Cultura e religione a Padova tra Cinque e Seicento*. Padova: LINT, 2001.

Sàntha, Georgio. "L'opera delle Scuole Pie e le cause della loro riduzione sotto Innocenzo X." In *Monumenta Historica Scholarum Piarum*. Rome: Apud Curiam Generalitiam, 1989.

Santoro, Mario. *Opere di Ludovico Ariosto Carmina, Rime, Satire, Erbolato, Lettere*. Torino: UTET, 1962.

Sasso, Maria Renata. "Dal leone marciano all'aquila bicipite. Il caso della scuola elementare di Palmanova." *Annali di storia dell'educazione e delle istituzioni scolastiche*, 15, (2008): 193–201.

Saulini, Mirella. *Bernardino Stefonio S.J. Un gesuita sabino nella storia del teatro*. Rome: Edizioni Espera, 2014.

Scaduto, Mario. *L'epoca di Giacomo Lainez 1556–1565: Il governo*. Rome: La Civiltà Cattolica, 1964.

Scaduto, Mario. *L'epoca di Giacomo Lainez, 1556–1565: L'azione*. Rome: La Civiltà Cattolica, 1974.

Scaduto, Mario. *L'opera di Francesco Borgia, 1565–1572*. Rome: La Civiltà Cattolica, 1992.

Scaduto, Mario. "Le missioni di A. Possevino in Piemonte. Propaganda calvinista e restaurazione cattolica 1560–1563." *Archivum Historicum Societatis Iesu*, XXVIII (1959): 51–191.

Scaduto, Mario. "Le 'visite' di Antonio Possevino nei domìni dei Gonzaga (contributo alla storia religiosa del tardo Cinquecento)." *Archivio storico lombardo* 10, LXXXVII (1960): 336–410.

Schmitt, Charles Bernard. *The Aristotelian tradition and renaissance universities*. London: Aldershot-Brookfield, 1998.

Schmitt, Charles Bernard. "Towards a Reassessment of Renaissance Aristotelianism." *History of Science*, 11, 3 (1973): 159–93.

Scroope, Martin. *Mission Formation Education: A Framework for Formation of Persons and Communities in Ignatian Education*. Pimble, Loyola Institute, 2006.

Seneca, Federico. *La politica veneziana dopo l'interdetto*. Padova: Liviana, 1957.

Sharrat, Michael. *Galileo: Decisive Innovator*. Cambridge: Cambridge University Press, 1994.

Signaroli, Simone. *Maestri e tipografi a Brescia 1471–1519*. Brescia: Eduzioni Torre d'Ercole, 2009.

Signorotto, Gianvittorio ed. *Ferrante Gonzaga. Il Mediterraneo, l'Impero 1507–1557*. Rome: Bulzoni Editore, 2009.

Sindoni, Angelo. "Le Scuole pie in Sicilia. Note sulla storia dell'ordine scolopico dalle origini al secolo XIX." *Rivista di storia della Chiesa in Italia* XXV, (1971): 375–421.

Smail, Daniel. *On Deep History and the Brain*. Oakland: University of California Press, 2007.

Sonnet, Martine. "L'educazione di una giovane." In *Storia delle donne in Occidente. Dal Rinascimento all'età moderna*, edited by Georges Duby and Michelle Perrot: 119–55. Rome-Bari: Laterza, 1991.

Sorbelli, Albano. *Il comune rurale dell'Appenino emiliano nei secoli XIV e XV*. Bologna: Zanichelli, 1910.

Spalla, Annibale. "Le Missioni teatine nelle Indie Orientali nel sec. XVIII e le cause della loro fine." *Regnum Dei* 27–28, (1971–1972): 1–76; 265–305.

Spessot, Francesco. "Primordi, incremento e sviluppo delle istituzioni gesuitiche di Gorizia (1615–1773)." *Studi Goriziani*, 3, (1925): 83–142.

Spinelli, Mario. *Giuseppe Calasanzio: il pioniere della scuola popolare*. Rome: Città Nuova, 2001.

Stella, Pietro. "Michele Casati." *Dizionario Biografico degli Italiani*, vol. 21 (1978).

Strazzullo, Franco. *Edilizia e urbanistica a Napoli dal '500 al '700*. Napoli: Berisio Arturo Editore, 1958.

Strazzullo, Franco. "La Chiesa e Casa dei SS. Apostoli di Napoli dopo la soppressione del 1809." *Regnum Dei* 13, (1957): 278–87.

Tabanelli, Mario. *Una città di Romagna nel Medioevo e nel Rinascimento*. Brescia: Magalini Editrice, 1980.

Tacchi Venturi, Pietro. *Storia della Compagnia di Gesù in Italia*, 2 vols. in 4 parts. Rome: Civiltà Cattolica, 1910–1951.

Taccone-Gallucci, Domenico. *Regesti dei romani pontefici per le chiese di Calabria*. Rome: Tipografia Vaticana, 1902.

Tambelli, Roberto. "Le missioni popolari dei teatini a Napoli." MBA diss., Università degli Studi di Napoli "Ferderico II," 2011.

Tamborini, Alessandro. *La compagnia e le scuole della dottrina cristiana*. Milan: Daverio, 1939.

Tanturri, Alberto. "Il collegio degli scolopi a Posillipo. Metamorfosi di una struttura educativa." *Campania Sacra* 31, (2000): 5–28.

Tanturri, Alberto. "Ordres et congrégations enseignants à l'époque de la Contre-Réforme. Barnabites, Somasques, Scolopes. " *Revue Historique* (2011): 811–52.

Tanturri, Alberto. "Scolopi e gesuiti all'epoca di S. Giuseppe Calasanzio." *Archivio italiano per la storia della pietà* 13, (2000): 193–216.

Tentorio, Marco. "In merito alle istituzioni somasche 'Orfanotrofio-Collegio-Convitto'." *Somascha* XXVI, (2001): 1–10.

Testa, Luca. *Fondazione e sviluppo del Seminario romano (1565–1608)*. Rome: Pontificia Università Gregoriana, 2002.

Timon-David, Joseph-Marie. *Une victime des Jésuites. Saint Joseph Calasanz*. Paris: Librairie Moderne, 1922.

Toffolo, Attilio. "Percorsi spirituali ed educativi nella Milano del XVI secolo. Ludovica Torelli tra chiostro e collegio." *Rivista della storia della Chiesa in Italia*, 2, (2012): 431–65.

Tomea, Paolo. *Tradizione apostolica e coscienza cittadina a Milano nel medioevo: la leggenda di San Barnaba*. Milan: Vita e Pensiero, 1993.

Toscani, Xenio. "Le Scuole della Dottrina Cristiana come fattore di alfabetizzazione." *Società e storia*, 26, (1984): 757–81.

Toscani, Xenio. "Ruoli del clero, canali e strumenti di apprendimento nella Lombardia dei secoli XVI–XIX." In *Formare alle professioni. Sacerdoti, principi, educatori*. Edited by Egle Becchi and Monica Ferrari, 70–118. Milan: FrancoAngeli, 2009.

Toscani, Xenio. *Scuole e alfabetismo nello Stato di Milano da Carlo Borromeo alla Rivoluzione*. Brescia: La Scuola, 1993.

Tosti, Osvaldo. "Ancora sulle Scuole Pie in Dalmazia." *Archivum Scholarum Piarum* XX, 31 (1996): 121–92.

Tronti, Mario, "Baranzano Redento," *Dizionario Biografico degli Italiani*, vol. 5, (1963).

Tuniz, Dorino. *Carlo Bascapé. Un vescovo sulle orme di san Carlo*. Novara: Interlinea, 2015.

Turchini, Angelo. *Sotto l'occhio del padre: società confessionale e istruzione primaria nello Stato di Milano*. Bologna: Il Mulino, 1996.

Turrini, Miriam. "Catechismi e scuole della dottrina cristiana nell'Italia del Cinquecento." In *L'educazione religiosa in Russia e Europa. XVI secolo*. Edited by Evghenia Tokareva and Marek Inglot, 60–80. Saint Petersburg: Casa editrice dell'Accademia russa cristiana umanistica, 2010.

Van Horn Melton, James. *Absolutism and the eighteenth-century origins of compulsory schooling in Prussia and Austria*. New York: Cambridge University Press, 1988.

Vanni, Andrea. *"Fare diligente inquisitione." Gian Pietro Carafa e le origini dei chierici regolari teatini*. Rome: Viella, 2010.

Varanini, Gian Maria, ed. *Storiografia e identità dei centri minori italiani tra la fine del Medioevo e l'Ottocento*. San Miniato: Firenze University Press 2013.

Veny-Ballester, Antonio. "S. Ignacio de Loyola y el retorno de los Clirigos Regulares a Roma." *Regnum Dei* 9, (1953): 19–25.

Venturi, Franco. *Settecento Riformatore*. Vol. I, *Da Muratori a Beccaria*. Torino: Einaudi, 1969.

Venturi, Franco. *Settecento Riformatore*. Vol. II, *La chiesa e la repubblica dentro i loro limiti, 1758–1774*. Torino: Einaudi, 1976.

Venturi, Franco. *Settecento Riformatore*. Vol. III, *La prima crisi dell'Antico Regime*. Torino: Einaudi, 1979.

Vigotti, Gualberto. *S. Carlo Borromeo e la Compagnia di S. Orsola. Nel centenario della ricostituzione in Milano della Compagnia di S. Orsola figlie di S. Angela Merici (1872–1972)*. Milan: Scuola tipografica S. Benedetto Viboldone, 1972.

Villanti, Nicolò. "Maestri di scuola a Ragusa (Dubrovnik) nel Medioevo 1300–1450." *Dubrovnik Annals* 22, (2018): 7–50.
Villari, Litterio. "I Padri teatini nella città di Piazza Armerina." *Regnum Dei* 40, (1984): 91–146.
Vinay, Valdo. "La Riforma in Croazia e Slovenia e il 'Beneficio di Cristo'." *Bollettino della società di studi valdesi*, 116, (1964): 19–32.
Volpi, Roberto. "Cortenovis Angelo Maria." *Italian Biographical Dictionary*, 29 (1983).
Walcher Casotti, Maria. "Il collegio e la chiesa dei gesuiti a Gorizia." *Studi Goriziani*, 71, (1990): 113–70.
Whitehead, Barbara J., ed. *Women's Education in Early Modern Europe. A History 1500–1800*. New York and London: Garland Publishing, 1999.
Whittle, Sean. *A Theory of Catholic Education*. London: Bloomsbury, 2015.
Woshinsky, Barbara J. *Imagining Women's Conventual Spaces in France, 1600–1800: The Cloister Disclosed*. New York: Routledge, 2010.
Zago, Giuseppe. "Maestri di Umanesimo in area veneta (XV secolo)." In *Maestri e pratiche educative in età umanistica (Italia settentrionale, XV secolo)*. Edited by Monica Ferrari, Federico Piseri and Matteo Morandi, 183–201. Brescia: Morcelliana, 2019.
Zambarelli, Luigi. *L'Ordine dei Chierici regolari Somaschi nel IV centenario della fondazione 1528–1928*. Rome: Tipografia Madre di Dio, 1928.
Zanardi, Mario, ed. *I gesuiti a Venezia: Momenti e problemi di storia veneziana della Compagnia di Gesù*. Padova: Gregoriana Libreria Editrice, 1994.
Zanelli, Agostino. *Del pubblico insegnamento in Brescia nei secoli XVI e XVII*. Brescia: Apollonio, 1896.
Zanelli, Agostino. "Maestri di grammatica in Foligno durante il secolo XV." *L'Umbria, rivista d'arte e letteratura* 2, 13/14 (July 1899): 102–03.
Zardin, Danilo. "Confraternite e comunità nelle campagne milanesi fra Cinque e Seicento." *La scuola cattolica* 112, (1984): 698–732.
Zardin, Danilo. "Scuola e accesso alla cultura nell'Italia della prima età moderna." *Annali di storia dell'educazione e delle istituzioni scolastiche*, 1, (1994): 253–64.
Zarri, Gabriella. "Aspetti dello sviluppo degli ordini religiosi in Italia tra Quattro e Cinquecento. Studi e problemi." In *Strutture ecclesiastiche in Italia e Germania prima della Riforma*. Edited by Paolo Prodi and Peter Johanek, 207–57. Bologna: Il Mulino, 1984.
Zarri, Gabriella. "Living Saints. A Tipology of Female Sanctity in the Early Sixteenth Century." In *Women and Religion in Medieval and Renaissance Italy*. Edited by Daniel Bornstein and Roberto Rusconi, 219–304. Chicago and London: The University of Chicago Press, 1996.

Zarri, Gabriella. "Ursula and Catherine: The Marriage of Virgins in the Sixteenth Century." In *Creative Women in Medieval and Early Modern Italy: A Religious and Artistic Renaissance*. Edited by Ann J. Matter and John Coackley; 237–78. Philadelphia: University of Pennsylvania Press, 1994.

Zovatto, Pietro, ed. *Storia della spiritualità italiana*. Rome: Città Nuova, 2001.

Index

Abbiategrasso 81
Abruzzo region 120
Acquaviva, Claudio 134
Acqui 97
Adria 114
Affò, Ireneo 6, 140, 144
Agnesi, Maria Gaetana 75–76
Aguzzani, Carlo 142
Alacchi, Giovanni 178
Alba 102, 151
Albenga 57, 102
Albinelli, Giacomo 21
Aldobrandini, Pietro 108
Aldobrandini-Farnese, Margherita 108
Alessandria 97, 101n12, 148
Ambrosi, Ambrogio 163
Amelia 102
    Somascan school 102
Anabaptism 29n50
Ancona 113
Anfora, Cesare 110
Angelic Sisters 12, 48n18, 48–49, 77, 84–87, 89
Angera 81
Annecy 97–98, 167–168
Antonini, Prospero 126
Aosta 98
Appiano 81, 147
Aquileia 128
Arcetri 64, 162
Arcimboldi, Giambattista 51, 97, 152–153
Ariosto, Ludovico 27
Aristotelianism 2, 58, 73, 75, 162, 167
Arnauld, Antoine 59
Arno 21
Arona 81–82, 97
Arpino 97, 153
    Barnabite College 153
Arsago 33, 81
Ascoli 36
Assisi 119
Asti 36, 97
Austria 4, 69, 129, 170–171, 179–180
Avignon 101, 119

Bacci, Porzia 89
Baldini, Ugo 174
Baliani, Giovanni Battista 164
Bangert, William 7
Baranzano, Redento 42, 42n2, 54, 167–169
    Uranoscopia seu de Caelo 168
Barbarigo, Marcantonio 12, 91–93
Barberini, Maffeo. *See* Urban VIII pope
Barletta 110
Barnabites 3, 5, 9, 12–13, 38–39, 41, 44, 48n18, 47–54, 62, 67, 69, 75, 77, 83, 85, 89, 96–99, 101, 101n14, 103, 115, 118, 122–123, 126–130, 133, 136, 152–154, 167–168, 172, 174, 178–179, 182
    Constitutions of 1579 49–50
    Exterarum Scholarum disciplina 52
Barthélemy-Gabriel Rolland d'Erceville 171
Barzazi, Antonella 58
Barzizza, Gasparino 26, 177
Bascapé, Carlo 50–51, 97
Basilicata region 121
Bassano 19, 114
Bazas 97
Belgioioso 36
Belinzaghi, Gaspare 81
Belluno 129
Bembo, Pietro 20
Benedict XI pope 70
Benedict XIV pope 49n20, 76, 168
Bergamo 34, 36, 81, 98, 101n12, 101–102, 109, 129
Bernardino of Siena 118
Berro, Vincenzo 65
Besozzi, Giovanni Pietro 49
Besozzo 21, 83
Bianchi, Angelo 52, 152
Bianchi, Maria Teresa 158
Biella 56, 102, 148
Bisignano 113
Bitonto 109
Blaisdell, Charmarie 80
Blanco, Giuseppe Antonio 110
Boddi, Francesco 99, 154
Boiardo, Matteo Maria 137
Bollate 33

Bologna   31, 70–72, 82, 98, 107, 113, 118–121, 133
   San Luigi College   99
   University of Bologna   3n4, 75
Bologna, Antonio   62n60
Bonaparte, Joseph   181
Bonifacio de' Colli   73
Bonneville   97, 154
Bonvesin de la Riva   25
Borelli, Giovanni Alfonso   164
Bormio   98–99
Borromeo Trivulzio, Margherita   82
Borromeo, Barbara   133
Borromeo, Carlo   37, 49, 81, 88, 97, 133, 146
Borromeo, Federico   82
Bosco, Giovanni   176, 183
Bourbon dinasty   143
   Ferdinand (Duke of Parma)   143
   Ferdinand IV (King of Naples)   173
   Henry IV (King of France)   167
   Louis XV (King of France)   143
Brebbia   147
Brescello   136
Brescia   11, 19, 31, 34, 36, 57, 76, 79–82, 101n12, 101–102, 118–120, 129
   Somascan College   57
Budapest   114
Budrio   71
Burke, Peter   3
Busachi   21
Busto Arsizio   81
Butzer, Martin   72

Cagliari   21, 65, 66n67, 66–67, 119, 121
Calabria   110
Calabria region   110, 118
Calasanz, Joseph   3, 11, 60–65, 111, 135–136, 160, 164, 178
Calvinism   29n50, 31, 72, 96, 162, 167
Campanella, Tommaso   63, 114, 160
Campanelli, Marcella   106
Campania region   109, 120
Campi Salentina   113
Campi, Domenico   141
Campoformio (treaty in 1797)   129, 180
Candelari, Chiara   93
Canisius, Peter   28
Canneto Sull'Oglio   35

Canobio   147
Cantù   81
Capodistria.   *See* Koper
Capua   109
Caracci, Persio   144
Caracciolo, Filippo   110
Carafa, Carlo   93
Carafa, Gian Pietro   73–74, 76, 105
Caravate   21
Carcare   112
Carinthia   126
Carioni, Giovanni Battista   12, 38–39, 47–48, 48n18, 51, 78, 85–86
Carnago   21, 33
Carpi   133, 136–137, 175
Cartesianism   59, 75, 165
Casale Monferrato   30, 102
Casali, Margherita   93
Casalini, Cristiano   7
Casalmaggiore   20, 97, 158
Casati, Michele   75–76
Caserta   151
Casorate   33
Casotti, Giovanni   155
Castelli, Benedetto   164
Castellino da Castello   33n61, 35–36, 38, 80
Castelseprio   147
Castiglione Olona   21
Castile   5
Catania   20
Catanzaro   110
Cateau Cambrésis (treaty in 1559)   4
Catherine II (Tsarina of Russia)   171
Catholic Reformation   16, 73, 160
Cavallermaggiore   102
Ceneda   114
Cento   102
Cesena   18, 119
Chelucci, Paolino   166
Chiari   114
Chiavari   102
Chieri   98
Chieti   113
Chivasso   19
Cividale   102, 126, 129–130
Civita Castellana   91
Civita di Bagnoregio   91
Clement VII pope   47, 73, 105, 117, 120

INDEX

Clement VIII pope   31, 51, 56–57, 97
Clement IX pope   143
Clement XI pope   91, 93
Clement XII pope   68
Clerics Regular of Saint Paul.   *See* Barnabites
Cocastel family   154
Coeducation   37
Cologne   119
Coluzzelli, Gerolama   89
Como   34, 36, 54, 81, 101, 108, 150
Compagnia dei Servi dei Poveri di Cristo.   *See* Somascans
Compagnia dei Servi di Puttini in Charità   36, 78
Compagnia della Reformatione Christiana in Charità.   *See Compagnia dei Servi di Puttini in Charità*
Compendium rei grammaticae maxime ex Linacro   29
Conegliano   114
Congregation of the Pious Workers   93
Conservatorio delle Convertite della Carità   79
Consiglieri, Paolo   73
Constantinople   179
Constitutioni et regole della Compagnia et scuole della Dottrina christiana   37
Conti, Carlo   163
Copernicus   3n4, 42n2, 160–161
Corbetta   147
Cornaro, Francesco   80
Corneliano   33
Corradi, Sebastiano   27
Correggio   131–133, 135–137
    Pious School   137–139
Corsica   120
Corsini, Odoardo   166
Corte Maggiore   102
Cortenovis, Angelo Maria   130
Cortona   97
Cosenza   110, 113, 121
Costanza del Carretto   110
Council Lateran IV   146
Council of Basel   146
Council of Trent   12, 80, 146–147, 150, 160
Crema   97, 129

Cremona   20, 34, 36, 50–51, 57, 81, 97–98, 103, 108, 152
    Barnabite College   97
Croatia   114n48
Curti, Luigia   158

Da Correggio dinasty   131–132
    Giberto III   131
    Siro   132
Dalmatia   114n48, 114–115
Davini, Gaetano   166
Dax   97
De discipulorum preceptorumque moribus.   See *De vita scholastica*
De vita scholastica   25
Decimo   33
Delbecchi, Agostino   68
Delle Laste, Natal   178
Desenzano del Garda   11, 78, 178
Desio   36, 81, 147
Devotio Moderna   48
Dominicans   24–25, 61, 116, 136
Doria, Vittoria   155
Dossena, Cosimo   51–52
Du Tillot, Guillaume   174
Dubrovnik   19, 114
Dunieri, Paolo   153

Emiliani, Girolamo   54, 100, 150, 178
England   5, 31, 161, 170
Erfurt   71
Este dinasty   17–18, 22, 132, 137
    Cesare   133
    Ercole III   137, 139, 175–176
    Niccolò III   23
    Rinaldo   136–137
Etampes   97, 154
Eugène de Beauharnais   180

Fabriano   31, 118
Facciardi, Timoteo   97
Faenza   18
Fanano   112, 135–136
    Pious School   136
Fano   119
Farnese dinasty   45, 108
    Alessandro (cardinal)   107
    Ottavio   107

Ranuccio I 45, 108
Fathers of the Oratory 172
Felbiger, Ignatius 170
Feltre 82, 114, 129
Ferlan, Claudio 125–126
Ferrara 4–5, 22–23, 26, 31, 36, 65, 70–71, 75, 82, 101n12, 107, 113, 118–119, 133, 149
    Jesuit College 75
Ficino, Marsilio 47
Filangieri, Gaetano 173
Filippini, Lucia 12–13, 92–94
Finale Emilia 137
Finale Marina 98
Firmian, Carlo 54
Fleury, Claude 59
Florence 31, 63n63, 63–64, 66, 69–70, 98–99, 113, 118–119, 154, 167, 173–174
    Pious School 164
    San Carlo College 98
Foggia 109–110
Foligno 18, 82, 98
Fontana, Mariano 99
Fontanellato 175
Fontanini, Giusto 126
Forlì 18
Foscarari, Egidio 29
Foscarini, Sebastiano 178
Fossano 57, 60, 102
Fossombrone 97
Fouldier family 154
France 3, 5, 96, 98, 107n27, 129, 143, 154, 171–172, 174, 181
    Béarn region 97, 167
    French Empire 180
    French Revolution 6, 115, 131n24, 139, 159n1, 159–160
    Gironde region 97
    Ile de France region 97
    Landes region 97
    Pas De Calais region 97
    southern 115
Francesco from Parma, public teacher in Mantua 22
Francis of Sales 98–99
Francis Xavier 44, 99
Franciscans 11, 24–25, 30–32, 44, 57, 79–80, 96, 116–118, 120–122, 139, 141, 143

Capuchins 31–32, 41, 103, 115, 117–118, 120–122, 136, 140, 182
Conventuals 25, 30–32, 117–120, 122, 136
Observants 30–32, 70, 117–120, 122, 136, 140
Francisco de Borja 44
Frascati 107, 112
    Pious School 114
Frisi, Paolo 169
Friuli region 102, 114n48, 123n1, 126, 130

Gadaldino, Antonio 29
Gaetano da Thiene 12, 73–74, 105
Galiano 147
Galilei, Galileo 64, 67, 114, 159–164, 169, 182
    Dialogo sopra i due massimi sistemi del mondo 162
    Galilean heritage 69, 160, 167, 182
Gallarate 147
Gambara, Laura 79
Gandía 44
Gavanto, Bartolomeo 98, 154
Gavirate 21
Gemona 114
Geneva 28, 29n50, 96, 124, 126, 167–168
Genoa 4, 36, 57, 97–98, 101n12, 107, 119–120, 154, 164, 180
    Guild of Notaries 98
    Republic of Genoa 112
Genovesi, Antonio 53, 173
Gentili, Antonio Maria 51
Gerdil, Giacinto Sigismondo 76
Germany 5, 29, 31, 36, 70–71, 113, 115, 124, 161
Ghislieri, Carlo Agostino 154
Ghisolfi, Virginio 144
Giordano Bruno 160
Giustinian, Marco 150
Goa 44
Goito 35
Gonzaga dinasty 22–23
    Camillo I (branch of Novellara) 95n1, 133, 152
    Cesare I (branch of Guastalla) 140
    Ferrante I (branch of Guastalla) 12, 34, 48n18, 85, 139
    Ferrante II (branch of Guastalla) 109, 143–144, 155
    Ferrante III (branch of Guastalla) 141

INDEX 215

Francesco (branch of Guastalla)   145
Gianfrancesco I   22
Luigi I, lord of Mantua   22n28
Margherita   109
Gorgonzola   147
Gorini, Melchiorre   52
Gorizia   115, 125n4, 125–127, 190
　Jesuit College   125–126
　Princely County of Gorizia and
　　Gradisca   124
Govone, Rosa   176
Gozzi, Gasparo   177
Gradenigo, Giovanni Girolamo   75–76
Gradisca d'Isonzo   115
Grambini, Alessio   155
Grassi, Tommaso   20, 35
Gratis et Amore Dei schools   33
Gratuitousness of schools   14, 20–21, 33, 38, 45, 62n60, 61–63, 68, 83, 128, 152, 171, 181
Gravesande, Willem   166
Gravisi, Girolamo   166
Graz   126
　Jesuit College   126
Greengrass, Mark   2
Gregory XIII pope   39, 161
Gregory XV pope   111
Grendler, Paul   7, 23, 43–44, 46–47, 60, 62, 64, 77
Guarino of Verona   19, 22–23, 23n31, 26, 177
Guastalla   12, 34–35, 39, 62n60, 75, 85, 109, 133–136, 139, 141–144, 155–156
　Educandato of Saint Charles   156
　Jesuit College   143

Habsburg dinasty   14, 32, 79, 137, 139
　Charles V (Holy Roman Emperor)   74, 95n1, 139
　Charles VI (Holy Roman Emperor)   137
　Ferdinand I (Holy Roman Emperor)   95n1
　Francis II (last Holy Roman Emperor, first Emperor of Austria)   129
　John of Austria   110
　Joseph II (Holy Roman Emperor)   60, 68, 115, 171, 180
　Maria Theresa (Holy Roman Empress)   170

Peter Leopold (Grand Duke of Tuscany, Holy Roman Emperor)   174
Philip II (King of Spain)   87
Heliocentrism   42n2, 64, 67, 159, 162
Hobbes, Thomas   75
Hohenzollern dinasty
　Frederick II the Great   170
　Frederick William I   170
Honorius III pope   117
Hungary   180

Iesi   120
Ignatius of Loyola   3, 43–45, 80, 178
Imola   18
Incino   147
India   44
Innocent X pope   65, 67, 73, 101n14, 106, 114, 163
　Innocentian Inquiry   67, 101n14, 105–106
Inquisition (Holy Office)   64, 74, 159, 161–165, 168, 182
Istria   114n48, 124
Italy   14, 16–17, 19, 21, 23, 28–29, 31–32, 34, 84, 95, 105, 174
　central   36, 90, 92–93, 98, 102
　Italian Wars (1494-1559)   14, 32, 79, 85, 93, 95, 131, 183
　Napoleonic Cisalpine Republic (1797-1802)   180
　Napoleonic Italian Republic (1802-1805)   180
　Napoleonic Kingdom (1805-1814)   139, 180
　northeastern   26, 123n1, 123–124, 125n3, 125n4
　northern   5, 14, 26, 26n41, 36–37, 48, 57, 66, 78, 93, 101n12, 101–103, 111, 121–122, 131, 139, 180
　northwestern   28, 98
　Po River Valley (*Pianura Padana*)   5, 85, 89, 93, 131, 179
　southern   4–5, 20, 57, 75, 82, 89, 93, 97–98, 101n12, 101–102, 109, 111, 113, 122
Ivrea   19

Jerusalem   179
Jesuits   5, 8, 11, 13–16, 39, 42–47, 52–53, 56, 59–61, 63–64, 66–69, 75–76, 80, 86, 88–89, 93, 96, 99, 101, 105–106, 108, 111, 115,

121–122, 125–127, 129, 133–139, 142–144, 147, 152, 163, 171, 173–178
  Expulsion from France (1764)   171
  Expulsion from Naples (1767)   173
  Expulsion from Parma (1768)   174
  Expulsion from Portugal and Spain (1759, 1767)   53n34
  Jesuitesses (*Gesuitesse*)   88, 90
  Ratio Studiorum   7, 42, 46, 52, 58, 94, 176
  Suppression (1773)   99, 121, 172
Julius III pope   101n14

Koper   114, 129
Krakow   119
Krk   114

L'Aquila   119
Lalli, Giuseppe   68
Lancelot, Claude   59
Landriani, Marsilio   108
Lario   34
Lasallian Brothers   172
Lazio region   89, 107, 120
Lazzari, Pietro   168
Lecce   109
Lecco   33, 81
Legnano   81
Leo X pope   31, 117–118
Lescar   97
Liguria   57, 102, 107
Lithuania   180
Livorno   97
Loches   97
Lodi   36, 57, 81, 97–98, 102, 153
  San Giovanni delle Vigne College   153
Lombardy   5, 11, 34, 37, 48, 48n18, 62n60, 79, 81, 89–90, 98, 101n12, 100–102, 108, 115, 121, 148, 179–180
  Austrian Lombardy   54
  Spanish Lombardy   86–87
London Synod of 1556   147
Loreto   98, 109
Louis René de La Chalotais   171
Lucca   31, 118
Ludovic des Hayes   168
Lugano   57, 102
Lviv   119

Macerata   18, 50, 98, 102, 130, 151
Madrid   107n27, 114
Magiotti, Raffaello   164
Magliano   112
Malpangotto, Michela   168
Mandas   21
Manduria   113
Mantua   5, 22n28, 22–23, 26, 30–31, 34–36, 109, 118, 132, 152
  Ca' Zoiosa (court school)   22, 152
  Duchy of Mantua   5, 143
  University of Mantua   134
Manzoli, Benedetto   30
Manzoni, Alessandro   57
Maranello (school teacher).   *See* Giovanni Maria Tagliati
Marche region   91, 120
Marliano   33, 147
Martin Luther   24, 71–72, 161
  Lutheranism   31, 42, 72, 162
Martinelli, Ignazio   90–91, 93
Masaniello   4
Mascilli Migliorini, Luigi   150
Masini, Eliseo   28
Massaglia   147
Matteo da Bascio   117
Mazenta, Antonio   167
Mazzonis, Querciolo   84
McCoog, Thomas   7
Medici dinasty   51, 64
  Cosimo III   98
  Ferdinando I   51, 97
  Ferdinando II   63n63, 164
Melanchthon, Philip   72, 161
Melegnano   33, 81, 147
Melfi   57, 102
Mellino, Giovanni   82
Mentana   112
Mercurian, Everard   134
Merici, Angela   11, 78–84, 90, 178
  Ricordi (Memories)   80
  Testamento (Legacy)   80
Merolla, Desiderio   153
Merone   54, 101
Messina   20, 44, 74, 76, 102, 110, 113, 119
  Theatine school   111
  University of Messina   75
Michelini, Famiano   64, 163–165, 168, 182

INDEX

Trattatto sulla direzione de' fiumi 165
Miglio, Luisa 77
Milan 5, 12, 19–21, 26, 31, 33, 35–37, 48n18, 48–49, 52, 54, 75–76, 81, 85–89, 97–98, 101, 101n12, 108, 114, 118–120, 130, 148, 152, 167, 173, 178–179
    Arcimboldi schools 52, 97, 99, 152
    Cicogna schools 20, 35
    Duchy of Milan 4, 19n19
    Guastalla College 12–13, 84, 88–90, 92
    Imperial College 129
    Milanese city gates 81
    Piattine schools 20
    Schools of Charity 20
Miletus 20
Mirandola 133, 135–136
    Jesuit College 136
Missaglia 155
Modena 11, 14, 16–17, 21, 29, 82, 107, 132–134, 137, 175, 188
    College of Nobles 132
    Duchy of Modena 5–6, 11, 27, 67, 113, 132–137, 139, 163, 175–176
    Jesuit schools 15
Moncalieri 19
Mondovì 75
Monferrato 57, 98
    San Clemente College 57
Montargis 97
Mont-de-Marsan 97
Montecuccoli family 21
Montecuccolo 21
Montefiascone 91–93
Monteripido 31
Monza 36, 50, 81, 83, 147
Moravia 114
Morelli, Angelo 163
Moricone 112
Murano 114, 149
    Pious School 166
Murat, Joachim 181
Muratori, Giovanni Battista 168
Muratori, Ludovico Antonio 53
Muselli, Girolamo 101n14
Muzio, Lorenzo 80

Naples 31, 57, 74, 82, 93, 101n12, 101–102, 109, 113, 118–120, 148, 173, 178, 180–181

Caracciolo College 57, 180
Kingdom of Naples 4, 20, 173
Napoleon 6, 60, 99, 115, 131, 139, 159, 179–181, 183
Narni 112
Negri, Paola Antonia 48, 77, 85
Nerviano 21
Newtonianism 59, 69, 165–166
Niccolò V, pope 21
Nikolsburg 114
Nizzoli, Mario 136
Nollet, Jean Antoine 166
Nontrinitarianism 28–29, 29n50
Norcia 112
Novara 36, 81, 97, 102, 167
Novara, Domenico Maria 3n4
Novellara 23, 95n11, 101, 133, 137, 144, 152, 175
Novello, Felice 102
Novi 102
Novi Chavarria, Elisa 73
Nuoro 21

O'Malley, John 7
Ochino, Bernardino 32, 101n14, 120
Ognibene Bonisoli da Lonigo 19
Orzinuovi 57, 102
Osimo 119
Otranto
    Land of Otranto (*Terra d'Otranto*) 121

Paciaudi, Paolo Maria 174
Padua 19, 26, 70, 108, 119, 129, 166, 177, 179
    College of San Marco 178
    University of Padua 3n4
Palazzolo sull'Oglio 19
Palermo 20, 110, 113, 119, 173
    Educandato Carolino 173
Pantegola, Caterina 79
Paolo d'Alagona 75–76
Papal State 18, 19n19, 111, 180
Parenzo. *See* Porec
Paris 14, 31, 70, 76, 117, 154, 166
Parma 6, 20, 36, 69, 71, 73, 82, 108, 118, 131–132, 174, 176, 178
    College of the Nobles 108
    Duchy of Parma 19, 19n19, 143, 174–175
    Jesuit College 45, 56
    University of Parma 108, 133

Paul III pope   43, 85, 101n14
Paul IV pope   39, 105
Paul V pope   57, 103, 168
Paullo   102
Pavia   20, 31, 36, 49–50, 55, 70, 97, 101n12, 118–119, 148, 179
   Barnabite College   97
   University of Pavia   49
Pavone, Sabina   7
Pavullo   135
Pavur, Claude   7
Pelagianism   38
Pergola   82
Perugia   31, 70, 90, 119–120
Pescia   98
Peter Lombard   70
Piacenza   20, 36, 97, 107, 144
Piarists   3, 5, 9, 11, 13, 39, 44–45, 60–69, 75, 96, 103, 111, 113–115, 121–122, 129–130, 133–139, 150, 160, 163, 165, 167, 172, 174–175, 178, 180
   Decreto per il buon regime delle Scuole Pie   68
   Florentine schools   67
   Ratio Studiorum Pro Exteris   68
Piazza Armerina   110
Pico dinasty   47
   Alessandro   133
   Giovanni   133
Piedmont   19, 28, 32, 57, 98, 101n12, 101–102, 108, 115, 124, 148, 167, 180–181
Pieter Van Musschenbroek   166
Pietrasanta, Silvestro   64, 66–67, 113, 163
Pieve di Cento   65, 66n67, 113
Pinerolo   19
Pinguente   114
Pio dinasty   136–137
   Alberto III   136
Piran   115
Pirano.   *See* Piran
Pirroni, Giovanni Carlo   68
Pisa   51, 97, 119, 130
Pistoia   174
Pius IV pope   28
Pius V pope   39, 49, 100, 108
Pius VI pope   180
Pius X pope   49n20
Pizzighettone   34

Platonism   47
Poland   68, 180
Pole, Reginald   147
Poleni, Giovanni   166
   Teatro di filosofia sperimentale   166
Poliziano, Ludovico   30
Pontirolo   147
Pontremoli   62n60
Poreč   114
Porto Maurizio   98
Portugal   2, 31, 44, 107n27
Poscolonna, Candido   51
Posillipo   113
Possevino, Antonio   28, 30, 32, 96, 125, 167
Prague   114, 119
Prato   174
Prato, Elisabetta   79–81
Protestant Reformation   5, 16, 24, 27, 29, 29n50, 31, 40, 71
Prussia   170
Puglia region   109

Ragusa.   *See* Dubrovnik
Rambaldoni, Vittorino.   *See* Vittorino da Feltre
Rastatt   114
Rasy, Elisabetta   77
Ravenna   18, 69, 101n14, 101–102, 108, 119, 148
Recanati   18
Reggio Calabria   75
Reggio Emilia   5, 17, 27, 30, 34, 82, 101n12, 132–134, 137, 143–144, 163, 175
   Jesuit College   133
Rimini   18, 107, 119
Rinaldi, Francesco   145
Riva, Giovanni Battista   58
Rivolta d'Adda   57, 102–103
Roest, Bert   25, 119
Rollin, Charles   59
Romagna region   4, 18, 70, 82, 102, 107
Rome   3, 12, 18, 31, 36, 48, 50, 56, 58, 61–62, 64–66, 71, 73–74, 77, 89, 91, 93, 101n12, 101–102, 112, 118, 120, 143, 152, 159, 162, 164, 178–180
   Campidoglio (Capitoline Hill)   91
   Clementino College   56–58
   Collegium Sancti Bonaventurae   118
   Maestri rionali   61

INDEX

Pontifical Roman Major Seminary   147
Sacking (1527)   74
Rosate   33
Rospigliosi, Giulio   143
Rovereto   102, 115
Rovigno.   *See* Rovinj
Rovinj   114
Ruggeri, Orazio   34

Sabbatini, Giuliano   135, 137
Sabbioneta   102
Sacro Arsenale   28
Salamanca   14, 118
Salerno   119
Salò   57, 102, 129
Samuel von Pufendorf   75
San Donato   81
San Giuliano   81
San Martino in Rio   137
San Miniato   120
San Pier d'Arena   107
San Severino   98
Sangalli, Maurizio   7–8, 10, 129, 166
Santini, Antonio   164
Sanvitale, Stefano   175
Sarafellini, Ventura   164
Sardinia   4, 20–21, 66, 68, 120, 180
    Kingdom of Sardinia   5, 176, 179
Sarzana   102
Sassari   21
Sassuolo   137
Sauli, Alessandro   49
Savi, Cristoforo   23
Savona   36, 101n12, 112
Savoy dinasty   181
    Carlo Emanuele (Pio of Savoy branch)   107
    Carlo Emanuele I   98, 167
    Carlo Emanuele III   75, 176
    Emanuele Filiberto   28, 32
    Vittorio Amedeo I   109
Savoy region   96–97, 99, 115, 154, 167
    Duchy of Savoy   19, 96
Scandiano   137
Scandinavia   31
Schools of Christian Doctrine   33n61, 36, 38–39, 55, 61–62, 76, 80–81, 83
Scipion, Francisco   14

Scipione de' Ricci   174
Serravalle   114
Serveto, Miguel   29
Servites   69–71, 73, 136, 140–141, 182
    Constitutions of Bologna   71–72, 142n51
    Constitutions of Budrio   71–72, 142n51
    Constitutions of Florence   142n51
    Constitutions of Parma   71, 73, 142n51
Settala   33
Settimi, Clemente   163
Sicily   4, 20, 68, 74, 110, 139, 181
Siena   31, 71, 101n12, 119
Sixtus V pope   118
Slovenia   114n48, 125
Solbiate   21
Somascans   3, 5, 9, 13, 39, 41, 44, 54–60, 62, 67, 69, 75–76, 83, 96, 100–104, 122, 126–127, 129–130, 143, 148–151, 164, 172, 178–180
    Expulsion from Venice (1769)   53n34
    Le regole circa lo studio   58
    Methodus studiorum ad usus Congregationis de Somascha   58
Somma   33, 81
Soncino   102
Soragna, Jacopo   144
Sormani, Paolo   155
Sorrento   110
Sozzi, Mario   64, 163–164
Spain   2, 4, 31, 48n18, 68–69, 89, 107n27, 174, 180
    Spanish governorate over Milan   4
Spalato.   *See* Split
Split   115
Stefonio, Bernardino   143
Strada, Famiano   143
Studenz   126
Styria   126
Suriano, Domenico   108
Sutri   91
Switzerland   31–32
Syracuse   110

Tagliacozzo   120
Tagliati, Giovanni Maria   29
Tanucci, Bernardo   173
Tarquinia   92
Tavazzi Catenaga, Camilla   98

Theatines   9, 12–13, 39, 69, 73–76, 96, 101, 101n14, 103, 107n27, 106–108, 110, 121–122, 136, 140–142, 174, 178
   Missionaries   107n27
Thonon   97–99, 167
Ticino   34
Tiraboschi, Girolamo   6, 15–16, 18n13
Toffolo, Attilio   87
Tolentino   151
Tolmezzo   114
Tolosa, Francesco   144
Tommaso da Viterbo   67n70
Torelli, Guido   85
Torelli, Ludovica   12–13, 39, 48, 48n18, 77–78, 85–90, 173
Tornielli, Agostino   50
Torricelli, Evangelista   164
Tortona   98, 101n12, 101–102, 148
Tosi, Giovanni Maria   36
Tradate   21
Tre Valli   33
Trentino region   102, 114n48
Treviglio   102
Treviso   19, 82, 102, 114, 119, 129, 150
Trezzo   83
Tribraco, Pomponio   21
Tron, Andrea   178
Turchini, Angelo   146
Turin   19, 36, 75, 98–99, 108–109, 119, 176
   Barnabite College   99
   University of Turin   176
Tuscany   20, 70, 107
   Grand Duchy of Tuscany   4, 51, 99, 180
   Kingdom of Etruria (1801-1807)   180

Udine   5, 97, 102, 123, 126–130, 136, 139, 150
   Barnabite College   124, 128, 131
   Society of Practical Agriculture   130
Umbria region   70, 91, 102
Urban VIII pope   57, 67, 114, 119, 162
Urbino   119
Ursulines   3, 11, 13, 78, 80–84, 88–89, 173, 178

Valencia   114
Valois dinasty   14, 32, 79
Valtravaglia   147
Varese   34, 36, 81, 147
Veglia.   *See* Krk

Velletri   57, 102
Venafro   120
Venerini Schools   12, 91–93
Venerini, Goffredo   89
Venerini, Rosa   12, 89–94
Veneto region   48, 76, 82, 101n12, 101–102, 108, 114n48, 124, 180
Venice   4–5, 27, 31, 33, 48, 55, 74–75, 78, 82, 93, 101n12, 108, 113, 115, 118–119, 128–129, 149–150, 177–179
   Interdict of 1606   127
   Morean War of 1695   128
   Patriarchal Seminary   149
   Republic of Venice   19, 26, 48, 60, 76, 114, 123–124, 127, 129, 131, 149, 177, 179
   Venetian *Stato da Mar*   19
Venturi, Franco   178
Venturino, reader of Virgil   22
Verbano   34
Vercelli   19, 28, 31, 101n12, 118, 167
Verona   19, 31, 36, 74–75, 82, 101n12, 101–102, 108, 129, 177
Vezzani, Giacomo   143–145
Viadana   20, 136, 143
Vibo Valentia   119
Vicenza   19, 101n12, 109, 129, 148
Vienna   119
Vigevano   20, 36, 97
Vignola   137
Vilnius   114
Vimercate   81, 147
Visco, Alessandro   110
Visconti dinasty   20
   Filippo Maria   85
Visconti-Sforza dukedom.   *See* Duchy of Milan
Viterbo   12, 18, 89–92
Vittorino da Feltre   19, 22–23, 26, 132, 152, 177
Vittorio Veneto   98
Voghera   102

Warsaw   69, 114

Zaccaria, Antonio Maria   12, 39, 47
Zagarolo   50
Zampichetti, Marzia   90
Zanon, Antonio   130
Zaragoza   114

Printed in the United States
by Baker & Taylor Publisher Services